To Christina

Ofla [illegible]

Hope you enjoy this
book & I underline the offer
to get you up the Cave-hill.

42-97862

THE STORY OF A B-17 FLYING FORTRESS CRASH AND THE LOSS OF HER CREW ON BELFAST'S CAVE HILL DURING THE SECOND WORLD WAR

ALFRED MONTGOMERY & WILLIAM LINDSAY

STATION 597©
PUBLICATIONS

First published in the United Kingdom in 2019 by
Alfred Montgomery & William Alan Lindsay

ISBN 978 0 95739 933 4

Typeset in Palatino Linotype

Contents

Introduction

Just days prior to the allied invasion of Europe, the crash of an American bomber on Belfast's Cave Hill during the Second World War, would forever be shrouded in myth and speculation. After the discovery of a wedding ring belonging to one of the crew members, the story was the focus of various books, newspapers, magazine articles, radio interviews, a television documentary and a Hollywood film over the years, such has been the interest.

The authors have endeavoured to explain the circumstances behind the crash in a well researched and logical fashion, leaving no stone unturned in their search for the truth, the basis of which, has been many years of researching official archives, interviewing eye-witnesses and examining wreckage which remained at the crash site.

75 years in the making, the true story of how ten young American airmen came to loose their lives on a cloud-enveloped hillside in Belfast, can now be told for the first time.

Alfred Montgomery

Glengormley, Co. Antrim, Northern Ireland

William Lindsay

Crumlin, Co. Antrim, Northern Ireland

Chapter One

A brief history of the Third Air Force

One of the four original numbered air forces, the US Third Army Air Force was activated as the Southeast Air District of the GHQ Air Force on 18 December 1940 *(which became Air Force Combat Command on 20 June 1941),* at MacDill Field, Florida. It was re-designated Third Air Force on 26 March 1941 with a mission for the defence of the Southeast and Gulf of Mexico regions of the United States.

MacDill Field was one of two major Army Air Corps bases established in the Tampa Bay area in the build-up prior to World War II. Tampa's Drew Field Municipal Airport, established in 1928 was leased by the Air Corps in 1940. A major expansion of the airport was initiated and Drew Army Airfield was opened in 1941. Two secondary Army Airfields, Brooksville Army Airfield and Hillsborough Army Airfield were built and opened in early 1942 to support the flight operations of MacDill and Drew Fields. The Bonita Springs Auxiliary Field, located near Fort Myers provided an additional emergency landing field for MacDill. All of these airfields came under the jurisdiction of the Third Air Force. III Fighter Command, the fighter arm, was head-quartered at Drew Field.

The Third Air Force initially provided air defence for the south-eastern United States *(1940–1941)* and flew antisubmarine patrols along coastal areas of the Atlantic Ocean and Gulf of Mexico, after Pearl Harbor. In January 1942, the command was withdrawn by Air Force Combat Command from the Eastern Defence Command and assigned operational training of units, crews, and replacements for medium bombardment, fighter and reconnaissance operations. In 1942, the antisubmarine patrols were turned over to the Coast Guard and other agencies and the command was engaged primarily in training replacements for combat units and operational training of units, crews, and individuals for bombardment, fighter and reconnaissance operations. It received graduates of Army Air Forces Training Command flight schools; navigator training; flexible gunnery schools and various technical schools, organized them into combat groups and squadrons and provided operational unit training (OTU) and replacement training (RTU) to prepare groups and replacements for deployment overseas to combat theatre's.

The Third Air Force primarily trained B-25 Mitchell and B-26 Marauder medium bomber groups and A-20 Havoc and A-36 Apache light bomber groups. It also trained replacement fighter pilots, initially using P-39 Airacobra and P-40 Warhawks in 1942, later with P-47 Thunderbolts and P-51 Mustangs beginning in 1943 and 1944 as they became available. The Third Air Force also provided support to the Army Air Forces School of Applied Tactics in Florida. By 1944, most of the Operational Training of groups ended, with the command concentrating on RTU training using Army Air Force Base Units (AAFBU) as training organizations at the airfields controlled by the Third Air Force.

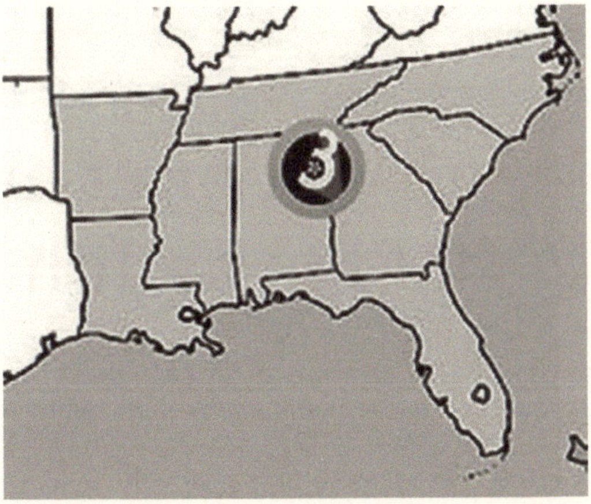

***Above**, Third Air Force Insignia and illustration showing the Third Air Force region of the United States, during World War II*

Chapter Two

A brief history of the Eighth Air Force

The Eighth Air Force was a United States Army Air Forces combat unit, which was based in England. It was originally designated as VIII Bomber Command, on 19 January 1942 and re-designated as the Eighth Air Force, on 22 February 1944. The Eighth engaged in operations primarily in Northern Europe, carrying out strategic bombing of enemy targets in France, the low countries and Germany. It was the largest of the deployed combat Army Air Forces in numbers of personnel, aircraft and equipment.

Prior to Pearl Harbor and the American involvement in the war, Royal Air Force Bomber Command, had concentrated on a doctrine of precision bombing in daylight. When the German defences inflicted costly defeats on RAF raids, in late 1939, a switch to night bombing was forced upon the command.

Upon the involvement of the United States into the war and the activation of VIII Bomber Command, strategic daytime bombing was adopted, assured of accuracy in hitting their targets, due to the highly secretive and successful Norden bombsight. The Royal Air Force had their doubts that daytime bombing could be successful and effective without large losses of aircraft and men, hence why the RAF opted to fly at night.

In January 1943, it was agreed that RAF Bomber Command raids in Germany would be reinforced by the U.S. Army Air Forces, in a Combined Operations Offensive plan called Operation Pointblank.

At the beginning of March 1943, 669 RAF and 303 USAAF heavy bombers were available. In late 1943, the 'Pointblank' attacks manifested themselves in the infamous Schweinfurt raids. Despite the use of combat boxes and the assembly ships to form them, formations of unescorted bombers were no match for German fighters, which inflicted a deadly toll. In despair, the Eighth halted air operations over Germany until a long-range fighter could be found, in 1944; it proved to be the P-51 Mustang, which had the range to fly to Berlin and back.

On 22 February 1944, VIII Bomber Command was re-designated as the Eighth Army Air Force. A prelude to the invasion of Europe was "Big Week", which was a sequence of raids by the USAAF and RAF Bomber Command, from 20 to 25 February 1944. The plan was to attack the German aircraft industry to lure the Luftwaffe into a decisive battle where the Luftwaffe could be damaged so badly, that the allies would achieve air superiority, which would ensure the forthcoming success of the invasion of continental Europe. Losses were heavy, the U.S. Eighth Air Force lost 97 B-17's, 40 B-24's and another 20 aircraft were scrapped due to damage, during the "Big Week raid". Big Week proved a success and bolstered the confidence of U.S. strategic bombing crews. Until that time, U.S. allied bombers avoided contact with the Luftwaffe, now the Americans used any method at their disposal to draw the Luftwaffe out into combat.

Less than a week after Big Week, Over 700 bombers along with 800 escort fighters of the Eighth Air Force, hit numerous targets within Berlin, dropping the first American bombs on the capital of the Third Reich. On 1 May 1944, over 1,300 Eighth Air Force heavy bombers made an all-out attack on the enemy's rail network, striking at targets in France and Belgium. On 7 May , another 1,000 bombers hit additional targets along the English Channel coast, hitting bridges, fortifications and marshalling areas. During the initial build up to D-day, new bomber crews were being dispatched to Europe from the US on a daily basis, having completed their training within the Third Air Force, to bolster the numbers of personnel in support of the allied invasion of Europe. This publication is the focus of one new Eighth Air Force crew, a crew of ten men, who were prepared to fight and if necessary, sacrifice their own lives in the pursuit of freedom.

Insignia of the Eighth Air Force

Chapter Three

An introduction to the Crew

At the age of 23, Lester Bryan Brooks, of Carrollton, Ohio, enlisted in the US Army Air Corps Reserves. Employed as a door to door insurance salesman in his home town, he was engaged to his high school sweetheart, Genevieve Rutledge. Accepted into the Aviation Cadet Training Program, as an Aviation Cadet, he began his Primary Flying Training in May-June, 1943, as a student pilot. Subsequently, he was assigned to the 69th Flight Training Detachment, which was stationed at Clarkesdale, Mississippi.

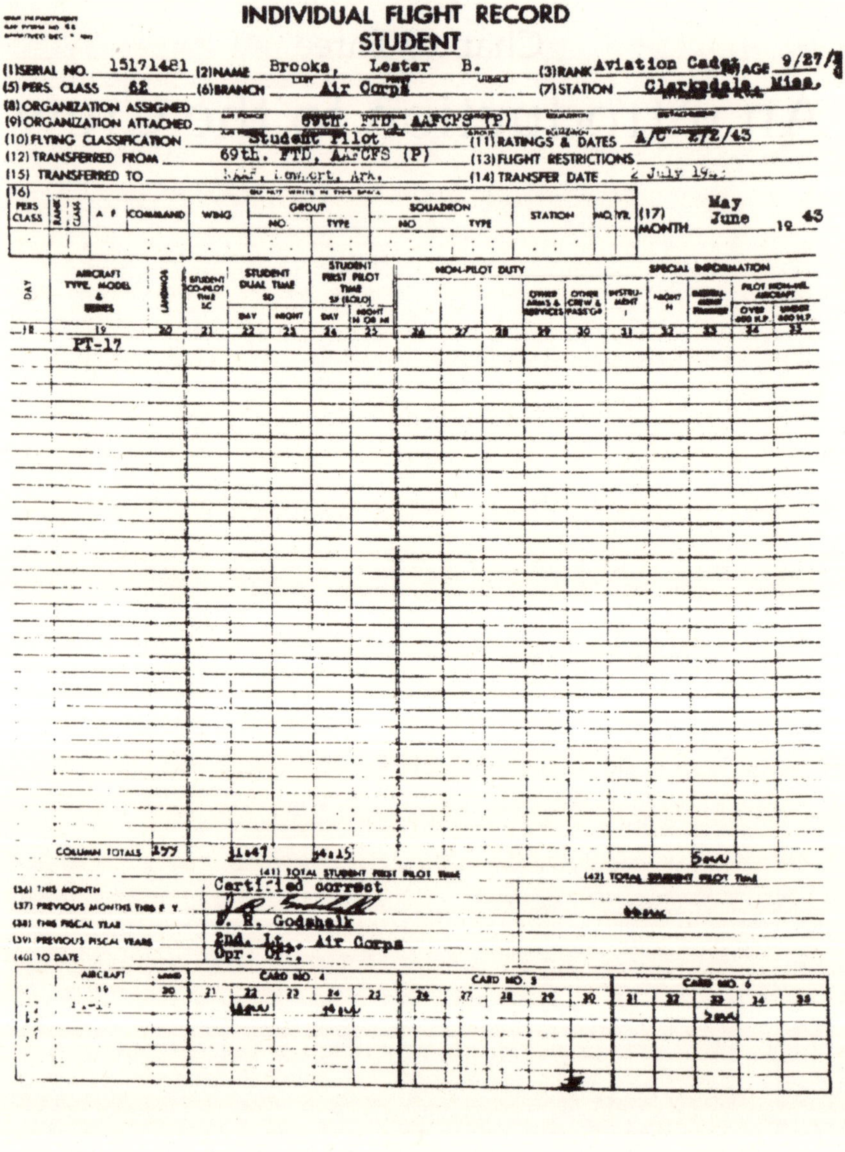
INDIVIDUAL FLIGHT RECORD
STUDENT

(1) SERIAL NO. 15171481 (2) NAME Brooks, Lester B. (3) RANK Aviation Cadet (4) AGE 9/27/
(5) PERS. CLASS 62 (6) BRANCH Air Corps (7) STATION Clarksdale, Miss.
(8) ORGANIZATION ASSIGNED
(9) ORGANIZATION ATTACHED 69th. FTD, AAFCFS (P)
(10) FLYING CLASSIFICATION Student Pilot (11) RATINGS & DATES A/C 2/2/43
(12) TRANSFERRED FROM 69th. FTD, AAFCFS (P) (13) FLIGHT RESTRICTIONS
(15) TRANSFERRED TO [illegible] (14) TRANSFER DATE 2 July 194[illegible]
(17) MONTH May June 1943

PT-17

COLUMN TOTALS

Certified correct
J. R. Godshalk
2nd. Lt., Air Corps
Opr. Of.

He completed 34 hours and 15 minutes flying time, in the Boeing PT-17 Stearman Trainer type aircraft, accomplishing his first solo flight during the month.

On 2 July 1943, Lester was transferred to Newport Army Airfield, in Arkansas to begin Basic Flying Training. At the end of August, he had accumulated 143 hours and 27 minutes flying time. During his time in Arkansas, he married his high school sweetheart, Gennie, on 23 July.

Transferring to George Field, in Illinois, he began his Advanced twin-engined Flying Training, in September, on the Beechcraft AT-10 Wichita, type aircraft. He had now accumulated a total of 257 hours, and 37 minutes total student pilot time, of which, 130 hours, and 20 minutes, were solo hours, additionally this total time consisted of 125 landings, 35 hours and 55 minutes of night flying, 22 hours and 15 minutes, instrument flying and 17 hours 20 minutes Link Instrument Trainer hours.

On 3 November 1943, after successfully completing his Primary, Basic and Advanced Flying Training, Cadet Brooks, was awarded his pilots wings and was assigned the rank of Flight Officer.

Jeremiah C. Murphy, grew up in New York City. His parents, Cornelius and Jane, were both born in Cork, Ireland and had emigrated to the States, in the late 1880's. Sadly, Jeremiah's parents both died, when he was still in school and he went to live with his uncle, John Walsh, in Albany, New York. John, was his mothers brother and had a family of his own, a wife, Anna and a daughter, Mary. In 1940, having completed three years of high school, he was working as a Gas Attendant, for a local Gas Station, in New York.

With war being declared, in the aftermath of the tragedy at Pearl Harbor, in December 1941, like many young patriotic Americans, Jeremiah enlisted to join the fight. He enlisted in the US Army, at Albany, New York, on 8 July 1942 and was assigned to the Air Corps, as a Student Pilot, within the Aviation Cadet Training Program.

Jeremiah began his Primary Flying Training at Dorr Field, which was located close to Arcadia, Florida, in August 1943. Dorr Field, was operated by the Embry-Riddle Corporation, under the 54th Flying Training Detachment, primarily as a training airfield for Royal Air Force flying cadets.

At the end of the month, he had completed his Primary Flying Training, in the Boeing PT-17 Stearman type aircraft. He logged a total of 65 hours flying time, of which 38 hours and 11 minutes, was student dual time. 26 hours and 49 minutes, was student first pilot time (solo).

In September, Jeremiah transferred to Greenville Army Airfield, in Mississippi, to begin his Basic Flying Training. At the end of October, he had accumulated 33 hours and 15 minutes student dual time, of which, 72 hours, was student first pilot time (solo).

Within this time, he had logged 14 hours and 5 minutes, instrument flying time, 8 hours, 20 minutes, night flying time and 10 hours of instrument flying ground instruction, on the Link Trainer.

PT-17 Stearman's on the flight line at Dorr Field, Arcadia, Florida.

Jeremiah transferred from AAF Greenville during November, to start his Advanced twin engine-type Flying Training, at AAF Seymour, which was located in the State of Indiana. He was assigned to the 30th Flying Training Wing, of the Army Air Forces Eastern Training Command and he began building up flying hours, in the Beechcraft AT-10 Wichita type aircraft.

The A-10, was a small twin-engined aircraft, suitable for use in training student pilots, in the handling of multi-engined retractable landing gear type aircraft. Beechcraft, terminated production in 1943, after it had delivered 1,771 AT-10's.

On 23 November 1943, Jeremiah married Norma Mercer, in Indiana.

A Beechcraft AT-10 Wichita twin engined trainer, in flight.

He had become acquainted with and dated Norma during his time at Dorr Field, which was close to Arcadia in Florida, where Norma lived with her parents.

In January, 1944, Jeremiah completed his Advanced Flying Training. In total, he acquired 71 hours, 25 minutes flying time, of which, 29 hours, 50 minutes, was Student Dual Time and 41 hours, 35 minutes, was Student Solo Time. In total, he had logged 244 hours and 20 minutes flying time, from Primary, Basic and Advanced Flying Training, of which, 101 hours and 40 minutes was Student Solo Time. On 7 January 1944, Cadet Murphy, was awarded his pilots wings, and assigned the rank of, Flight Officer.

Joseph V. Nobilione, was raised in the borough of Manhattan, in New York City. His mother, Palmina and father Mattea, were natives of Italy. He had two sisters and three brothers, one of whom, was born in Naples, Italy. During the great depression of the 1930's, his father had worked as a Long-shore-man for a local steamship company.

Completing four years of high school and working as an office clerk, he enlisted in the US Army Air Corps, on 17 July 1942.

He was accepted into the Aviation Cadet Training Program and subsequently, in May 1943, he began his Primary Flight Training as a student pilot, with the 71st Flying Training Detachment, which was located at Harrell Field, Camden, Arkansas.

Harrell Field opened in August 1942 and began training Army Air Corps Flying Cadets, under contract, to Wiggins-Marden Aero Corp. It was assigned to the US Army Air Forces Gulf Coast Training Centre, as a Primary Flying Training airfield.

In late June, Cadet Nobilione had logged a total of 66 hours and 5 minutes, in the Boeing PT-27 Stearman type aircraft, of which, 32 hours and 6 minutes was dual instruction time and 32 hours, 59 minutes was logged as Student Solo Time.

Cadet Nobilione, during his training.

Sitting centre, cadet Nobilione, presumably with friends, who are also cadets.

Additionally, he completed 5 hours ground instruction on the Link Instrument Trainer.

During the month of August, at Grenadier Army Airfield, Cadet Nobilione was eliminated from Student Pilot Flying Training, due to failing to meet the prescribed standard of training. At this time, he had accumulated a total of 116 hours and 15 minutes total Student Pilot Flying Time. Subsequently, he was accepted for training as a Student Navigator and began his training in October.

The training was provided by Pan American Airways, at their PAN AM training school, which was located at Coral Gables, in Florida. PAN AM provided instruction, facilities and aircraft. Navigator School lasted 18 weeks and consisted of 500 hours of ground instruction in the duties of a navigator *(charting, directional bearings, computed headings, airspeed, radio codes, celestial navigation, etc.)*. This was combined with familiarity of the duties of a pilot or radioman, in case of emergency.

A portrait photograph of cadet Nobilione, taken during his training, the winged propeller on his peak cap, signifies that he is a cadet.

Lieutenant Nobilione, proudly wearing his Navigators wings on his class-a uniform.

After four weeks of training he would have acted as a navigator, in day and night flights, flying in the Consolidated Commodore type aircraft. From 9 October to 11 February 1944, upon completion of his training, he had logged a total of 54 hours and 15 minutes flying time as a Student Navigator. On 12 February 1944, he was assigned the commissioned rank of 2nd Lieutenant.

Lieutenant Nobilione was now a qualified Navigator and he was awarded his Navigators Wings.

During his training, he was praised for an having an excellent character and an unusual devotion to all assignments.

After graduating from Coral Gables, it was remarked that he became resourceful and extremely accurate, proving himself to be a valuable Navigator.

A Pan American Airways Consolidated Commodore aircraft in flight.

In 1942, a young Leighton B. McKenzie of Mill Valley, California, graduated from Tamalpais High School. He had been active in sports and was remarked to have been proficient in hurdles and the high jump, on the school c track team.

In the early 1920's, his mother, Guinevere Zaun Robinson, had studied music at the University of California, in Berkeley. At University she dated Malcolm Durham McKenzie, who would later become his father. They were married on 11 February 1924, but soon thereafter their marriage would unfortunately lead to divorce. Leighton and his mother moved into the Robinson family home, which was located at 123 Edgewood Avenue, in Mill Valley, California. There, he lived with his mother, grandparents and uncle Shayer.

Leighton's grandfather, Leighton Robinson, was a native of Cornwall, in England and was a former sea captain. From 1905 until 1941, he was the Deputy Shipping Commissioner for the Port of San Francisco. Leighton Robinson was a father figure to young Leighton and many troubled youths in the San Francisco area, who he attempted to help guide, through scouting and sailing activities.

Left to right, Leighton Robinson, Alex Barr, Leighton McKenzie and Arthur Brodeur, November 12 1939.

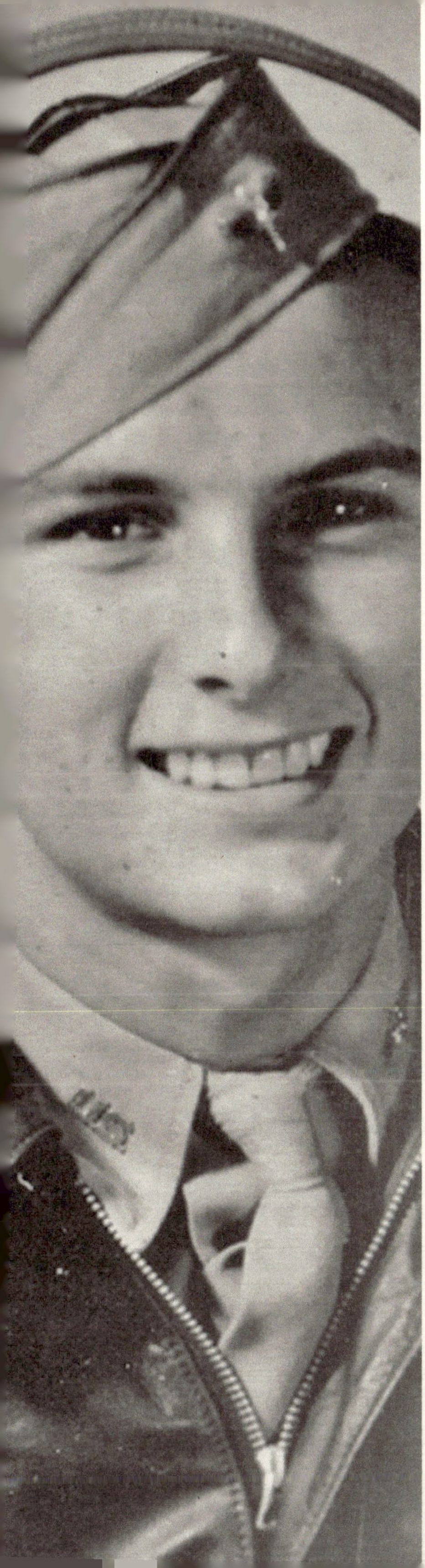

On 12 November 1939, Leighton's grandfather was commissioned by the Library of Congress, to record some old Sea-Shantys from his seafaring days. Many songs were recorded, of which, his grandson, young Leighton, participated in.

Leighton was drafted into military service, registering on 11 December 1942, at the age of 18. He was assigned to the Air Corps and subsequently accepted into the Aviation Cadet Training Program, as a Student Bombardier. He began his flexible gunnery training at Laredo Army Air Field, located in Laredo, Texas, in July 1943, completing 16.7 hours.

On 24 July, he was transferred to Killington Field, Texas.

On 6 August, he began his Bombardier training at Childress Army Airfield, Texas. His training would also consist of dead-reckoning navigator training time, in the event that the Navigator was injured during a flight.

He logged, 61 hours, 35 minutes, as a Student Bombardier and 37 hours, 45 minutes, as a Student Navigator.

In total, at Childress, he logged 128 hours, 35 minutes, total student time and completed 425 hours of ground instruction.

In December 1943, Cadet McKenzie completed his training and was awarded his Bombardiers Wings. Rated as a Bombardier-Navigator, he graduated from class 43-17 and was assigned the rank of Flight Officer.

In 1939 at the age of 19, Howard A Hibbler, of Wichita, Kansas, graduated from El Dorado High School. He was the stepson of Mr. Wilson Efaw and Mrs. Susie Efaw. He had a younger sister, Ruby, who was also adopted by the Efaws. Their birth father was a native of Australia. In 1940 he was employed by the Boeing Aircraft Company, at their Wichita plant, as a sheet metal worker. At the Wichita plant, PT-17 Stearman training aircraft and sub-assemblies for the B-17 Flying Fortress were constructed.

In November 1941, when Howard was 21, he was eligible to be drafted into military service. On 16 February 1942, he registered for military service and subsequently he was assigned to the Air Corps, as an Enlisted Man. He was assigned to Sheppard Field, in Texas, where he received five months of Basic Training. On 12 January 1943, Howard was assigned to the 11th Photographic Squadron, which was located in Colorado Springs, Colorado.

The squadron trained crews and technicians photographic reconnaissance and mapping.

After successfully completing his training at Colorado Springs, Howard was transferred to the 3rd Air Force Personnel Depot, located at Plant Park, in Florida. He was awarded the wings of an Aerial Gunner.

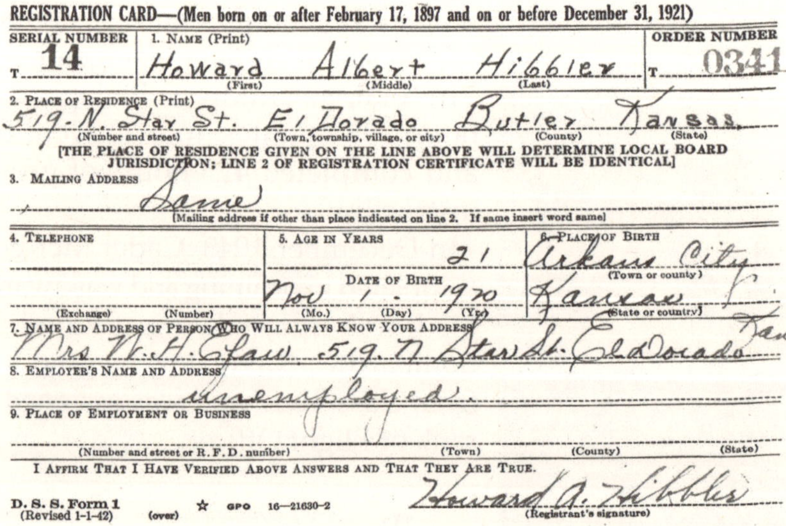

REGISTRATION CARD—(Men born on or after February 17, 1897 and on or before December 31, 1921)

SERIAL NUMBER T 14 | 1. NAME (Print) Howard (First) Albert (Middle) Hibbler (Last) | ORDER NUMBER T 0341

2. PLACE OF RESIDENCE (Print) 519-N. Star St. (Number and street) El Dorado (Town, township, village, or city) Butler (County) Kansas (State)

[THE PLACE OF RESIDENCE GIVEN ON THE LINE ABOVE WILL DETERMINE LOCAL BOARD JURISDICTION; LINE 2 OF REGISTRATION CERTIFICATE WILL BE IDENTICAL]

3. MAILING ADDRESS Same
[Mailing address if other than place indicated on line 2. If same insert word same]

4. TELEPHONE (Exchange) (Number) | 5. AGE IN YEARS 21 DATE OF BIRTH Nov (Mo.) 1 (Day) 1920 (Yr.) | 6. PLACE OF BIRTH Arkansas City (Town or county) Kansas (State or country)

7. NAME AND ADDRESS OF PERSON WHO WILL ALWAYS KNOW YOUR ADDRESS Mrs W. H. Efaw 519 N Star St. El Dorado Kansas.

8. EMPLOYER'S NAME AND ADDRESS unemployed.

9. PLACE OF EMPLOYMENT OR BUSINESS
(Number and street or R. F. D. number) (Town) (County) (State)

I AFFIRM THAT I HAVE VERIFIED ABOVE ANSWERS AND THAT THEY ARE TRUE.

D. S. S. Form 1 (Revised 1-1-42) (over) ☆ GPO 16—21630-2

Howard A. Hibbler
(Registrant's signature)

Lawrence R. McGrane, was born in New York and resided in New Rochelle, with his mother Mae, in 1940. He was employed, by White Cross Laboratories and had also worked as an automobile mechanic.

He enlisted in the New-York National Guard as an Enlisted Man, on 23 September 1940 and was assigned to the 105th Field Artillery Medical Detachment. He was stationed at Fort Mclellan, in Alabama, where he received his Basic Training, before being stationed in the Hawaiian Islands for 18 months.

Subsequently, he transferred to the Air Corps and began his Advanced Flexible Gunnery Training. His training included familiarisation with the duties of the Radio Operator, in the event the Radio Operator was injured. Upon completion of his training, he received the wings of an Aerial Gunner.

[redacted]

McGrane, Lawrence R. — 2/29/20
(Last name) (Other names) — (Date of Birth)

3706 Dyer Ave., N. Y. C. — N. Y. C.
(Home address) — (Place of Birth)

(Change of address)

20215468

(Change of address)

Med. Det. 105th F. A.	3	9/23/40
(Enlisted in)	(No. Yrs.)	(Date enlistment)
A-US (GO 36 AGO,NY) 15 OCT 40		
(How separated from active service)		(Date separation)
Died 1 Jun 44.		
(Reenlisted in)	(No. Yrs.)	(Date re-enl.)
(How separated from active service)		(Date separation)
(Reenlisted in)	(No. Yrs.)	(Date re-enl.)
(How separated from active service)		(Date separation)
(United States service)		(Continue on back)

Form AGO-PB-E-1. 7-9-37-100,000 (1B-214)

Edward Ewing McGill, a native of Nashville, Tennessee, was born on 14 December 1915, to Robert and Della McGill. His fathers parents were of English heritage, having both been born in England.
Known to his friends as Buck, he attended East Nashville High School and Austin Peay State College were he excelled in Football. Upon graduating from high school in 1939, he was employed as a baker in the cake department of a local bakery. Changing profession,

he was employed as a shipping clerk at the Graham Paper Company.

With the outbreak of war in Europe and the US a neutral entity, Edward went to Canada and enlisted in the Royal Canadian Air Force. He completed a number of operational combat missions with the RCAF and transferred to the US Army Air Forces in December 1942.

He was assigned to the 427th Bombardment Squadron, of the 303rd

ALEXANDER C. STRICKLAND CREW - 427th BS Stric-Nine B-17 #42-5392 (427BS) GN-X, Crew assigned 427BS: 20 Mar 1943. Staff Sergeant McGill is kneeling, centre, holding a small dog.

Bombardment Group, Eighth Air Force. The 303rd was a heavy bombardment unit who were based at AAF Station 107, Molesworth, England. They flew the B-17 Flying Fortress type aircraft and were known as the infamous "Hells Angels". As a Staff Sergeant, he completed 28 missions, 27 of which, were with the Alexander C. Strickland crew. On the nose of their B-17, the name *"Stric-nine"* was applied as nose-art.

The following, are details of one of Edwards operational combat missions with the 303rd;

303rd BG (H)
Combat Mission No. 66
3 September 1943
Target: German A/F Aircraft Repair Depot, Romilly-Sur-Seine, France
Crews Dispatched: 19
Length of Mission: 5 hours, 25 minutes
Bomb Load: 12 x 500 lb H.E. M-43 G.P. bombs
Bombing Altitude: 22,000 ft
Ammo Fired: 15,056 rounds
Enemy Aircraft Claims: 1 Destroyed

Major Walter K. Shayler, 360BS Commanding Officer again flew on the mission as co-pilot in Capt. Stalling's 360BS #42-5854 Alley Oop. Four aircraft were abortive: #41-24587Bad Check 427BS (Hullar) - supercharger failed. #42-5221 Son 427BS (Cardwell) - No. 3 engine failed. #42-5257 Miss Bea Haven 359BS (Brown) and #42-5434 Lady Luck 360BS (Cogswell) - Waist gunners became ill. Major Kirk R. Mitchell proceeded to the target with his 15 remaining B-17s and dropped 45 tons of M-43 500-lb. bombs on the target from 22,000 ft. Weather was fair with two to five miles visibility and 8/10 to 9/10 cloud cover over the target. The bombardier 1Lt. Jack B. Fawcett had a good bomb run. He reported, "I saw the target all right and set my sight on it. Just as I was to release our bombs, a cloud rolled right under us and I dropped the bombs right through the middle of it. I had plenty of time to aim however, so there wasn't any reason why we shouldn't have hit." Maj. Mitchell commented, "The mission was only fair. We went in with P-47s all the way and nothing bothered us much. We had a three-minute bomb run." P-47 Thunderbolts gave perfect escort all the way to the target and on the return. Crews expressed admiration for the fighter cover and claimed that they saved a lot of casualties. S/Sgt. Kenneth W. Hull on The Duchess claimed one FW-190 destroyed. Several aircrews finished their operational tours: Capt. Alexander Strickland, pilot of Winning Run stated, "There was nothing to it. A good way to finish up." 1Lt. Joe Bradbury, pilot of Thumper Again added, "I've had it. But it wasn't too bad. Flak was accurate but we didn't get hit. A few fighters attacked us but didn't hurt us. Those

P-47's really saved the day." T/Sgt. Arnold Doran, top turret gunner on The '8' Ball MK II said, "It was a good trip but I kind of wondered about making it back when I saw all those fighters come after us before we hit the coast. But they peeled off and went after the Group behind us." Mission 066 - 2 S/Sgt. William Fleming, waist gunner on Winning Run said, "It wasn't too rough and not too easy and the bombing was pretty good. Three fighters that I saw were eager beavers. They came in to about 50 yards but didn't stay around." S/Sgt. Edward McGill, the other waist gunner on Winning Run added, "It wasn't so bad. A few fighters made a pass at us but the P-47s kept them pretty busy." S/Sgt. Anthony Sherg, tail gunner on Winning Run said, "We had one pretty vicious attack but they looked like they were more scared than I was."

Upon completion of his missions, S.Sgt. McGill was awarded the Distinguished Flying Cross and received three oak leaf clusters.

In Europe, the DFC, was awarded to some crews, for their performance throughout a tour of duty. An Oak Leaf Cluster, was commonly placed on military awards and decorations, to denote those who have received more than one bestowal of a particular decoration.

In early 1944, S.Sgt. McGill returned to the US on a four month furlough to spend time with his family, before being assigned to a Replacement Training Unit, to train newly formed aircrews that were ready to depart for Europe.

Edward McGill Awarded D. F. C.

Staff-Sgt. Edward E. McGill, 26, son of Mrs. Della McGill, 804 Boscobel Street, has been awarded the Distinguished Flying Cross, it was announced yesterday by the War Department.

McGill is stationed in England and has taken part in many raids over enemy territory as a crew member of the Flying Fortress, "Vicious Virgin." In a raid August 27 over Northern France, the Fortress was hit squarely by an anti-aircraft shell, but managed to make its base safely without the loss of a man.

McGill was formerly a member of the Royal Canadian Air Rorce and was transferred to the U. S. Army Air Forces last December. He has received three oak leaf clusters.

Lawrence E. Dundon, was born on 12 June 1912, in Louisville, Kentucky. His father Lawrence Sr., was a Policeman and his mother Daisy, was a homemaker. He had two half brothers, Russell and Hollie Hough.

He attended Western Junior High School in Louisville, graduating in 1930.

In the years that followed, he gained employment as an apprentice, with the Western Recorder, a local Newspaper, where he trained as a lithographer-printer. At the Western Recorder, Lawrence met and began dating Miss Ruth Taylor, in the fall of 1933. In 1934, Larry, as he was known to his friends and family, took Ruth to her prom as her date, in July. He gave her a wristwatch, as a graduation gift.

Ruth and Larry, during the 1930's.

Larry and Ruth on their wedding day.

On 21 October 1939, Ruth and Larry were married at the Baptist Tabernacle, which was located at 26th and Market Street. Helen King, was the maid of honour and Larry's brother Hollie, was his best man. They spent their honeymoon in Lexington and upon their return, they made their first home in an apartment, at 2547 West Market Street.

On 16 October 1940, Larry was registered as a draftee, for future military service.

In the spring of 1941, Larry and Ruth drew up plans and constructed their own home, at 219 North 33rd Street and moved in on Ruth's birthday, 19 November 1941. A particular feature of the house that Larry wanted, was a wooden staircase. Now new homeowners, the couple constructed a picket fence around the house and erected storm windows, in Spring, the following year.

In 1942, Larry was inducted into military service and subsequently he was assigned to the Air Corps. In January 1943, he departed on a troop train for Miami Beach, Florida, where he conducted his Basic Training with the 933 TSS. After Basic, in June, he was transferred to the 811 TSS, located in Chicago. Their headquarters were located in the Stevens Hotel, which was right in front of Lake Michigan. Most of their training and manoeuvres were conducted in Grant Park, which was just across the street.

Ruth visited Larry over several weekends during his training in Chicago and stayed at the YMCA, who had made lodging available to soldiers wives on the top three floors of the building. From here, Ruth and the other men's wives watched their husbands marching down the street as they proudly sang marching songs, with their eyes focussed straight ahead.

From Chicago, Larry was transferred to Sioux Falls, South Dakota, before transferring once again to the 1027th F.G. Training Squadron, in Laredo, Florida, for Aerial Gunnery Training. In early 1944, Larry was awarded his Radio Operator-Aerial Gunners wings. He would soon begin his advanced training on the B-17 Flying Fortress, as part of a crew that would soon be ready to head overseas to take the fight to Europe.

Ruth and Pvt. Dundon, during his early days of training, presumably in Chicago.

Corporal Dundon, proudly wears his wings on his class-a uniform.

Larry's graduation photograph at Sioux Falls. He is wearing his class-a uniform.

Corporal Dundon and Ruth, Larry is wearing the type M-41 field jacket, which was a popular jacket that could be worn all year round by enlisted men and officers alike.

Wilbur D. Brewer, was born in DeWitt County, Illinois. He was one of six siblings who were all brothers, Amos, Alden, Charles, Floyd and Roger. They lived with their parents, Charles and Verna, at 316 Maple Street, Wapella, just outside the town of Clinton, in Illinois. Charles worked as a Conductor for the Illinois Central Railroad.

Wilbur, attended Clinton Community High School in 1937 and would later transfer to Wapella High School, where he excelled in athletics. He graduated, in the class of 1940.

In the months that followed leaving school, he was employed by the P.H. MaGirl Foundry and Furnace Works, as a Stenographer.

On 28 October 1942, he enlisted in the Air Corps and subsequently began his Basic Training in November, at Sheppard Field, Texas. At this time, he was dating Eileen Burns, who also attended Wapella High School. In April the following year, Wilbur and Eileen were married in California, where he was stationed in Inglewood, with North American Aviation. Shortly thereafter he completed his Basic Training. On 8 May 1943, Corporal Brewer transferred to a base in Kansas City, for Flight Engineer Training. To celebrate his graduation from Basic, Wilbur's wife Eileen, his mother, father, three brothers and one of their wives, decided to drive up to Fort Riley in Kansas City for the weekend to see him. They left Clinton at 2am on Saturday. Early Monday morning, on their way home, in heavy rain, another motorist who was driving a truck, overtook another vehicle, on their side of the road. To avoid a head-on collision, the Brewers swerved off the road and crashed into a telegraph pole. Wilbur's wife Eileen and his mother and father, tragically, were killed in the accident. His three brothers and sister-in-law were severely injured. They were rushed to Research Hospital.

Eileen Burns, Corp. Brewer Are Married

Wapella Couple Wedded Saturday In California

Miss Eileen Burns of 607 East Washington street, daughter of Mrs. Elsie Peters of Wapella, became the bride of Corp. Wilbur D. Brewer, son of Mrs. Verna Brewer, Wapella, on Saturday. The ceremony was performed by Judge Frank Parents of Inglewood, Calif.

The couple was attended by Miss Mariam Builta of Bloomington and Corp. Robert Beard of Inglewood. The bride wore a gold jersey suit with black accessories and a corsage of white orchids. Miss Builta wore a brown wool suit with beige accessories and a corsage of white gardenias.

Corp. Brewer is attending school at the North American aviation plant in Inglewood. Mrs. Brewer is employed at the State Farm insurance companies, where she will remain for the present.

The crash occurred near Oak Grove, on US Highway no. 40. There were conflicting reports surrounding the circumstances of the crash, some news reports stated that the cause of the accident was due to a head on collision with the truck.

After the accident, his brothers and sister-in-law were discharged from hospital and made their way back to Clinton, to a home that would never be the same again. Poor Wilbur, was devastated, in the blink of an eye, he had lost half of his family. He and Eileen had been married just two weeks when the tragedy occurred.

Wife, Parents of Pvt. Wilbur Brewer Killed After Visiting Camp

Clinton, Ill., May 21—(AP)—Triple funeral services were held today for C. C. Brewer, 56, Illinois Central railroad conductor, his wife, Mrs. Verna Brewer, 55, and their daughter-in-law, Mrs. Wilbur Brewer, 19, a bride of three weeks.

They were killed in an automobile-truck accident Monday near Kansas City when returning to Clinton from Ft. Riley, Kans., where they had visited Private Wilbur Brewer.

On 21 May, a triple funeral service took place in Clinton. Eileen was laid to rest at Memorial Park Cemetery, which was located on the outskirts of Clinton. His parents, were laid to rest at Woodlawn Cemetery. The two cemeteries shared the same plot of land.

On 30 June, Wilbur was transferred to Love Field, Texas and later, Harlingen Army Airfield, in Texas, where he would begin Aerial Gunnery Training.

In August he returned to Clinton on a 10 day furlough, which he spent with his brothers, Charles and Amos.

He was promoted to the rank of Sergeant, in November.

During January, Wilbur completed his Aerial Gunnery Training and returned home to Clinton, were he spent time with his brothers, on furlough. Through the hardships he had encountered in his young life, Wilbur had completed his training and he was now ready to begin his advanced training as part of an aircrew. He would soon be ready to head off to war.

Robert Lee Graves Jr. was born in Arkansas, on 28 August 1917. He lived in El Dorado, Arkansas, with his mother Maggie and Father Robert Sr. on the family farm.

On 26 March 1938, he was married to Ola Landom. In June, Ola gave birth to a boy, who they called Billie J. Graves. Within a matter of months the marriage unfortunately failed and they subsequently divorced. Robert, was granted custody of their son and they continued to live on the family farm with his parents.

On 11 November 1942, Robert enlisted for military service and subsequently reported to Camp Robinson in Arkansas, for Basic Training. Upon completion of Basic, Robert was assigned to the Air Corps.

He was stationed in Florida, California, Colorado and Nevada, where he received his Aerial Gunnery Training and basic Bombardier training.

In February 1944, Robert was awarded his Aerial Gunners Wings and he was now ready like the rest of the men, to come together for advanced training as an aircrew.

Chapter Four

Advanced Training

In February 1944, the men were assigned to a Replacement Training Unit *RTU* which was located at MacDill Field in Florida. They were assigned to the 488th Bombardment Group, 3rd Air Force.

Subsequently, combat crews consisting of ten men were formed from the pool of newly qualified trainees. They were to receive advanced training and work as a combat crew in the B-17 Flying Fortress type aircraft. The "Brooks" crew consisted of Lester, as Airplane Commander, Jeremiah - Co-Pilot, Joseph - Navigator, Leighton - Bombardier, Lawrence Dundon - Radio Operator, Wilbur - Flight Engineer-Top Turret Gunner, Howard & Edward - Aerial Gunners, Lawrence McGrane - Ball Turret Gunner and Robert as the Tail Gunner.

As the weeks progressed the men became a tightly knit aircrew and had become proficient in their jobs.

The duration of the flying training at MacDill consisted of 120 flying training hours for each combat crew, over a period of 10 weeks, or 70 days in total.

Larry's wife Ruth, did not know that their posting at MacDill would be their last, before heading overseas. She went down to spend two weeks with Larry and ended up staying three months.

Gennie, Lester's wife, got to know all of the crew very well and she was looked upon by them as a mother figure.

488TH BOMBARDMENT GROUP (H)

DAILY SCHEDULE

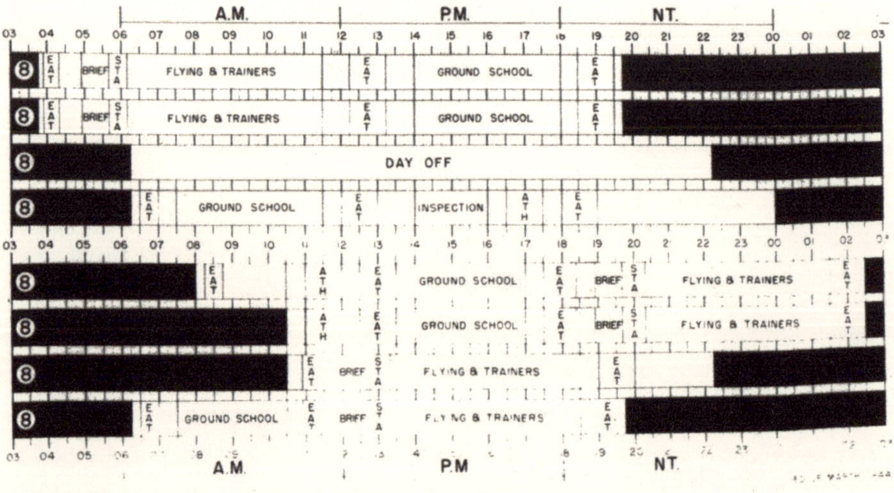

THE 488TH
BOMB BURST
VOL. 1, NO. 1 MACDILL FIELD, FLORIDA THURSDAY, MARCH 16, 1944

Published Exclusively in the Interests of the Personnel of the 488th Bombardment Group (H) MacDill Field, Florida

LT. COL. MARTIN NEW GROUP C. O.

Lt. Col. Watson Spent Year In the Aleutians On Temporary Duty

Lt. Col. Ansley Watson, former 31-year-old Commanding Officer of the 488th Bombardment Group, is a regular guy who has earned the respect and admiration of every man in the Group.

An amazingly accurate memory enables him to work with the aggressiveness and efficiency of a city editor. He knew the 488th inside and out and, of more importance, he has the best interests of the men at heart.

Col. Watson was born and raised in Anderson, S. C., and graduated from Boys' High School there in 1929. Four years later, when the depression had hit a new low, he received his degree from Davidson College, in Davidson, N. C.

From there he took a course in aeronautics at the famed Massachusetts Institute of Technology and then spent several months in South America in experimental and research work. He returned to the States in the spring of 1935 and was employed by Jefferson Medical College and the United Air Lines in New York City before he decided to enter the service.

In June of 1936 he began his training as a flying cadet at Randolph and Kelley Fields and received his commission and wings as a pursuit pilot a year later.

His first assignment was at Langley Field, Va., with the 36th Pursuit Squadron, and he remained with that outfit until January, 1938, when he went to work as first officer for the United Air Lines, with a regular run between San Francisco and San Diego.

Seven months later, he took an examination for a regular commission and received it on Oct. 1. He was ordered back to duty with the 32nd Bomb Squadron (H) at March Field, Cal., and remained with the 19th Bombardment Squadron (Queens Die Proudly) until June of the following year.

His next assignment took him to New Orleans, with the 30th Bomb Group, 21st Bomb Squadron, and six months later he was assigned to a B-24 Group stationed at Muroc Lake, Cal., with long open moter patrol duty along the west coast.

Shortly after the Japs struck at Pearl Harbor, Col. Watson was transferred back to March Field and then went on detached service with the Navy in the Pacific. When the Japs invaded the Aleutians, his squadron was sent there on temporary duty and remained there until June of last year. The outfit was sent out on several combat missions during that

(Continued on Page 3)

Bomb Burst Will Publish Bi-Weekly

The BOMB BURST is to be published exclusively for the personnel of the 488th Bombardment Group and devoted primarily to military interests.

This first issue was published with limited facilities and it is the desire of the Special Service Office to soon increase the paper to eight pages. It will be distributed every other Thursday.

Opinions expressed in this newspaper are those of the individual writers and under no circumstances are they to be considered those of the United States Army. A majority of the stories will be initialed.

It's your newspaper and each member of the 488th is urged to cooperate in making it the best possible.

At Long Last . . . Real Live Ghosts!

We stopped in at the Base theater Monday night to see the movie thriller, "The Uninvited." We want to take this opportunity to throw a bouquet toward Paramount for finally producing ghosts that were really ghosts—and not the usual fictional ghosts that turn out to be an unsuspecting butler, lovable caretaker or a conveniently mad scientist. The fact that we don't believe in them didn't prevent our temperatures from dipping below normal at the proper moments.

818th Proves Best At Retreat Parade

The 818th Squadron was awarded the "E" banner following last Friday's Retreat Parade on the MacDill Parade Ground. The 841st was runner-up.

The "E" banner is awarded to the squadron which shows up best in attendance, response to commands, appearance, military bearing, distance, intervals and alignment by flights when they are marching past the reviewing stand.

Lt. Col. Watson

'Pistol Packing Mama' Crew Sad When World's Record Holds Up Only Two Days

Members of the crew of "Pistol Packin' Mama," current pride of the 843rd Bomb Squadron, are wearing long faces these days—and with good reason.

Last week, the steady, unheralded "Pistol Packin' Mama" was landed after establishing a world's record for B-17s. She flew a toal of 975 hours and 40 minutes without changing any of her original four engines.

Two days later, word was received that "Good Conduct," a Flying Fortress at Hendricks Field, Sebring, reached 1,000 hours to break "Pistol Packin' Mama's record by a comfortable margin.

Capt. John C. Thrift, Commanding Officer of the 843rd; Lt. Nelson D. Koplin, engineering officer and the crew all agreed that their Fortress could have gone another 200 hours with ease. Crew chief S/Sgt. J. T. Jones stated that "she wasn't even puffin' after 975, and if she could have received an extension, she'd still be flying her original engines."

When "Mama" had completed her 975 hours, Wright Field refused to extend any more time, so the crew took her in for a bath and engine change. The time represents more than 40 days of round-the-clock flying.

The B-17 arrived here from Wendover Field, Utah, on Dec. 31 of last year, with a total of 545 hours and 20 minutes under her belt. She became one of the regular training ships, shooting landings and going cross-country —many times with student officers at the controls.

"Mama" 'went through the usual maintenance routine — a change of oil every 100 hours after 650 had been completed, the necessary precautionary checks, and particular attention was given to the flexible hose. The ship was never in trouble.

The rest of the crew includes Sgts. R. Hayward and K. T. Brown; Cpls. M. J. Maroney, C. H Hallobough, L Mann, F. E Gaudio and R. Gluckman; Pfc. J. Katz and Pfc. M. Sande.
—R. J. W.

Succeeds Lt. Col. Watson, Who Moves To Avon Park

Lt. Col. Robert K. Martin, former Provisional Group Commander of the 88th Bombardment Group at Avon Park, is the new Commanding Officer of the 488th, having assumed his duties Tuesday. He succeeds Lt. Col. Ansley Watson, who has been assigned to the same Group at Avon Park.

Lt. Col. Martin, who is 33 years of age, is a native of Dayton, Ohio. He is a graduate of Butler High School there and received his degree from the University of Dayton in 1933, having majored in Mechanical Engineering.

He received his commission and wings on June 23, 1934, after training at Randolph and Kelly Fields.

On Oct. 10, 1935, he was sent to Hawaii and remained on duty there until December 12, 1937, when he returned to the States.

Exhibit # 27

Soldier Deserves An 'A' for Trying

Red Cross workers come across many humorous stories in their particular type of work, but this one tops 'em all as far as we're converned. It was told by Mr. Ray Ellis, who is now with the 397th Bombardment Group, which was originally activated here at MacDill Field.

One day, back in early 1943, when Mr. Ellis was stationed out in Texas, a forlorn looking Negro soldier came into his office.

"Sir," he stated, "I've just received a wire that my father is dead and my Commanding Officer said that I'd have to get permission from you to get an emergency furlough."

Mr. Ellis was very sympathetic and explanied that he would check with the Red Cross office in the soldier's home town and would notify his squadron when the connection was made.

So Mr. Ellis sent out a wire for confirmation and the reply came back in les than two hours:

"Pvt. M ——'s father is dead all right—and has been for the past five years." — R. J. W.

WE DON'T GET IT

Riding Enthusiasts— Although they are dressed for a formal evening, Mr. and Mrs. Sherwin Trent, 425 South Drive, Miami Springs, are often seen in riding clothes as they are equestrian enthusiasts. They have their own horse.—(Picture cutline in the Miami Daily News.)

Ed. Note: The cutline writer must sell oats!

The 488th BOMBBURST

Official Publication of the 488th Bombardment Group (H)
MacDill Field, Florida.

BOMB BURST STAFF

Commanding Officer .... Lt. Col. Robert K. Martin
Officer in Charge .... Lt. Robert J. Wood
Editorial .... Cpl. Irving Levine
Artist .... Pvt. Allan P. Lewis
Photographer .... Cpl. J. E. Hornstein

Printed by The Commercial Printers.

IS IT WORTH IT?

The Army proudly announced last week that during 1943 only 27 out of every 1,000 men caught a venereal disease—the lowest infection rate ever recorded. The 1942 rate was 40.5.

Despite this impressive figure and the miraculous sulpha drugs which science has placed at the Army's disposal, venereal disease rates can be reduced even more, and the goal for the 488th is a large "goose egg."

The soldier who goes out carelessly and contracts a venereal disease is of no value to the Army, but a decided handicap. His treatments are taking up the time of doctors and nurses who might be free to handle more worthy cases.

If a soldier would only stop to consider the serious consequences and heartache which might result from a venereal disease — the blindness, paralysis, insanity, heart disease, locomotion and other infections which may ruin his life, as well as others—he would be a little more careful when he stepped out.

Few soldiers get into much trouble when they're sober. They can think clearly and they know what they're doing. But the man who goes out and doesn't know when he's had enough to drink—keeps pouring it down until he loses his senses, is only sticking his own chin out. He isn't capable of taking care of himself and leaves himself wide open for trouble.

When a member of a bomber crew—whether he's a pilot or navigator or bombardier or gunner—contracts a venereal disease, he is grounded while taking curative sulpha drugs. During this medication, his reactions can't be trusted. This means the loss of a man in a highly trained bomber crew—and readjustments and replacements have to be made. Things like that put a heavy-footed brake on the war effort.

A great nation-wide drive on venereal disease is planned this year, and 50 of the largest and hardest-hit cities are ready to start campaigns. But to make it really effective, they need the full cooperation of every man and woman in the armed services.

So you can be doing yourself and the Army a favor by using your head. The war isn't going to last forever and it won't be too long before you'll be returning to your families and friends. Don't have the fear of a recurring venereal disease on your mind when that day comes.—R. J. W.

FALSE TEETH NEED OWNER

Laundry Workers Find Choppers of Unhappy Officer

Somewhere in these United States and perhaps right here on MacDill Field, an officer is having difficulty with his steaks and pork chops (if he's able to get any).

Because on February 25th last he inadvertently walked out of the post laundry without his false teeth (see cut) and the choppers have been hanging there ever since—waiting to be identified. A dentist estimated the teeth are worth approximately $100.

So if you happen to see an officer who looks a bit disgruntled over a bowl of soup, you might show him the picture. (Personnel working in the laundry also want it known that there is no extra charge for cleaning the teeth.)

Also among the articles left in the laundry is a little note book containing the names, addresses and phone numbers of more than 30 gals in practically every section of the United States. (Only a member of the Air Forces could accumulate such a tempting list.)

The original owner of the book might be even more miserable than the missing owner of the false teeth—'cause several officers have been bringing their own pencils and note books to the laundry.

Laundry workers have also found dog tags, receipts of all kinds and a baby sock—the last article was placed in a captain's return laundry and he sent it back with a curt note: "What kind of soap do you use over there?"—R. J. W.

In Syracuse, N. Y., George Scott received court permission to change his name to Wojciech Kuc . . . which is even stranger than the story about Joe Stink, who wanted to change his name to Mike Stink.

NEWS Significance

BATTLE OF THE PACIFIC: For 19 bloody months Rabaul has been the main objective of Gen. Douglas MacArthur's slow campaign across the eastern end of the New Guinea Peninsula and of the Allies' converging drive up the ladder of the Solomons. Rabaul, one of Japan's greatest (or ex-greatest) naval and air bases, 830 mile south of Truk, may be Gen. MacArthur's next target.

From the time Allied forces occupied Bougainville and brought Rabaulwithin easy bombing range, the Jap-held base has been subjected to an almost daily pounding from the air—it was hit by nearly 3,000 tons in February alone. No other Jap base in the Pacific has taken such a beating and even U. S. surface craft have sneaked up to shell it.

Allied fliers have reported that all Jap ships had left and that Jap planes were no longer in the area to cause any trouble. Although the deserted Jap garrison would probably resist to the bitter end—Rabaul appears to be wide open for an amphibious invasion.

LOS NEGROS INVASION: The sudden attack on Los Negros in the Admiralty Islands by U. S. forces moved closer to the mainland of Japan and further isolated some 72,000 Japs—22,000 in the Solomons, 50,000 in New Britain.

When U. S. destroyers moved along broadside to the low-lying coast of Los Negros and broke the silence with five-inch guns, it was inconsistent with the noraml Allied island invasion. This was not a landing on an enemy beach which had been saturated by bombardment—success this time depended up surprise. And the Japs were surprised. When they discovered what was taking place, their resistance was disorganized.

But they were still very troublesome. Wrote Cpl. Bill Alcine, Army correspondent:

"By the faint light of the moon, the Americans watched the Japanese creep toward them from the edge of the air strip. Sometimes the Japs crawled to the very edge of the cavalrymen's foxholes before they were killed. One major told me he was going to sleep in his hammock that night and suggested that I do the same. During the night, however, troops nearby heard a commotion and the major called out: "Don't shoot, boys, it's Major ——!" Nothing more was heard. The next morning they found the major dead, his head nearly severed from his body and with several bayonet wounds."

It was the same kind of warfare which unnerved U. S. troops on New Georgia last July.

BATTLE OF RUSSIA: With Red Army troops battling on the doorsteps of Estonia, Latvia and Poland—and pointing a new drive toward the Rumanian frontier, the weather stepped in, bounced up 40 degrees and the magnificent winter campaign on the Eastern front was nearing its end.

The winter had been highlighted by many a glorious victory for the Reds, but according to Moscow's "Red Star," the objective was not merely to roll the Nazi hordes back—but to destroy them. In that, the campaign of the short winter had failed.

Military men, however, were not so pessimistic. They totaled up the results of the three-monhs offensive and found them very satisfying. In that period the Russians had:

1) Regained rich grain lands; coal, iron, nickel and manganese; millions of working hands for the manpower pool.

2) Killed, wounded or captured hundreds of thousands of Germans, taken vast booty.

3) Captured a dozen major cities and lifted the siege of Leningrad. (Last week freight began to shuttle between Moscow and Leningrad over a direct railway.)

4) Virtually freed the Dnieper.

BATTLE OF ITALY: As the Fifth Army fronts around Cassino and the Nettuno beachhead hung in stalemate last week, a group of U. S. infantrymen fought in streets and buildings in Cassino for 17 nightmarish days and nights . . . as bitter as any in the war.

On the first day, the Americans drove into a northern edge of town. They dug in and soon an order came through: "Tanks will leave, infantry will stay." Then began fierce fighting that was measured by the loss or capture of a single house, or even a single room in a house. Sometimes No-Man's land was only a strip 10 yards wide.

MAIL COMES IN

Finally, on the morning of the seventeenth day, mail came in. Some of the men had been eating, sleeping and fighting in the same room for eight days . . they had just about given up hope for relief by fresh troops. The men were summoned from their houses that had been chewed apart by artillery shells, grabbed their packs and dragged themselves back for a much-deserved rest.

The relief had moved up, but the incredible battle for Cassino continued. Soldiers went on fighting from house to house and room to room.—R. J. W.

Chaplain's CORNER

By CHAPLAIN GRAHAM

Hi Soldier!

Thanks for your attention.

Have you ever stopped to think that you aren't being properly trained for combat? That is, if you aren't giving full attention to your spiritual life.

Your training for physical combat is for a temporal warfare. This soon ends. But the warfare of spirit—right against wrong—is eternal.

The chapels and the chaplains are here to help you train spiritually for the hard times ahead. Make use of them.

Be seeing you in chapel.

842nd Has Good Time Despite Rain

A steady all-day downpour failed to dampen the spirits of members of the 842nd Squadron last Saturday and those who turned out at Sunset Beach in St. Petersburg were enthusiastic in their praise at the way things turned out.

The rain eliminated the sunbathing, softball and swimming, but there was plenty of good dancing, good conversation and not-so-good harmony.

The committee in charge of entertainment arrangements were First Sgt. Travis Gibson, M/Sgt. Jack W. Gardner, M/Sgt. Gillian G. Padgett, Kenneth Thurber, S/Sgt. Boyd Howe, Sgt. Andrew J. Magee, Jr., and Sgt. Charles Floyd.

Extensive Summer Athletic Program Is Being Planned for 488th Group

Plans are now underway to provide the 488th Bombardment Group with one of the most extensive summer athletic programs in the entire Third Air Force — including softball, base ball, tennis, golf, volleyball and a sprinkling of table tennis and pocket billiards thrown in. The program will be on an inter-squadron basis.

There will be three softball and volleyball leagues—both on the same order. Three leagues are to be formed in both sports, one for the permanent party officers, one for the permanent party enlisted men and one for the combat crewmen. The two circuits are expected to start during the first week of April.

Each squadron and group headquarters will be represented in the permanent personnel leagues, while the BC detachment will be made up of five teams.

SPLIT SCHEDULE

Present plans call for a split schedule, with the first half winding up in June and the second half in September. The winners of each half will meet in a best-of-seven series for the 488th championships—and there will be plenty of prizes for the winners.

One baseball team will be organized to represent the entire group and they will probably be able to play at least once a week. against other MacDill teams.

GOLF TOURNAMENT

Plans are also being discussed to conduct an officers' and an enlisted men's golf tournament at a nearby course, with a qualifying round followed by match play to determine the best in the group. The top five players will represent the group as a team.

And the same in tennis. An elimination tournament will be conducted and the eight men who reach the quarter-finals will represent the group against other teams.

In table tennis and pocket billiards, each squadron will conduct its own eliminations and the winners will meet for the group championships

Lt. Earle W. Brown, physical training officer, will appoint an athletic director for each squadron and headquarters, but it will be up to the personnel of each outfit to cooperate.

With a little effort on each man's part, the program can be successful and interesting without the usual drawbacks.—R. J. W.

818th and 843rd Seek Base Basketball Title

By Cpl. Irv Levine

Two members of the 488th Bombardment Group, the 818th and 843rd basketball teams, will be seeking their second consecutive victories over the 962nd Signal Company and the Base Hospital, respectively tonight when they clash in a double bill at base gymnasium No. 1. The first encounter will start at 1930.

A victory for the two group teams will clinch the second round titles for the two base leagues—the 818th in the "B" circuit and the 843rd in the "A" loop. By winning, they will be eligible for the play-offs which will decide the base-wide basketball championship of MacDill.

In Monday night's action, the 818th staved off a fourth-period rally by the 952nd to eke out a [illegible] victory, while the 843rd outscored the Base Hospital quintet, 31-25.

The 818th got off to a fast start and at the half had piled up a 16-6 lead, but the scrappy team found the range in the fourth quarter and started chopping down the lead . . . falling three points short as the final whistle blew.

S/Sgt. Tom Swift and Pvt. Walter Roberts, former Holy Cross College athlete, set the scoring pace for the winners, each tallying eight points.

In the nightcap the Base Hospital jumped off to a quick 6-0 start in the opening moments of play only to see their lead evaporate as the 843rd moved into furious action. Coming from behind in the second quarter, the 843rd took their second triumph in three games from the losers.

Lt. John Harvey and Cpl. Jim Kirchner accounted for 19 of the winning points between them, while giant center Wehurst dumped in 11 for the losing cause.

843rd (31)	G	F	P
Harvey	5	0	10
Thrift	1	0	2
Anderson	0	1	1
Berien	0	0	0
Lorenz	2	1	5
Bograkos	1	2	4
Nolan	0	0	0
Kirchner	3	3	9
Green	0	0	0
Totals	12	7	31

Hospital (25)	G	F	P
Snyder	1	0	2
Thompson	0	0	0
Cooper	0	1	1
Newhouse	0	1	1
Wehurst	4	3	11
Stromdahl	2	0	4
Manderfield	1	0	2
Vaughan	2	0	4
Totals	10	5	25

Score at halftime: 843rd, 17; Base Hospital, 13.

818th (28)	G	F	P
Roberts	4	0	8
Kozakiewiecz	1	0	2
Tuttle	2	0	4
Swift	4	0	8
Quinn	1	0	2
Jenkins	1	0	2
Henry	1	0	2
Harter	0	0	0
Totals	14	0	28

952nd (25)	G	F	P
Cowan	[illegible]	[illegible]	[illegible]
Boga	2	0	4
Ingram	1	0	2
Beiner	1	1	3
Mishler	2	0	4
Tillery	0	0	0
Corchera	0	0	0
Totals	12	1	25

Score at halftime: 818th, 15; 952nd, 6.

488th Quiz...

This is the first quiz in a regular series that will be published with each edition of the BOMBURST. For each correct answer, five points will be given and the 15 members of the 488th who collect the highest number of points will be awarded prizes in the way of theater tickets and cigarettes

All answers may be turned in to the squadron mail room or Group Special Service Office, Bldg. T-236. Winners' names and answers will be published in the next edition. Deadline for answers is 1800, Friday, 17 March.

1. Which one of the following names is out of place in the group? 1) Sam Snead, 2) Byron Nelson, 3) Fred Perry, 4) Horton Smith.

2. Which one of the following names is out of place in this group? 1) Stan Hack, 2) Pete Reiser, 3) George Gipp, 4) Joe Gordon.

3. What former heavyweight boxing champion was incorrectly reported killed in action on the island of Crete?

4. Who made the following statement and to what organization was he referring: "Never before in military conflict have so many owed so much to so few."

5. Who is commander of the Allied Air Forces in the Southwest Pacific?

6. What was the Kellogg-Briand Pact designed to do?

7. What Army Air Forces plane, which has an excellent record in combat was formerly referred to by some as the "Incredible Prostitute?" And what does the expression mean.

8. What city in Russia marked the deepest penetration of the German army?

9. Who was commanding general of the British First Army in the North African campaign?

10. How many Britons are reported to have been killed as the result of Nazi bombs over England?

Nine Boxers From 488th In Tourney

Nine members of the group are among those battling in the MacDill Field Golden Gloves and Base Championship tournament at gymnasium No. 1.

Leading the 488th contenders is Sgt. Lou Lazzera (Lou Dundee), BC Detachment, who opposes Pvt. Joey Smithers, of the Base Detachment, in the final bout for the middleweight title of the Third Air Force tonight.

Two other BC soldiers, Cpl. Frank Falvey and Sgt. Wendell Wilkinson, are rated strong contenders for the welterweight championship.

KNOW YOUR OUTFIT

The 488th Bombardment Group (H) was activated at Geiger Field, Washington, October 7, 1943, and moved to MacDill Field early in November.

A list of the group and squadron commanding officers and first sergeants is listed:

Group

Commanding Officer: Lt. Col. Robert K. Martin; Deputy Commander: Major James H. Thompson; Executive Officer: Lt. Col. Rudolph B. Robeck; Adjutant: First Lt. Richard P. Skelton; Sergeant Major: Tech. Sgt. Harvey Hale.

818

Commanding Officer: Capt. Arnold T. Phillips; Executive Officer: Major Charles H. Harper; Adjutant: Second Lt. Willard E. Wentz; Firs tSergeant: Martin P. Howard.

841

Commanding Officer: Major Wilson Moore; Executive Officer: Major Adrian P. Downing; Adjutant: First Lt. John S. Farrington; First Sergeant: Tech. Sgt. Max W. Carman.

842

Commanding Officer: Major Raleigh A. Shoemaker; Adjutant: Second Lt. John S. Thomas; First Sergeant: Travis J. Gibson.

843

Commanding Officer: Capt. John C. Thrift; Executive Officer: Major Harry B. Wright; Adjutant: Second Lt. James R. Bailey; First Sergeant: Arch H. Scruggs.

BC

Commanding Officer: Lt. Col. William L. Koob; Executive Officer: Capt. William L. Ball; Adjutant: First Lt. James A. Nolan; First Sergeant: Fred H. Linder.

Lt. Col. Watson

(Continued from Page 1)

time and they aided in the preparations for the invasion of American troops on Attu and Kiska.

Col. Watson returned to March Field and joined the 383rd Bomb Group as Deputy Commanding Officer. Three months later, he was sent on special duty as commanding officer of the 398th and came to the 488th in October. He was Deputy Executive under Col. Gerry Mason and assumed the duties of commanding officer when the latter went overseas.

Col. Watson was married in December, 1938, but a tragic airplane accident in October of last year cost Mrs. Watson her life. He has no children. — R. J. W.

Good Story

There was a young lady named
Hall,
Who wore a newspaper dress to
a ball;
Her costume caught fire—
Burned out her entire
Front page, sports section and all!

PVT. RAJAH

818 HQ 841 COLUMN WRITE! 842 843

Cpl. Jackson Now Experimenting With Mental Telepathy

By Sgt. John Russo

My experience with newspapers has been practically nil . . . sure, I worked for one once, but I'll have to admit that it wasn't exactly on the editorial end of it. It was more on the distribution line—to be frankly explicit, I did have one of the best corners to sell my papers in the whole city of Boston, exclusive of Scollay Square and the Boston Common, but I don't suppose any of you fellows are familiar with that part of the "Old Beantown." In any event, I shall make a gallant attempt to keep you all (that's the southern influence on me) informed on what "makes" with the boys from Group Headquarters.

The Red Cross is really missing out on a good bet unbeknownst to them. Maybe we should tip them off that we have an unlimited supply of pure grade A fighting blood (with red corpuscles too) going to waste daily. Yep, the local blood bank should declare a dividend and their troubles would be over, for their stock would be amply replenished every 24 hours. Come to think of it, "Little" MacArthur, you don't shave more than once a day, do you? Mac, alias T.W.O. (Teenie Weenie Operator) from Operations is a sight to behold as he wields the old chin scraper every morning—should we say, with reckless abandon. Many a patient onlooker (get in line, please) is seen to flinch and turn pale as the red pool widens and swirls around Pee Wee's feet, But not so MacArthur. He doesn't bat the proverbial eyelash as he unconcernedly proceeds about his operation. It is a known fact that new troops are green and inexperienced, regardless of the amount of training they've had, until they've been "blooded" in battle. . . . The boys in Bldg. T-149 have passed the test with flying colors. One was heard to like this.

A beautiful friendship is on the verge of coming to a sad end one of these fine days. (Tampa Chamber of Commerce, please note.) We call them the Smith brothers. They eat together, work together and are the typical inseparables. One sleeps in the lower bunk, the other in the upper . . . both share the same window. Upper wants it open, but Lower insists on having closed for, he claims: "I don't like drafts—I got caught in one not so long ago, and I haven't gotten over it yet."

The Group S-2 office recently moved to Hangar No. 4, into spacious new quarters. How do you get there? That's easy. Just take any bus going in the direction of Drew Field. You can't miss it.

Pfc. Jim Weathers (they call him "Stormy" because of his sunny disposition) tells this one about his pal, Cpl. Jim "Stonewall" Jackson. It seems that Jackson corresponds with one of the other sex, a cute little Wave, stationed approximately 300 miles from here. Our boy, the message center impresario, a student at all times, is now delving into the mysteries of mental telepathy. That accounts for the blank expression on his face every day promptly at 10 o'clock when he goes into his strange interlude trying to contact his honey through space. "So far he hasn't had any luck," confides Weathers, "Personally, I think he's tuning in on the wrong Wave length."

Famous last words: "What DID they have for chow today?"

WINNER REWARDED — Lt. James C. Bynum, Group Special Service Officer, congratulates S/Sgt. Willis VanDyke, 841st Quiz winner. Seated left to right: Lt. John Kretzmer, Chaplain Richard M. Graham, Lt. Robert J. Wood and Lt. Bynum. Standing: S/Sgt. Fred Blanck, Sgt. Quiz; S/Sgt. VanDyke and Sgt. Earl Sacks, of the 818th, runner-up.

S.Sgt. Fowler Has 843rd Guessing--And Girl Too

By Pfc. Paul Rosen

Sound a louder note on the trumpet and beat the drums just a bit stronger, for it's the 843rd Squadron reporting upon its activities.

S/Sgt. George Fowler has all the boys guessing. Will he become engaged, or won't he? Several weeks ago while on detached service at instructors school, he appeared on the "Vox Pop" radio program, receiving for his efforts, a diamond ring, wrist watch and a long distance telephone call to his girl back home. The call was to have cinched the "knot," but until he returns from furlough, his buddies are wondering.

Something new has been added. Pfc. Gerald Michelman is now wearing a "neon" hash stripe. down with the ... and one

The ice has finally been broken, and in Florida, of all places. Sgt. Taylor Babee, the statistical genius of the orderly room, who hadn't quit working for a day or night either finally relented and went to town one evening last week.

Cpl. Irving Fried, his harmonica apparently missing, now entertains at the dayroom each noon with piano solos. Getting back into form is Constantine Jemiola, the man of a million musical instruments, who returned last week from a furlough spent in Chicago.

Pfc. Tom MacArthur still teases Sgt. Burton Jones with that memorable remark, "When is your wife sending you a chocolate cake?"

Jones' answer is still that silent glare.

841st Squadron Is Proud of Its Quiz Champions

By Pfc. Bernard Rosenblatt

The 488th has finally gone to press. The officers and men of the 841st offer their best wishes in this undertaking.

For weeks the men in the orderly room have wondered what was the cause of S/Sgt. John Cooper being slightly bald; after watching F/Sgt. Max W. Carman work on the morning report while Sgt. Cooper is on furlough, we have found the answer. F/Sgt. Carman has been advised to use Kremel before it is too late.

Talking about the 841st being the best, last Saturday morning at the Base theater, Group Special Service had a quiz contest in which two members of each squadron in the 488th participated. Not only did S/Sgt. Willie Van Dyke of our squadron take first place, but four out of five other men of the 841st that went ... them right. We really showed the other squadrons what kind of men we have in the 841st.

COMPLAINT SECTION

The two gripes of the week — The raise in the price of sandwiches in the PX. The empty coke machines in the hangar whenever you want a coke.

A certain corporal in Engineering whose initials are E. G. W. had the colossal nerve to stand up a gal that came from a distant city to see him. Shame on you, Corporal.

Here's one the big wheels cannot answer: Who is the Commanding General of 16th Air Force? Maybe one of you spokes can.

Some fellows say Pvt. Clark wasn't very sober, others say he just didn't see the door, but we know the truth. A mosquito bit him on the chin.

When is S/Sgt. John Lawrenson of the Medics going to get his certificate so that he can get his right size of GI shoes?

All's Fair

Mary had a little lamb,
Whose fleece was white as snow;
Mary passed a butcher shop—
But the lamb went by too slow!

Pacific Veteran of 842nd Is After Softball Position

By Pvt. Lou Loures

These are news and views of the 842nd Squadron compiled by this reporter between physical training sessions. Any resemblance between this and T. C. 87 is purely coincidental.

Pvt. Harold E. Patterson has returned to the orderly room staff after spending a week as a patient at the Base hospital. Glad to see you back, Pat. . . Wedding bells will be ringing soon for Sgt. James Kimbrough. The happy event will take place March 22. Best wishes to you and your bride-to-be from the squadron, Sergeant.

The little "iron" man of the squadron is James E. McRoberts, squadron chef par de excellence. The 842nd lads call him "Shrapnel," due to the various injuries he received in the South Pacific campaign. A veteran of many battles, McRoberts has been awarded the Purple Heart by the War Department. Right now he's concentrating upon fully regaining his health and also is ready to claim a first team berth on the squadron softball team.

The bowling team with M/Sgt. Gillian S. Padgett, Sgt. Sam A. Hambian, Sgt. James E. Ross, Sgt. James M. Bichers, Pfc. F. E. Fredericks, Sgt. Donald G. McKay, has been going great guns in MacDill Field competition In the last match they took over the 843rd Squadron in all three games. Thus far, they have won five of six contests and will soon be leading the league.

Talking of hard workers, Pfc. Carmine Harari, of the orderly room, is attending a course in psychology at Tampa University.

EINSTEIN BAFFLED

Don't feel too badly if you were forced to call in outside help to complete your income tax form. Because none other than the internationally famous Professor Albert Einstein finally gave up and sought the aid of a tax expert.

It has been said that no one will understand the form that's being prepared for next year.

Rumor Mongers Are Wide Awake 24 Hours a Day

By Pvt. Carl Lunstedt

We pile out of our beds and hit the latrine to start a new day. It's too early in the morning to talk about anyhing and most of us are too full of sleep to pay much attention to what is happening.

However, the lads with the rumors are wide awake. They didn't sleep the night before, their time having been spent concocting new wrinkles on the old theme to circulate the following morning.

One says, "Forty WACS are coming into headquarters to take over all desk jobs."

Another states, "No. 60 WACS are joining headquarters to do all the clerical duties."

A third reports, "Three hundred basics are coming here for us to train. We'll show them how and then they'll get our jobs when we ship out to Borneo."

Still another comes up with this, "The 488th is going to be split up into two groups."

Someone disputes this with, "The 488th is going to be split up into several cadres to start new groups at B-29 air bases."

The last one says, "By April 1 we'll all be overseas."

So, the rumors whirl around our brains while we shave, eat, and attempt to do our regular tasks.

Thus, by the time we are ready to hit the sack at night, our thoughts are more than slightly confused and somewhat distorted. So we are kept awake puzzling over the entire situation.

"Let's see," we mutter, half aloud, "Joe's a good guy, he's in the know and he's telling the straight story."

Joe's fanciful rumor we are convinced comes direct from the powers that be and we decide that comes tomorrow morning, we'll wear that new tie and brand new set of khakis to impress the WACS when they arrive at the office.

Yet, while we figure the problem is solved and drift off to dreamland, the boys who make the rumors are lying awake, their minds manufacturing a brand new series to use the next day.

The moral: Youth wil be served, frequently stuffed with bologna!

Medics Delight in 'Giving the Needle'

By S/Sgt. Frederick Blanck

This should be titled "Shot by the Medics," but we've reconsidered and leave the title in public domain.

Answers to our inquiries, when we, the willing workers at the dispensary, ask soldiers about their immunization records.

"I haven't got my record with me, but I don't need any 'shots' anyway."

"I got everything in the place, including yellow jaundice, in 1942."

However, despite the protests they usually get the injections in six delicious flavors.

Our boy, T/Sgt. Bob Runnels seems to be out of his office working in other parts of the dispensary the last few days. What's the matter, too much pressure working in attractive feminine surroundings

Sergeant Hibbler, mans the starboard side waist gun, during a practice mission, in a B-17 Flying Fortress.

Presumably Edward McGill or Robert Graves, mans the same waist gun as Howard Hibbler, during a training mission in a B-17 Flying Fortress.

With bomb-bay doors open, dummy bombs are about to be dropped from the bomb-bay of a B-17 Flying Fortress, during a training mission.

Edward McGill, holds his parachute and poses for a photograph, he is wearing an A-2 leather flying jacket with a yellow Mae West life preserver.

Larry holds the photographers headset, as he is photographed in front of a B-17 during his training at MacDill.

The Brooks crew, presumably at Hunter Field, Georgia, prior to their departure. Standing, are the officers, from left to right; Leighton McKenzie, Joseph Nobilione, Lester Brooks and Jeremiah Murphy. Sitting, are the enlisted men, from left to right; Lawrence Dundon, Howard Hibbler, Robert McGrane, Wilbur Brewer and Edward McGill.

Presumably at Hunter Field, Georgia, prior to their departure, the crew pose for a group photograph in front of a B-17 Flying Fortress. From left to right; Robert Graves, Lawrence Dundon, Leighton McKenzie, Joseph Nobilione, Lester Brooks, Jeremiah Murphy, Wilbur Brewer, Howard Hibbler and Edward McGill.

At MacDill, the crew practiced simulated bombing missions, using practice bombs and would become proficient in formation flying, flying similar distances, as that of, England, to Germany. This would test their endurance, under simulated combat conditions and prepare them for the reality they were soon to encounter. Edward was all too familiar with the reality of flying in combat, having previously completed tours with the USAAF and RCAF. Having a combat veteran on-board would certainly have prepared the men for the reality that they were soon to encounter, over the FLAK filled skies of Europe.

After four months of training, the Brooks crew were ready for overseas deployment. They were all given a fourteen day furlough and many returned home to be with their families. Ruth, Larry, Lester, Gennie and her cousin, drove home from Florida to Louisville, Kentucky. Gennie's cousin was also a pilot and in the same squadron as the crew. They departed from Florida early in the morning and drove continuously until around midnight. Larry, Lester and Gennie's cousin took turns driving. They arrived at Larry and Ruth's home in the early hours of the morning. It was a welcoming and warm site to them, as they had been away from their home for so many months. Lester, Gennie and her cousin, went to bed for a while, but Ruth and Larry went down to her parents house to wake them up and ask for some eggs, bacon and bread. They also got a quart of milk from a neighbour. Before returning home they paid Larry's mother a visit and returned to their home to freshen up. They made sure that Lester, Gennie and her cousin, were well fed before they departed for Carrollton, Ohio, that morning.

Leighton McKenzie made his way home to California with Robert Graves and passed through Arkansas. During that trip he signed the Centerville Township Pollbook in Little Rock.

Chapter Five

Farewell

On 21 May, at around 08:30 in the morning, Ruth said goodbye to Larry at Union Station. Larry and his crew were making their way back to MacDill Field in Florida, in preparation to transfer to the Third Air Force Staging Wing, which was located at Hunter Field in Georgia. Hunter Field was a staging area for newly assembled combat crews. At Hunter, crews would collect an aircraft and depart the US for the European Theatre of Operations.

Upon arrival at Hunter Field, the crew were sent to the Personnel Processing Centre, where they would be issued new type intermediate winter flying clothing. Their old winter clothing, if they still had it with them, would have been handed in, in exchange. Individual crew records were processed and then corrected in preparation for departure. M-3 pistols with holsters and trench knives, were issued to the crew and they were measured for their parachutes.

During their stay at Hunter Field, the crew likely made the most of the large Post Exchange that was on the station. Crew members such as the aerial gunners and the bombardier, would have required some form of entertainment for the long flight ahead. The PX supplied goods that the crew could purchase at their own expense, that were usually not readily available in such remote locations such as airfields. Entertainment usually came in the form of playing cards, reading comics, magazines and newspapers.

At Hunter, the Brooks crew were assigned an aircraft, a new metal finish, fresh from the factory, Boeing B-17G Flying Fortress, Army Air Force Serial Number, 42-97862.

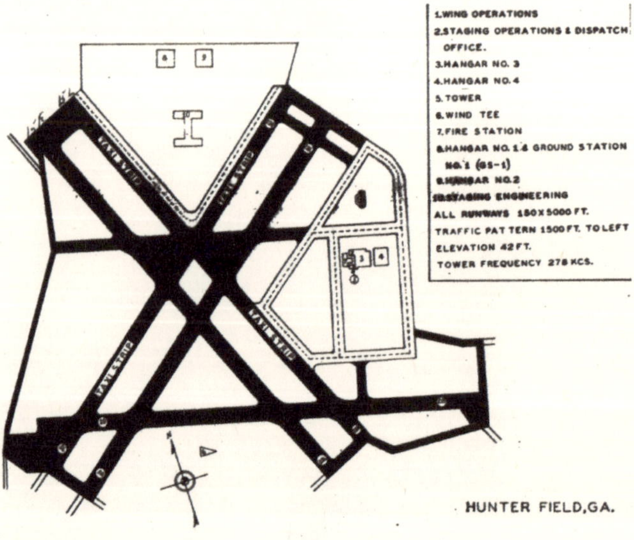

Boeing B-17G Flying Fortress bombers are assembled on the production line at the large Boeing plant, in Seattle.

Another view of the B-17 assembly process, shows forward fuselage sections on the assembly line, at the Boeing Seattle assembly plant.

B-17G 42-97862 was built under contract at the Lockheed-Vega plant in Burbank, California. The aircraft was accepted into the USAAF inventory on 21 March 1944 and subsequently on 22 March, the aircraft departed Burbank for Tulsa, Oklahoma, to await modification. The modifications required to make aircraft ready for current combat conditions, were unable to be applied on the production line which necessitated that the aircraft were to be flown to modification centres.

Departing the modification centre, 42-97862 arrived at Hunter Field on 22 May. The aircraft was inspected and serviced by ground crews. All necessary equipment that would be required for the forth-coming transatlantic flight, that was missing, needed to be acquired, before the aircraft could be signed off to a new crew.

The B-17 did not have the sufficient range to travel across the Atlantic ocean without refuelling, therefore, it was required that additional bomb-bay fuel cells were fitted to the aircraft. These two fuel cells were installed on each side of the bomb bay. This increased the range of the aircraft, by a few hundred miles, which provided enough endurance to reach Europe. After inspection a test flight was performed on the aircraft by base test pilots and a familiarisation flight would later be conducted by the crew in preparation for their departure.

***Above**, with the bomb-bay doors open, the bomb-bay fuel cells can be clearly seen.*

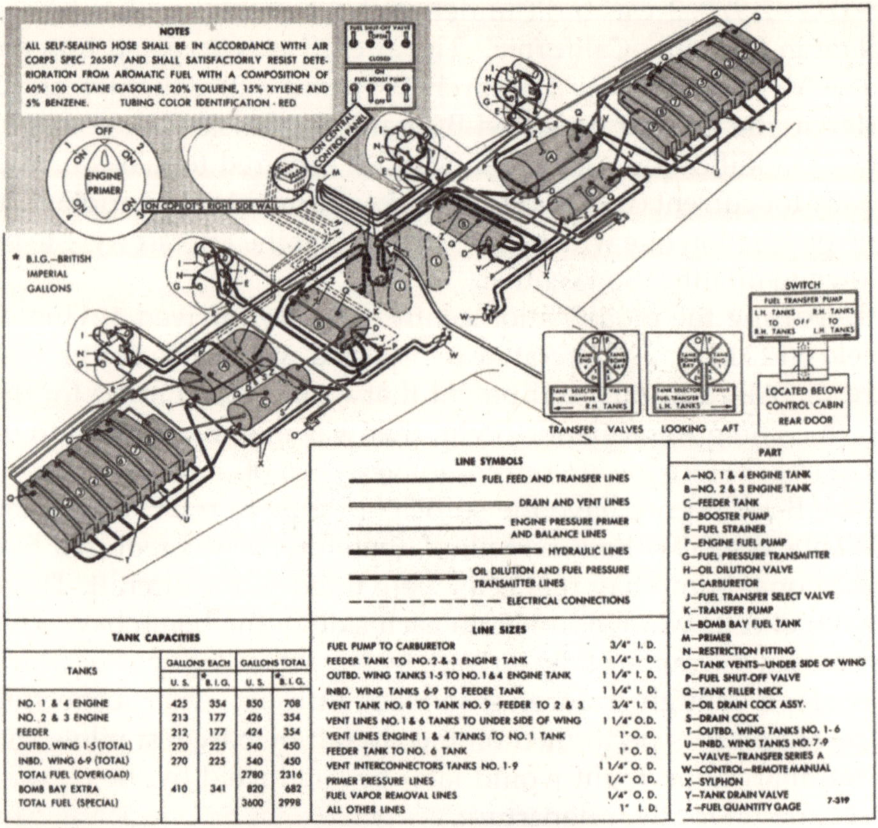

TANK CAPACITIES

TANKS	GALLONS EACH		GALLONS TOTAL	
	U. S.	*B. I. G.	U. S.	*B. I. G.
NO. 1 & 4 ENGINE	425	354	850	708
NO. 2 & 3 ENGINE	213	177	426	354
FEEDER	212	177	424	354
OUTBD. WING 1-5 (TOTAL)	270	225	540	450
INBD. WING 6-9 (TOTAL)	270	225	540	450
TOTAL FUEL (OVERLOAD)			2780	2316
BOMB BAY EXTRA	410	341	820	682
TOTAL FUEL (SPECIAL)			3600	2998

LINE SIZES

FUEL PUMP TO CARBURETOR	3/4" I. D.
FEEDER TANK TO NO. 2 & 3 ENGINE TANK	1 1/4" I. D.
OUTBD. WING TANKS 1-5 TO NO. 1 & 4 ENGINE TANK	1 1/4" I. D.
INBD. WING TANKS 6-9 TO FEEDER TANK	1 1/4" I. D.
VENT TANK NO. 8 TO TANK NO. 9 FEEDER TO 2 & 3	3/4" I. D.
VENT LINES NO. 1 & 6 TANKS TO UNDER SIDE OF WING	1 1/4" O.D.
VENT LINES ENGINE 1 & 4 TANKS TO NO. 1 TANK	1" O. D.
FEEDER TANK TO NO. 6 TANK	1" O. D.
VENT INTERCONNECTORS TANKS NO. 1-9	1 1/4" O. D.
PRIMER PRESSURE LINES	1/4" O. D.
FUEL VAPOR REMOVAL LINES	1/4" O. D.
ALL OTHER LINES	1" I. D.

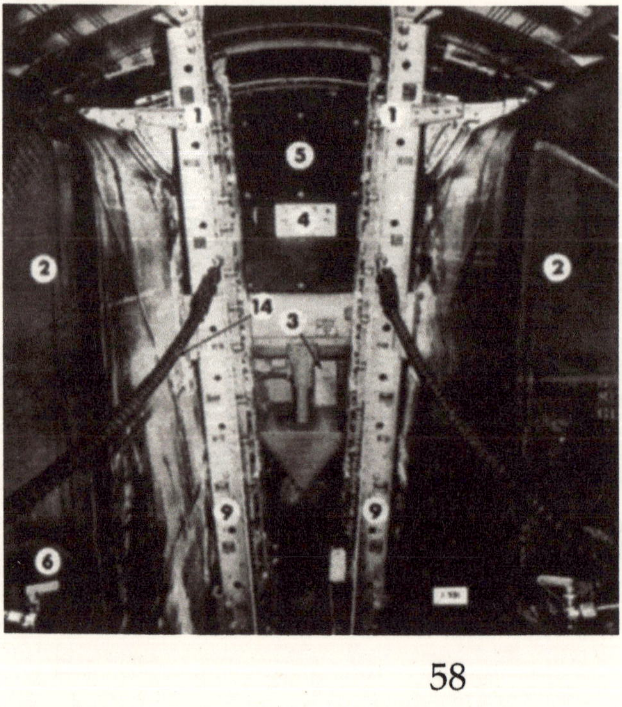

***Above**, the B-17 fuel cell layout, the bomb-bay tanks, can be seen in the centre of the fuselage. **Left**, the bomb-bay tanks, as seen from the bomb-bay catwalk.*

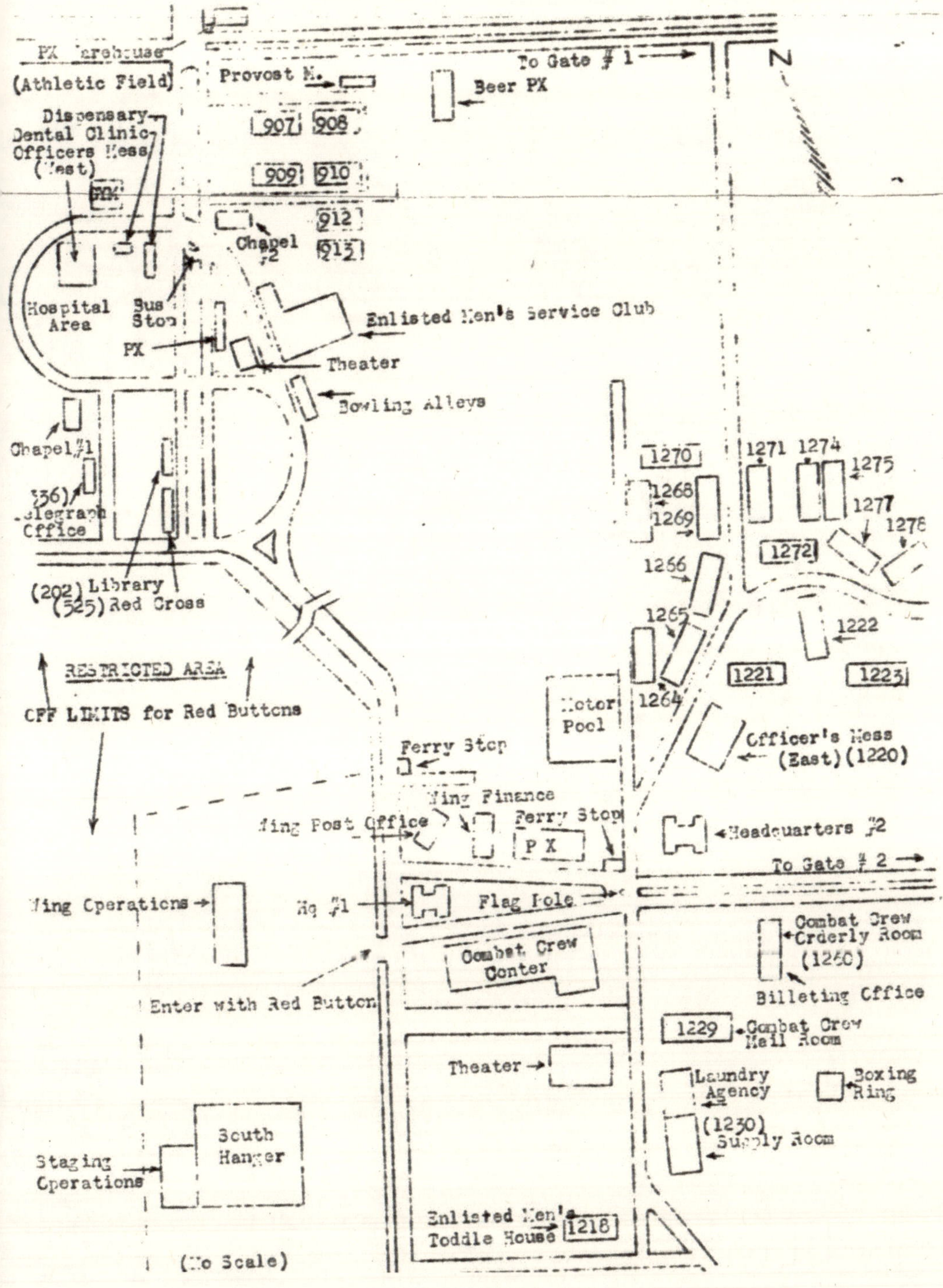
PX Warehouse
(Athletic Field)
Provost M.
To Gate # 1
N
Beer PX
Dispensary
Dental Clinic
Officers Mess (West)
907
908
909
910
912
913
Chapel #2
Hospital Area
Bus Stop
Enlisted Men's Service Club
PX
Theater
Bowling Alleys
Chapel #1
(336) Telegraph Office
(202) Library
(525) Red Cross
RESTRICTED AREA
OFF LIMITS for Red Buttons
1270
1271
1274
1275
1268
1269
1277
1278
1272
1266
1265
1222
1221
1223
1264
Motor Pool
Officer's Mess (East) (1220)
Ferry Stop
Wing Finance
Wing Post Office
Ferry Stop
P X
Headquarters #2
To Gate # 2
Wing Operations
Hq #1
Flag Pole
Combat Crew Center
Combat Crew Orderly Room (1260)
Billeting Office
Enter with Red Button
1229
Combat Crew Mail Room
Theater
Laundry Agency
Boxing Ring
(1230) Supply Room
South Hanger
Staging Operations
Enlisted Men's Toddle House
1218
(No Scale)

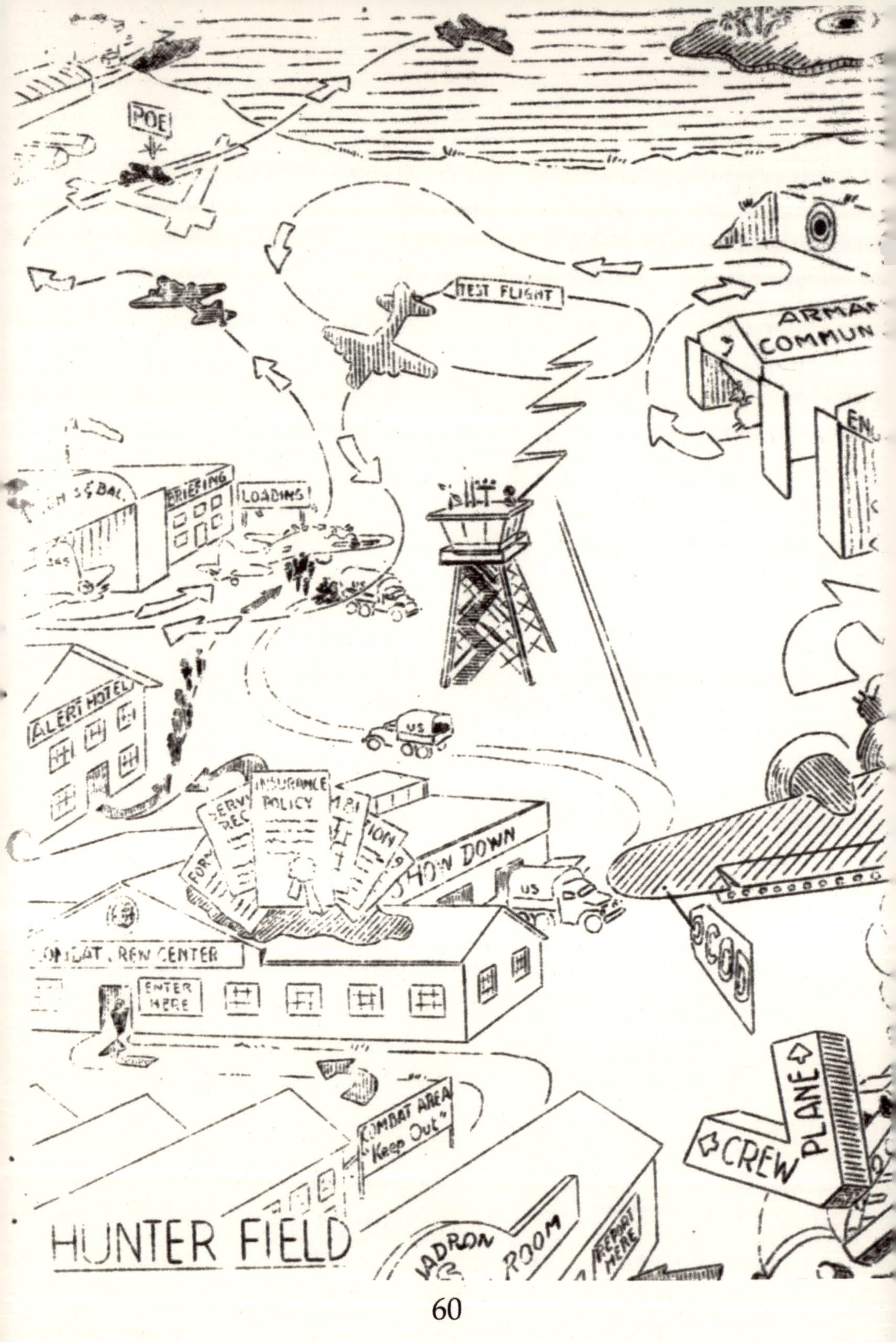
POE
TEST FLIGHT
BRIEFING
LOADING
ALERT HOTEL
INSURANCE POLICY
ENTER HERE
COMBAT AREA "Keep Out"
CREW
PLANE
ROOM
REPORT HERE
HUNTER FIELD

In the early hours of 29 May, the crew of 42-97862, departed Hunter Field for Dow Field in Maine, which would be their Port of Embarkation from the US. They were required by Air Transport Command to arrive before 3pm that afternoon.

Before departure, the crew were given a briefing which consisted of last-minute instructions on routes to be traversed and explanations on the contents of flight kits. Flight Kits, contained maps, charts, technical orders, route information, radio and flight data, contact and communication regulations, cruise charts, check sheets and a terse article on security discipline. The Brooks crew were one of 693 combat crews that were processed at Hunter Field during the month of May.

Departing Hunter Field, the crew made their way along the east coast through the states of South Carolina, North Carolina, Virginia, Delaware, New Jersey and the State of New York. Joe, Lawrence, and Jeremiah were from New York, so they decided on a small detour along the way. At 1:30pm Lester and Jeremiah circled 42-97862 over Joe's family home, Joe, was anxiously waiting to see if anyone could see him. Afterwards, Joe wrote a letter home to his sister, that he had his fingers crossed that an engine would "konk out", so they could land at Roosevelt Field a short distance away.

They continued onward to their Port of Embarkation, arriving at Dow Field in the state of Maine, on the afternoon of 29 May. During the flight, the crew had travelled for four hours, and forty five minutes, covering a distance of over 1000 miles. Upon arrival at Dow, the aircraft and the crew, were officially transferred to the US Eighth Air Force.

An aerial view of Dow Field.

On 30 May, the crew departed the US for Gander, Newfoundland, in Canada, their last port of call before crossing the Atlantic. Joe, recalled *"the trip from Maine to Gander was pretty nice, and I had no trouble finding the place"*. The crew were flying the Northern Route across the Atlantic, direct to the UK without stopping, from Gander, to their intended destination, Valley, in Wales. There were a number of northern ferry routes via Goose Bay, Canada, via Bluie West 1 and Bluie West 8 in Greenland and a final stop in Iceland, usually at Reykjavik, Keflavik (Meeks Field), or Patterson Field. The smaller twin engined aircraft that did not have the endurance to fly the direct routes usually traversed the latter routes.

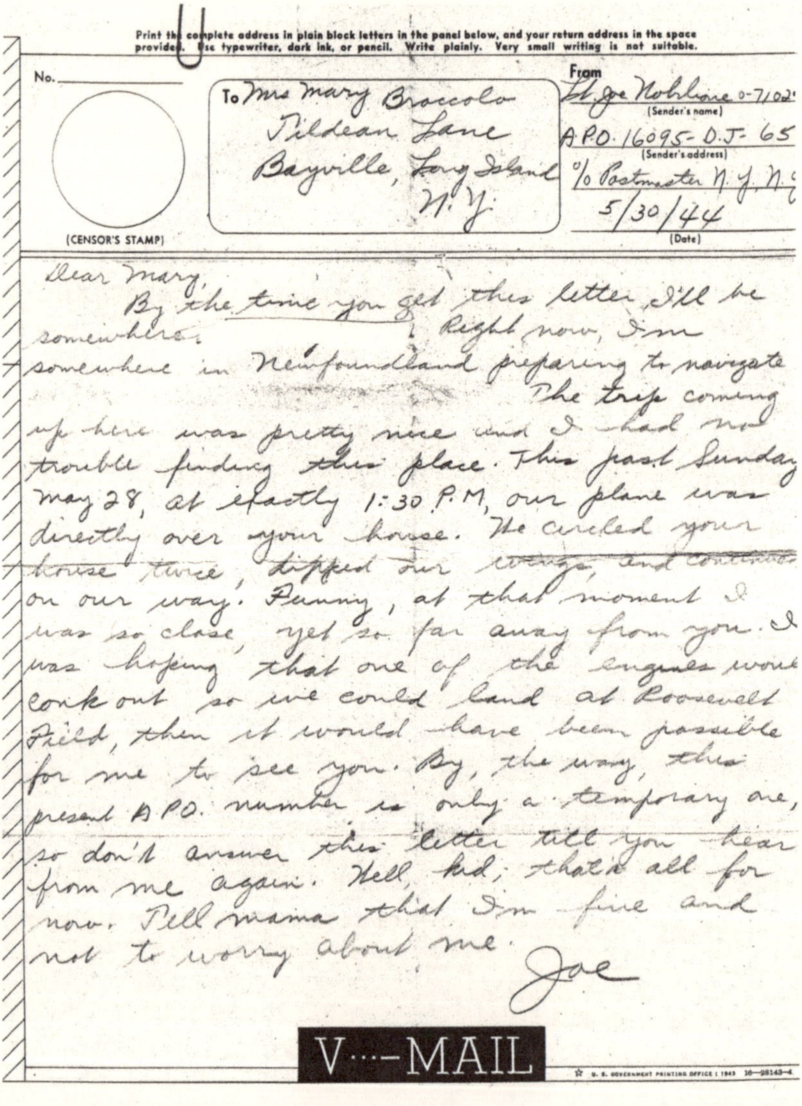

Print the complete address in plain block letters in the panel below, and your return address in the space provided. Use typewriter, dark ink, or pencil. Write plainly. Very small writing is not suitable.

No.

To Mrs Mary Broccolo
Tildean Lane
Bayville, Long Island
N.Y.

(CENSOR'S STAMP)

From Lt. Joe Noblione 0-7102
(Sender's name)
A.P.O. 16095-D.J-65
(Sender's address)
% Postmaster N.Y. N.Y.
5/30/44
(Date)

Dear Mary,
By the time you get this letter, I'll be somewhere. Right now, I'm somewhere in Newfoundland preparing to navigate. The trip coming up here was pretty nice and I had no trouble finding this place. This past Sunday May 28, at exactly 1:30 P.M., our plane was directly over your house. We circled your house twice, dipped our wings, and continued on our way. Funny, at that moment I was so close, yet so far away from you. I was hoping that one of the engines would conk out so we could land at Roosevelt Field, then it would have been possible for me to see you. By the way, this present A.P.O. number is only a temporary one, so don't answer this letter till you hear from me again. Well, kid, that's all for now. Tell mama that I'm fine and not to worry about me.
Joe

V···–MAIL

U. S. GOVERNMENT PRINTING OFFICE : 1943 16—28143-4

When there was inclement weather on the direct route and strong head winds, the heavier four engined aircraft would sometimes use the routes via Goose Bay and onward to Iceland. On other occasions aircraft would fly directly from Goose Bay to the UK.

Upon arrival at Gander on 30 May, the crew disembarked their aircraft and had a look around the station. Gander was a RCAF Station, which had a contingent of USAAF personnel assigned.

Many took the time to write letters home to their loved ones. The crew stayed overnight at Gander and prepared their aircraft for the long transatlantic flight ahead.

The next morning there was a heavy overcast and it was raining. The aircraft was refuelled and Lester made a good pre-flight external inspection of their aircraft for any damage.

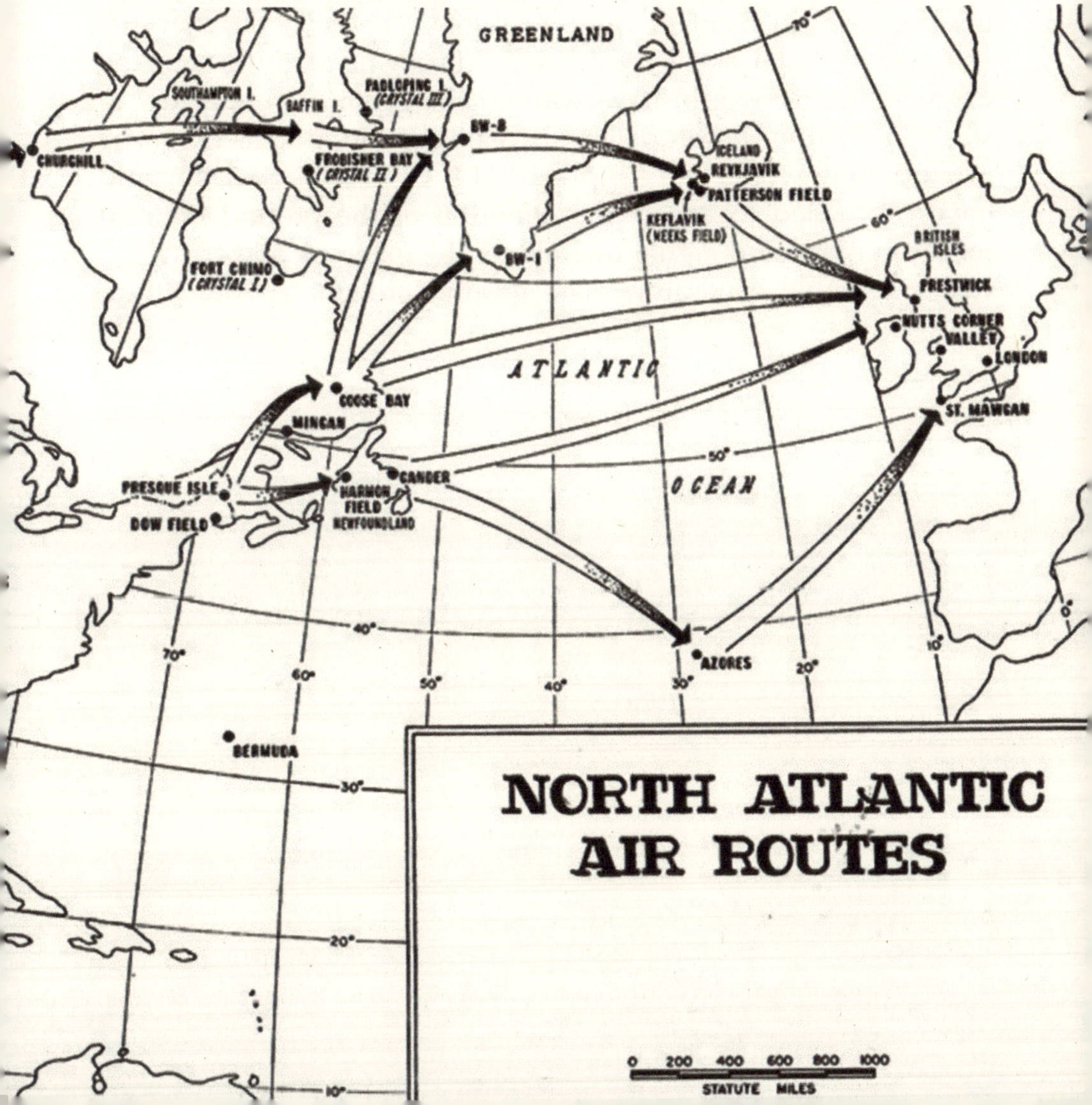

At this time, the ground-crew would have started to turn over the engines by hand, to lubricate the cylinder bores with oil, as the oil usually settled within the crankcase after a few hours. This was accomplished by three men turning the propeller blades by hand and was known as *"pulling the props through"*. The external inspection complete, Lester, Jeremiah and the crew entered the aircraft from the rear waist gunners entrance to make an internal inspection of the aircraft and upon completion, made their way to the cockpit. Lester, the airplane commander, sat in the left seat and Jeremiah, in the right seat, which was the co-pilots position. They would have strapped on their parachutes and Jeremiah would have began to read through the cockpit checklist before starting the engines. Joe, the navigator, would have crawled into the navigators compartment, which was located in the forward nose section, in front of the two pilots. The cockpit checklist completed, Lester and Jeremiah would now be ready to start the engines. Lester would have warned the ground crew below to stand back from the propellers, by calling "PROP CLEAR". The ground crew would have replied "ALL CLEAR". Lester would have proceeded to attract the attention of the ground crew in the form of a hand signal to connect the external power, which was a portable generator. The ground crewman would have

An aerial view of RCAF Gander.

acknowledged his signal and within seconds the hum of the generator would be heard throughout the aircraft. A quick hand signal to Lester would indicate that the generator had been connected.

In the cockpit, Lester and Jeremiah would have began their start-up procedure. It was the co-pilots responsibility to hold the starter switch for the number one engine for 15 to 20 seconds and at the same time, with his right hand, set the hand primer for the number one engine, pumping it a few times, to get the air out of the primer lines. At this time, the airplane commander, Lester, would have unlocked the mixture controls and Jeremiah would have pressed the starter and mesh switch. The propeller would begin to turn over as Jeremiah continued priming the engine. Within moments, the number one engine would have burst into life with a roar and a puff of smoke from the exhaust. At this time, Lester would have pulled back the mixture control and Jeremiah would have immediately focused on the oil pressure gauge for a rise in pressure. The throttle would be adjusted to read 1000 RPM on the RPM indicator gauge. Lester would then have signalled to the ground crew below that he was ready to start the number 2 engine and the same start-up procedures would be applied to the remaining engines.

Ready to taxii, Lester would have signalled to the ground crew to remove the external power and the wheel chocks. The ground crew would usually approach from beneath the fuselage to remove the power and under the wings behind the propellers, to avoid being struck and proceed to a safe distance in front of the propellers, to indicate that they were safely clear.

For taxiing, the two outboard engines, number 1 and number 4, were commonly used for directional control on the ground, as the rudder was ineffective.

Holding just short of the active runway, it was common practice to taxii the aircraft at a slight angle for the engine run-up, so that all of the propellers were over the concrete and any aircraft behind would not be damaged during the run-up of the engines, prior to take-off. The brakes would be set and the trim tabs adjusted to read 0. A quick radio call would be made to the tower for take-off clearance. When permission was granted, the tail wheel would be

The number one engine, of a B-17 Flying Fortress is in the process of being run up, with the assistance of a ground generator.

FLYING FORTRESS
WARNING
T-1
T-2

The cockpit of a Boeing B-17G Flying Fortress, the two control wheels can be clearly seen. Close to the floor, are two sets of rudder pedals. The throttle quadrant is located centrally and the instrument panel runs left to right, behind the control wheels. The left hand side was the airplane commanders side of the cockpit.

unlocked and they would taxii out to the active runway. Lining the aircraft up straight on the runway, Lester would have called for the tail wheel to be locked and the brakes applied, by using the toe brakes on the rudder pedals.

The Brooks crew were ready for take-off. Holding on the brakes, the throttles would likely have been advanced to 25 inches manifold pressure, at which time, the brakes would be released and the aircraft would begin its take-off roll. It was the co-pilots responsibility to focus closely on the engine instruments as the airspeed gradually increased. At 50 mph the rudder would become effective. Up until this time, Lester could keep the aircraft tracking straight using the throttles to manipulate power to the engines. At around 100 mph the aircraft would became airborne. A kick of the brakes would stop the wheels from spinning and the landing gear would be retracted. A quick check of the landing gear retraction light would confirm that the gear had retracted.

At around 130 mph the power would have been reduced for a cruise climb, reducing manifold pressure first and then RPM. Lester would visually inspect the left landing gear and Jeremiah, the right. The crew in the rear gunners area would confirm to Wilbur that the tail wheel had been retracted and the switch would then be returned to the neutral position. The aircraft would now be climbing to its cruising altitude and the crew would settle in for the long flight ahead, catching their last sight of land as it faded into the distance through the clouds.

They had expected to fly in formation with other crews but for reasons unknown, this was not permitted and presumably each aircraft took off separated by set time intervals. The Brooks crew were now on their way to the European Theatre of Operations.

The crew would have made good progress flying across the Atlantic into the East, with a strong tail-wind due to the prevailing winds.

A long flight, the aerial gunners likely climbed their way through the aircraft from nose to tail, asking the pilots and navigator for regular updates on their position. Wilbur, the Flight Engineer, would have performed hourly visual checks on the aircraft's instruments, engines, nacelles and fuel cells.

The flight was uneventful, but they had used more fuel than they had expected to. Seemingly, they would need to land at a diversionary airfield. Within their flight kit that was provided to them at Hunter Field, there were details on diversionary fields that could be used if required in the event of being low on fuel, or bad weather at their intended destination. The crew were now approaching the coast of Ireland and checked in with Transatlantic Control.

A Brooks squadron B-17, during a practice formation flight.

144° MAG
48 ST M
182° MAG
72 ST M
45 ST M
174° MAG
142 ST M
tell pilot
call pilot
tell carl
ETA 1152
GLASGOW
GREENOCK
DUMBARTON
FALKIRK
GRANGEMOUTH
PAISLEY
COATBRIDGE
HAMILTON
KILMARNOCK
SYMINGTON 227 276
LANARK
PRESTWICK TOWER 6440 126.18 Mc
AYR TOWER 6440 116.1 Mc
AYR
ISLAND of ARRAN
CAMPBELTOWN
MACHRIHANISH 20
MULL OF KINTYRE GGC 297.5
GIRVAN
TURNBERRY 35
DALMELLINGTON
NEW CUMNOCK
DUMFRIES
LOCKERBIE
STRANRAER
PORTPATRICK
GLENLUCE
WIGTOWN
LUCE BAY
Port William
WISTOWN BAY
Burrow Head
Mull of Galloway
SOLWAY FIRTH
SILLOTH TOWER 6440
MARYPORT
WORKINGTON
WHITEHAVEN
CLEATOR MOOR
MILLOM
BARROW IN FURNESS
DOUGLAS
CASTLETOWN
PEEL
RAMSEY
Point of Ayre
ISLE OF MAN
LARNE
BALLYMENA
NUTTS CORNER RADIO 326
Nutts Corner WYQQ 4220
NUTTS CORNER TOWER 6440 126.18 Mc
BANGOR
BELFAST
NEWTOWNARDS
LISBURN
LURGAN
PORTADOWN
BANBRIDGE
BELFAST W6C 333
BALLYHALBERT 25
BALLYHALBERT TOWER 6440 116.1 Mc
DOWNPATRICK
BISHOP COURT 50
Ardglass
St Johns Point
NEWCASTLE
NORTHERN IRELAND
NEWRY
GREENCASTLE 50
DUNDALK BAY
DROGHEDA
Balbriggan
COLLINSTOWN
220
DUBLIN
DUBLIN BAY
DUN LAOGHAIRE
BALDONNEL 300
BRAY
I R I S H S E A
SKERRIES GGK 306.5
VALLY GZ9 3425
Valley WYQU 4220
VALLEY TOWER 6440 126.18 Mc
WYQU 286 DN VALLEY RADIO 286
HOLYHEAD
AMLWCH
BEAUMARIS
BANGOR
CAERNORVON
CAERNORVON BAY
CONWAY
LLANDUDNO
RHYL
COLWYN BAY
ST ASAPH
DENBIGH
PRESTATYN
HOLYWELL
FLINT
MOLD
RUTHIN
BIRKENHEAD
HOYLAKE
WALLASEY
FORMBY
SOUTHPORT
SQUIRES GATE TOWER 6440
Squires Gate 3OY 3965
BLACKPOOL
FLEETWOOD

An AAF Aeronautical Chart of the United Kingdom and Northern Ireland, this is likely one of the charts that the crew had on-board their aircraft. The track to Valley can clearly be seen and was easily intersected via the Nutts Corner Radio Range if required.

An AAF Aeronautical Chart of Northern Ireland and EIRE. The Derrynacross Range is clearly marked, the western leg of which, can be seen extending out into the Atlantic Ocean, over the neutral country of EIRE.

Chapter Six

Hold on the Range

Due to their low fuel reserves and the possibility of bad weather at Valley, 42-97862 and a number of other American aircraft diverted to USAAF Nutts Corner, AAF Station 235, In Northern Ireland. AAF Station 235 was manned by British RAF and American USAAF personnel. It was designated as a diversionary station for aircraft arriving from the US that were unable to safely reach their destination on the British mainland. The control tower was jointly manned by the two air forces. Likely flying through the Donegal Air Corridor, 42-97862 would have proceeded to fly on the Derrynacross Radio Range, the western leg of which, extended across the Donegal Air Corridor out into the Atlantic Ocean. Upon overflying the Derrynacross Range which was located at Belleek and proceeding on the eastern leg, this would intersect with the western leg of the nutts corner

radio range, which would bring the aircraft over Lough Neagh during their approach to the range station. The flight tuned into the Nutts Corner Radio Range and contacted NAGAR *(Nutts Corner)* radio, through the radio range frequency, informing them of their change in flight plan and necessity to land at the airfield. NAGAR tower informed 42-97862 along with 15 other aircraft, to *"hold on the radio range"* and that each aircraft would be allowed to *"make their let down to land, in turn"*.

A Radio Navigation Aid, the Range Station was located at RAF Aldergrove airfield, in-between Nutts Corner and nearby Langford Lodge airfields. Flying on one of four legs of the range, an aircraft could be guided to within the vicinity of the airfield to make a safe landing, provided the airfield was visible upon flying over the Range Station.

The Derrynacross Radio Range, which was located at Belleek. This Range was what was known as a four-course range. The central equipment building, had a central mast. There were four outer masts, two of which emitted the morse letter N and the remaining two emitting the morse letter A, these were called quadrants. When aircraft flew over the central mast, this was known as the cone of silence, as the two morse tones emitting from the other masts, would fall silent over the headset, which would inform the pilot that he was directly over the range station.

The nutts corner range also facilitated instrument landings at nearby USAAF Langford Lodge and RAF Aldergrove airfields. It operated on a frequency of 353 Kilocycles and broadcast its station identifier, HU (Phonetic; HOW UNCLE), in audible morse code.

First contact with Nutts Corner, by the crew of 42-97862, would likely, have been, according to USAAF Radio Telephone procedures, as follows; "NAGAR Radio, this is ARMY 42-97862, over". The NAGAR Range, would have replied, ARMY 862, this is NAGAR Radio, over.

The controllers at RAF Nutts Corner, stacked the aircraft at varying altitudes, along the North-East and South-West legs of the radio range, separated at altitudes from 3000ft, down to 500ft. The aircraft would fly along these invisible legs of the range, at their assigned altitude and airspeed, for a specified amount of time, before

making a procedure turn and backtracking along the leg of the range they had just been flying on. This allowed the aircraft to stay airborne, within a safe distance of the airfield, conserve fuel at a cruise configuration and be separated from other traffic, until they were each given permission to approach the airfield to land.

With 16 aircraft holding on the range, at different altitudes and many with low fuel remaining, unfortunately the controller in the control tower had become confused and he was unable to let any of them down to land. This necessitated in the aircraft holding on the range for a number of hours, until more experienced controllers could take over and assess the situation.

Presumably the 16 aircraft would have been given one of two holds to fly, 1. the East leg of the range, flying at a specified altitude, airspeed and time, up and down the leg of the range, with a procedure

The remains of the Nutts Corner Radio Range equipment building. As of 2019, this building still remains, close to the main entrance to RAF Aldergrove airfield. The central and four outer course masts have long since been removed. 42-97862 would have flown directly over this buildings central mast many times, during its holding procedure.

turn, at either end of the leg. When the aircraft flew over the range station "Z" Marker and heard the "cone of silence" over their headsets, they knew their approximate position relative to the airfield. Initiating a procedure turn they would fly back down the leg of the range they had just been flying on, at a designated airspeed, altitude and for a specified time, using a stopwatch, before again, making a procedure turn and heading back towards the range station. 2. Flying both the East and the West legs of the radio range, would take the aircraft directly over Langford Lodge, where a radio range fan marker was located. After passing the Langford fan marker, travelling on course for 4 minutes, over the Lough, the aircraft would make a procedure turn, over Lough Neagh and fly back up the range, in the direction they had just come from, back over the range station and out towards the eastern leg. This procedure would have been repeated many times over and over, until control tower operators informed an aircraft to make their let down, to land.

The specified time that 42-97862 was requested to fly the legs of the range is unknown, but the duration could have been more or less than 4 minutes, as there is no official paperwork that verifies how many minutes they were requested to fly on the legs of the range, by the control tower operator.

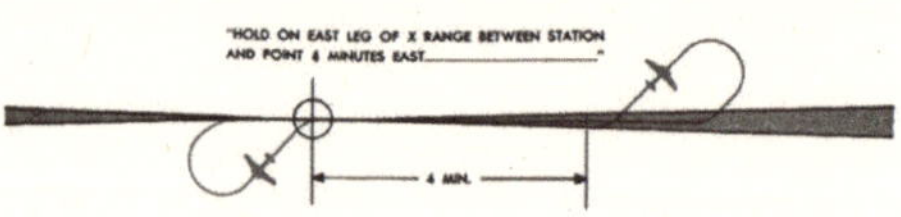

***Above and below**, examples from an official USAAF Instrument Flying training manual, showing the procedure for holding on the East leg of a radio range station, and holding on the East and West legs of a Radio Range Station, for a specified amount of time.*

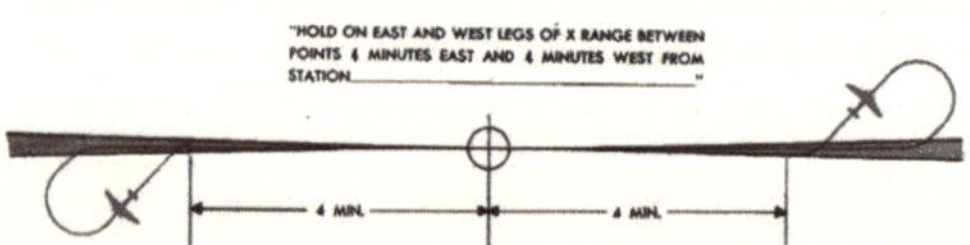

HOLDING PROCEDURES

a. In airways traffic control it is frequently necessary to hold aircraft over given points particularly when a number of aircraft approach the same airport for a landing under instrument flight conditions. Holding procedures will be conducted under Airway Traffic Control (ATC) instructions. The point on which to hold will be specified by ATC, and may be the intersection of two radio range legs, a fan marker or some other radio fix. For instance the instructions may be "Hold 4 Minutes East of station, at 5000 feet". When the aircraft arrives over the airport, it may be placed in a landing sequence, in which case an altitude will be assigned to the pilot. He will not change this altitude except when directed to do so by ATC. When instructed to hold, the pilot will receive the following directions: "You are number 3 to land, hold at 4000 feet on the west leg of the radio range. Expect approach clearance at 2240." As soon as the preceding aircraft lands he will be instructed to descend to 3000, when he becomes number two to land. When the next preceding aircraft has landed, he will be number one to land, and will be cleared to approach and to the tower frequency for landing instructions.

***Left**, from the official USAAF, Instrument Flying Training manual, a description of a holding procedure, on a Radio Range.*

***Right**, an original USAAF approach plate chart, for the Nutts Corner Radio Range.*

NUTTS CORNER, N. IRELAND

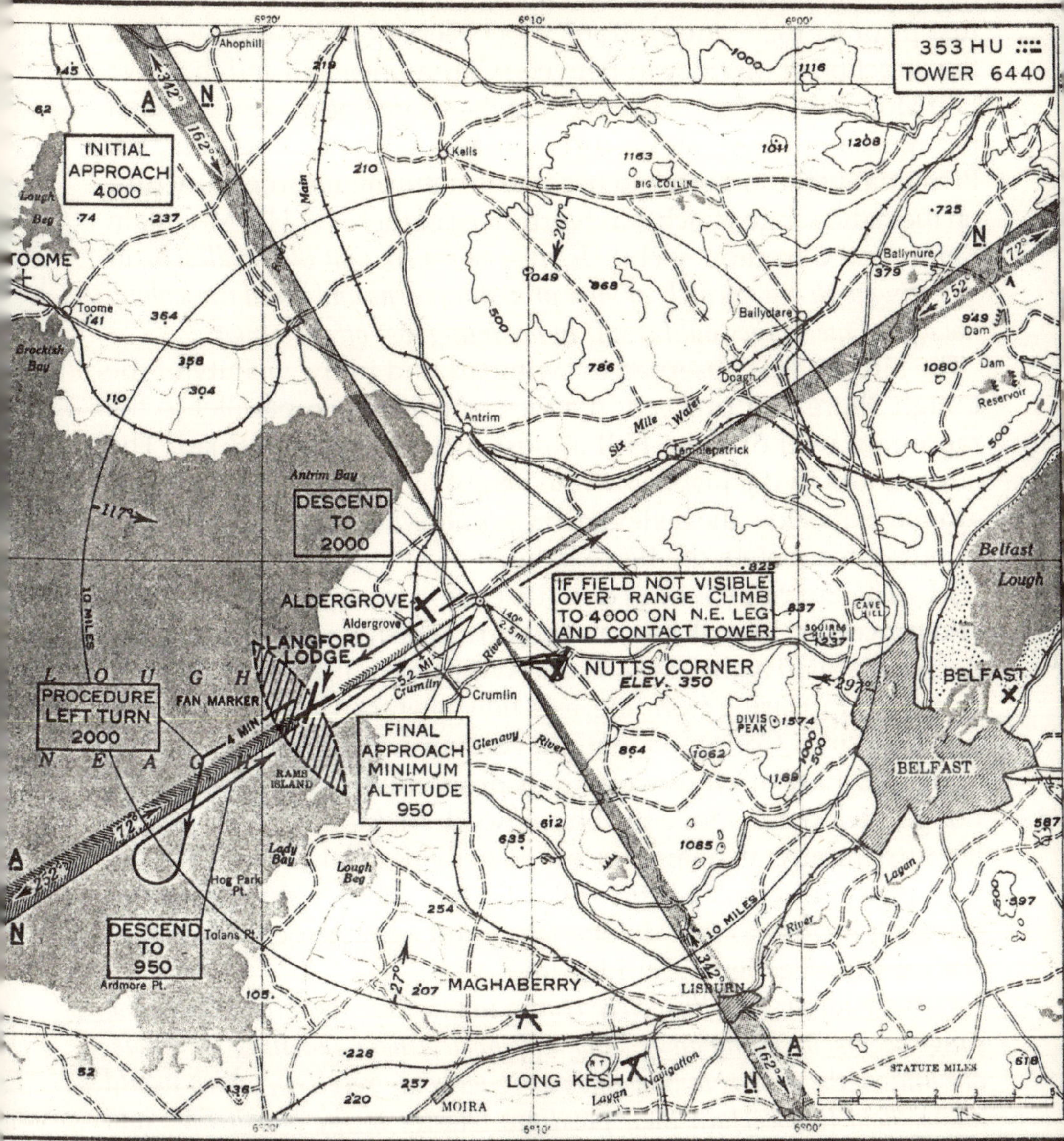

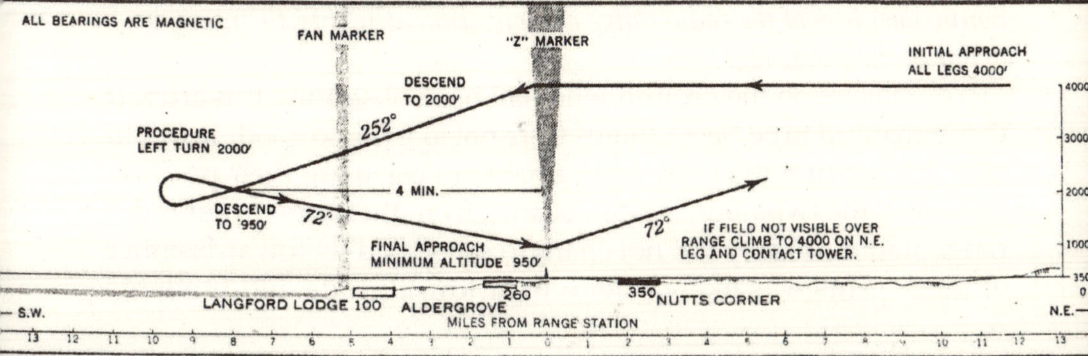

CEILING VISIBILITY MINIMUMS			TIME-DISTANCE STATION TO FIELD 2.5 MILES			
KE-OFF	DAY 500-2	NIGHT 500-2	100 M.P.H.	140 M.P.H.	160 M.P.H.	180 M.P.H.
NDING	DAY 800-2	NIGHT 800-2	1 MIN. 15 SEC.	1 MIN. 5 SEC.	56 SEC.	50 SEC.

Just prior to 10:30 am 42-97862 was observed to have come from the direction of Mossley in-between Carnmoney Hill and the Cave Hill Mountain Range. Approaching the shore line of Belfast Lough flying in a South-Easterly direction below the ceiling-overcast. Presumably the aircraft had become lost during its procedure turn on the radio range which was North-East of the Cave Hill Mountain Range and Carnmoney Hill. *It must be stated, that the smallest error in timing with a stopwatch, of their procedure turns and timed track along the legs of the range could result in becoming lost off the range.*

The aircraft was observed to swing around in the vicinity of the Lough Shore and proceed in a westerly direction parallel to the mountain wall of Cave Hill almost over the Antrim Road. The aircraft was flying just below the height of the ceiling, which was around 50ft below the Bellevue Ridge line, which, in turn, was a few hundred feet below the Ben Madigan mountain top and McArt's Fort. The aircraft continued on its course, passing Belfast Castle and proceeded to make a slow left turn which took it between the gantries located at the Harland and Wolff ship yard and the Malone Road. Disappearing from site, as it flew over the Castlereagh ridge line deep into County Down. Several minutes later the aircraft appeared East of Hollywood and proceeded to fly over Belfast Lough, to a point above the Shore Road. Making a ninety degree left turn the aircraft again proceeded to fly parallel to the mountain wall passing Belfast Castle and initiated another slow left turn, bringing it close to the Malone Road and again proceeded out of site over the Castlereagh Ridge line.

It would appear that they were trying to intercept one of the two radio range beams, by flying away from and toward them, listening for a fade, or build, of the A or N audible morse signal being received, which would allow them to ascertain their position, relative to the North-East and South-East legs of the radio range and subsequently, find their way back to one of the range legs.

To onlookers on the ground who had been observing this aircraft they perceived to be *"lost"*, things were not looking so good. It would now appear that the crew were unable to calculate their position relative to the two range station beams, from the nutts corner radio range station, as they did not change course and fly towards either of them. This was likely due to their low altitude and the large mountain range in their path which likely would have caused "Mountain Effect", which in turn, would have caused the reflection of radio waves. There was also the added issue of "Shore Line Effect" which would distort radio waves at the shore line of a large body of water such as Belfast Lough and Strangford Lough.

Flying over Belfast Lough from the direction of Hollywood, 42-97862 passed the navigation buoys which were situated in the middle of the Lough. At this time NAGAR Radio made radio contact with 42-97862, informing the aircraft that they were cleared to make their let down to land at the airfield. 42-97862 replied, stating that they were now flying *"Contact"*, over a lake. Observers on the ground noted that the landing gear was observed to have been extended in preparation for landing and at this moment in time, the engines appeared to sound normal, as if they were in a cruise configuration.

After failing to locate the beams it appears the crew used their direction finding equipment to locate the direction in which the radio signals from the NAGAR radio range were emitting. Using a device called a Radio Compass, once tuned into the correct frequency of the range, the radio compass would indicate what direction the transmissions from the radio range were emitting from on the instrument face of the pilots bearing indicator, which was located on Lester's side of the cockpit instrument panel. When the needle was lined up on the 0 of the bearing indicator instrument face, the aircraft was now on a direct heading for the radio range.

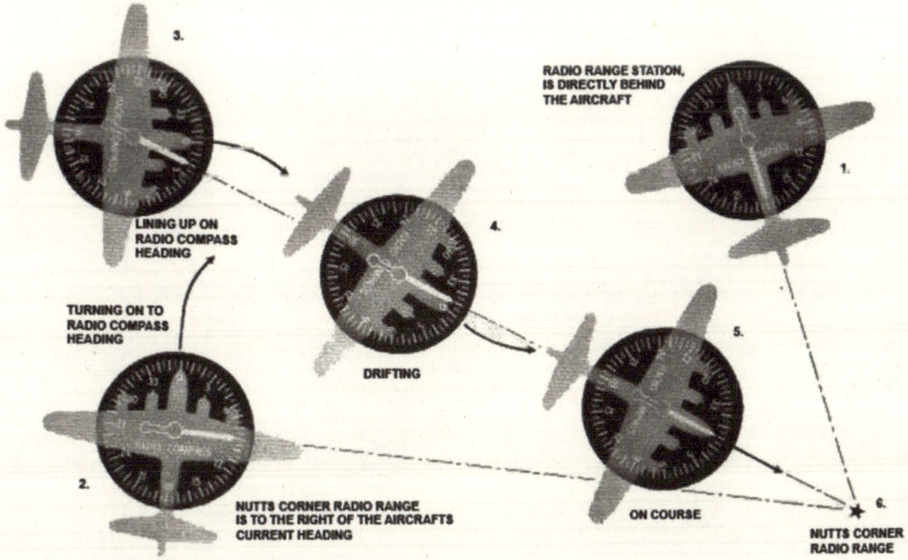

GIVE

A modern day recreation, depicts 42-97862, as it tracks parallel to the mountain wall of Cave Hill, in front of no.10 and no.13 Ben Madigan Park.

Automatic Radio Compass Control Box.

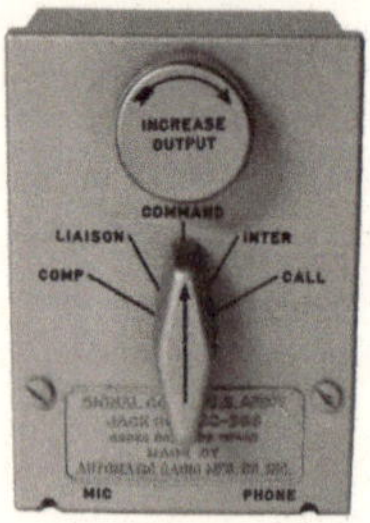

***Above left**, with the Radio Compass indicator now reading on 0, the crew were now on course for the Radio Range Station, at Nutts Corner. **Left**, Interphone-Radio Jack Box, it was typically positioned at the stations of the pilot, co-pilot, navigator, and radio operator. When placed in Comp position, the audio from the compass receiver could be heard. **Above**, The Automatic Radio Compass Control Box, there was one located at the Navigators station and one in the cockpit.*

A Navigator, at his station in the navigators compartment of a B-17 Flying Fortress. He is plotting a course on a chart.

A Radio Operator, in the radio room of a B-17 Flying Fortress aircraft, his parachute is placed on top of the BC-348 command receiver.

There would have been a concerted effort by the pilot, Lester, co-pilot, Jeremiah, navigator, Joe and radio operator Larry, to ascertain the direction of the radio range using all of their skill, training and hardware on-board the aircraft at their disposal, additionally the flight engineer, Wilbur, would have been up front in the cockpit with the two pilots, monitoring the engine instruments, keeping watch and monitoring the remaining fuel on-board, ensuring the aircraft was kept in balance by transferring fuel from one tank to another as required.

Had the crew mistook Belfast Lough for Lough Neagh, in which they had possibly just been flying over if they were flying both legs of the range?.

In the aircraft, all now must have appeared well, they had established their position relative to the airfield range station and they had configured the aircraft for landing, within minutes they will be ready to let down over the range and land at Nutts Corner.

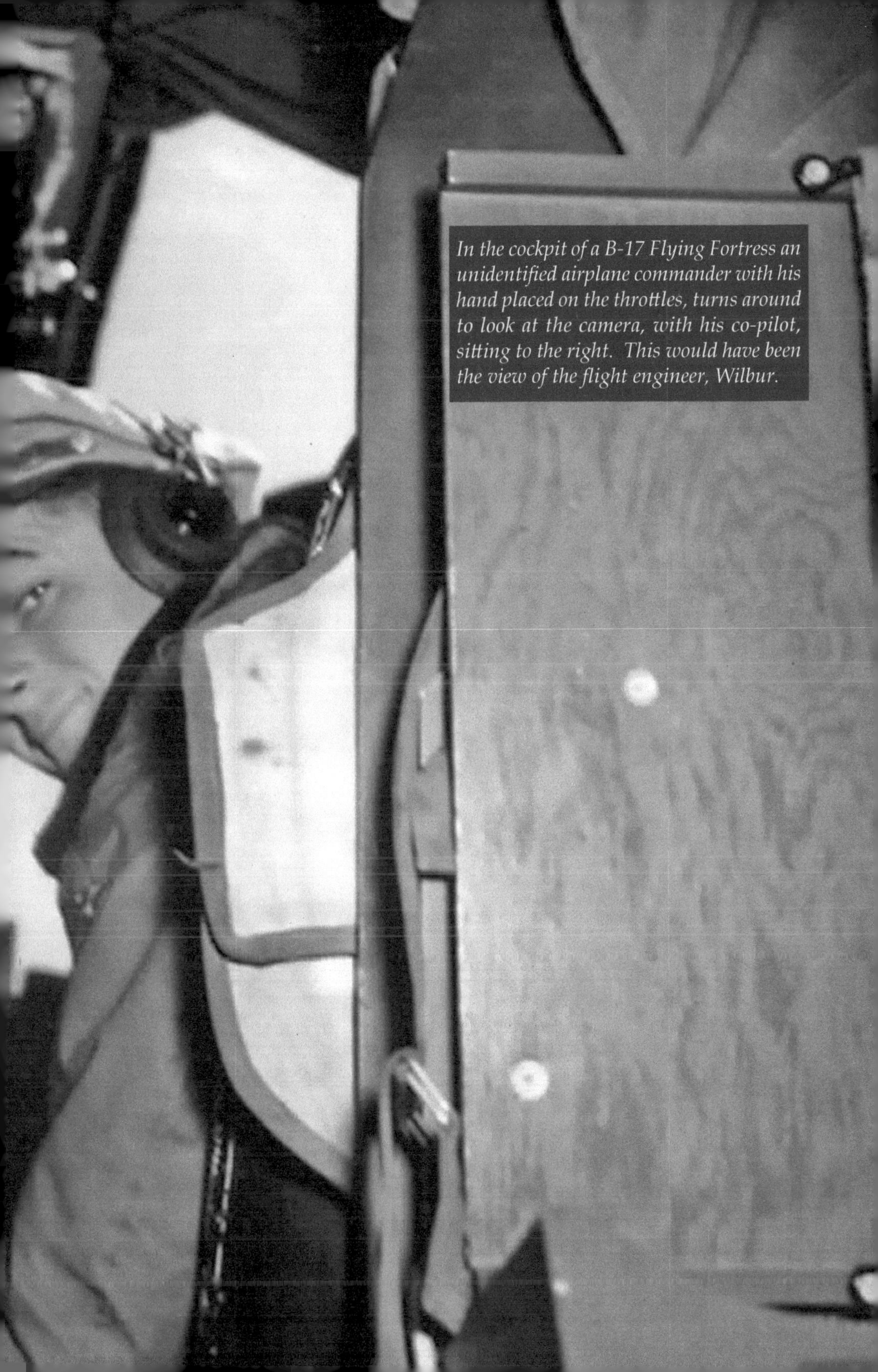

In the cockpit of a B-17 Flying Fortress an unidentified airplane commander with his hand placed on the throttles, turns around to look at the camera, with his co-pilot, sitting to the right. This would have been the view of the flight engineer, Wilbur.

In the rear gunners compartment of the aircraft, like the airman in this photograph, one of the crew would have been in this location waving down below to William Aiken and his mother, presumably from the right hand window.

Chapter Seven

Dear mother

Just before 10:30 am, 42-97862 flew over houses at the junction of Voltaire Gardens and Serpentine Road, just off the Whitewell Road, where nine year old William Aiken and his mother were standing. As they looked up at the roaring bomber flying directly overhead and very low, in the rear waist gunners window a crew member was waving down to them below, so they waved back. One of the crew had started to write a letter to his mother. The atmosphere in the aircraft must have been one of excitement and relief after their long transatlantic flight they were finally coming in to land, they had made it!.

At no.13 Ben Madigan Park, a young James Nolan and his colleagues were working on their first after school job, making ship model kits in a garage to the side of the house. They had been observing and discussing the aircraft's flight path for around ten minutes or so, from the driveway of the house.

At this time at no.10, Mrs. Woosnam-Jones, the wife of an RAF chaplain, was upstairs when she heard the sound of a low flying, large four engined aircraft passing by to the rear of the house. Presuming it was a Flying Boat preparing to land on Belfast Lough. To the shock of James Nolan and his colleagues, the aircraft was flying towards the mountain wall just above Ben

No.13 Ben Madigan Park.

Madigan Park. They shouted and waved, but to no avail. Moments later the sound of cracking timber could be heard as the aircraft began to tear a one hundred yard path through the trees. One of the engines began to trail blue smoke with wreckage and debris falling all around. James and his colleagues immediately began to run up to the top of Ben Madigan Park, momentarily stopping, they witnessed the moment of impact. Striking the rock face below the Bellevue Plateau, there was an intense blue-star shaped flash followed by a hot orange glow at the centre, which emitted from the nose and port side engines as the aircraft struck the rock face. Immediately, the aircraft came to a dead stop, mid air. The nose of the aircraft disintegrated as far back as the wings leading edge appearing intact thereafter, it bounced back along its flight path and dropped, tail first, through the remaining trees, crackling, as it fell to the ground.

A column of brown-grey smoke, tinged with blue streaks, ascended above the Bellevue ridge line and drifted eastwards on a light wind.

At the junction of Voltaire Gardens and Serpentine Road, William Aiken and his mother, who moments earlier had been waving to one of the crewmen, looked on in shock and horror as they heard the impact.

In this recreation, from the driveway of no.13, James Nolan would have seen the aircraft heading for the trees on the Bellevue Ridge, moments before impact.

Meanwhile, at no.10 Ben Madigan Park, Mrs. Woosnam-Jones immediately went to the telephone and within 15 seconds, she was through to her husbands office at RAF Dunlambert, informing him of the crash on the hill above their home, followed by an emergency call to the police. Her husband, Mr. Woosnam-Jones, immediately informed the controller at RAF Headquarters, which was located at Stormont and proceeded to drive to the crash site with the camp commandant of Dunlambert, Flying Officer Thompson. During her climb up the hill, which was around 2 to 3 minutes after the initial impact, the first gush of orange flames and black smoke began to billow out of the trees.

At the junction of Serpentine Road and Voltaire Gardens, William Aiken and his mother looked on in silence. The silence was broken by a cacophony of exploding ammunition, of which, the surrounding area was illuminated by streaks of light, followed by smoke trails, which were falling out of the sky. At this moment, his mother began to cry.

Mrs. Woosnam Jones finally arrived at the crash site and was met with an up-rush of flames, but the explosion of signal flares and ammunition made it impossible to get close enough to the remains of the aircraft to see if there were any survivors. She made a close visual inspection around the aircraft, but could see no members of the crew. To hasten the rescue attempt, she made her way back down the hill to the road, to direct ambulances and rescue parties to the crash site. At this time, on her way down the hill, around 15 minutes after the telephone call, she met her husband Mr. Woosnam-Jones, who along with F/O Thompson, began the arduous climb up the hill to the crash site.

They were the first service personnel to reach the crash site. Ammunition was exploding continuously. Several civilians were on the scene, taking cover behind a bank of earth, James Nolan, was amongst them. Believing there were bombs on-board, they were fearful of a huge explosion. They also stated, that they had seen several men in the aircraft and that no one had managed to make it out. Another, reported that they had seen one of the crew, hanging out of the aircraft, in the middle of the flames, but had since fallen back.

Believing that some of the crew might possibly still be alive and

At the junction of Serpentine and Voltaire, William Aiken and his mother would have seen the aircraft pass by, as it headed towards Cave Hill.

unable to extricate themselves, Mr. Woosnam-Jones crawled up the hillside alongside the lesser damaged tail section of the aircraft. Reaching a break in the fuselage, where the right waist gunners window was located, he was able to peer into the remains of the radio-room and the forward fuselage. By now, the fire had likely spread from the fractured bomb bay fuel cells and had spread to the radio room. A number of the crew were visible in the radio room, several in the heart of the fire itself, but there was no sign of life anywhere. All had likely been killed in the crash or the ensuing fire that engulfed the aircraft. The intense heat, choking fumes and the constant explosions of ammunition and signal flares, made it impossible for him to remain there for more than a very brief space of time.

The National Fire Service had arrived on the scene very quickly, but due to the steep nature of Ben Madigan Park, they were unable to drive their vehicle forwards and had to turn around and reverse up the road to access the site *(reverse gear, being a lower ratio, than first forward)*. Arriving around 10:40 and with the Royal Ulster Constabulary also on the scene, it took almost ten minutes before they could begin dousing the intense fire with only water, using sections of first aid hose.

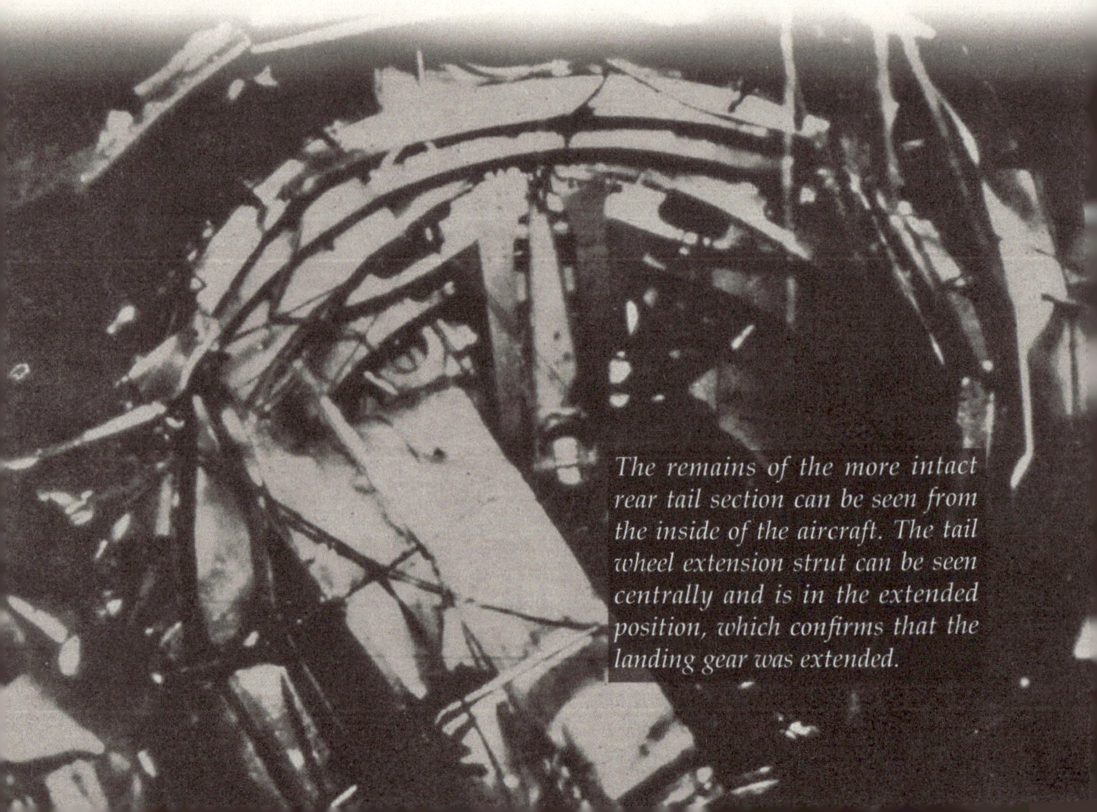

The remains of the more intact rear tail section can be seen from the inside of the aircraft. The tail wheel extension strut can be seen centrally and is in the extended position, which confirms that the landing gear was extended.

Another indication that the landing gear had been extended, is this photograph of one of the main landing gear legs. It has been clearly sheared off at its mounting point.

At 10:50, Mr. D.H. Elliott, who had heard the aircraft pass over Felden House moments before the crash, arrived on the scene with a rescue party. He enquired as to any casualties and made a good reconnaissance of the area but nothing could be done until the flames had been dampened down by the NFS.

When the flames had subsided the fire service hacked their way in to the remains of the broken fuselage section using axes. Mr. Elliott and a Mr. McKibbin, who was now on the scene, got to work on the recovery of the crew. Four were recovered and placed on stretchers by Mr. Elliott and R.V. Cooke. A soldier of the Royal Army Medical Corps and an NFS man, Bill Norris, gave valuable assistance. A band of willing volunteers assisted and six more were recovered and were lowered to the bottom of the field, the remaining four were transported to the top. During the recovery operation, one of the crew was found in the vicinity of the left wing.

Bill Norris, a fireman from Whitla Street Fire Station in Belfast, recalled that grey woollen blankets were placed on the bodies, of which, due to the intense fire that had taken place, steam could be seen rising through them. He was shocked, that the remains of a man, who likely

The remains of the burnt out tail section of the aircraft can be clearly seen in its bare aluminium finish. The serial number on the tail can also be clearly seen, it reads; 297862, in black stencilling. The remains are lying almost at the base of the hill at a steep angle. The small window near the break, was the rear waist gunners compartment window, likely the one that a crew member had been waving from just moments earlier. The remains of the US national insignia can be seen, to the right of the window, at the break in the fuselage. The right horizontal stabilizer-elevator has been severed in half. Underneath the tail, appears to be small sections of the right wing, which has moved from behind its normal position. Severed and burnt trees can be seen around the aircraft.

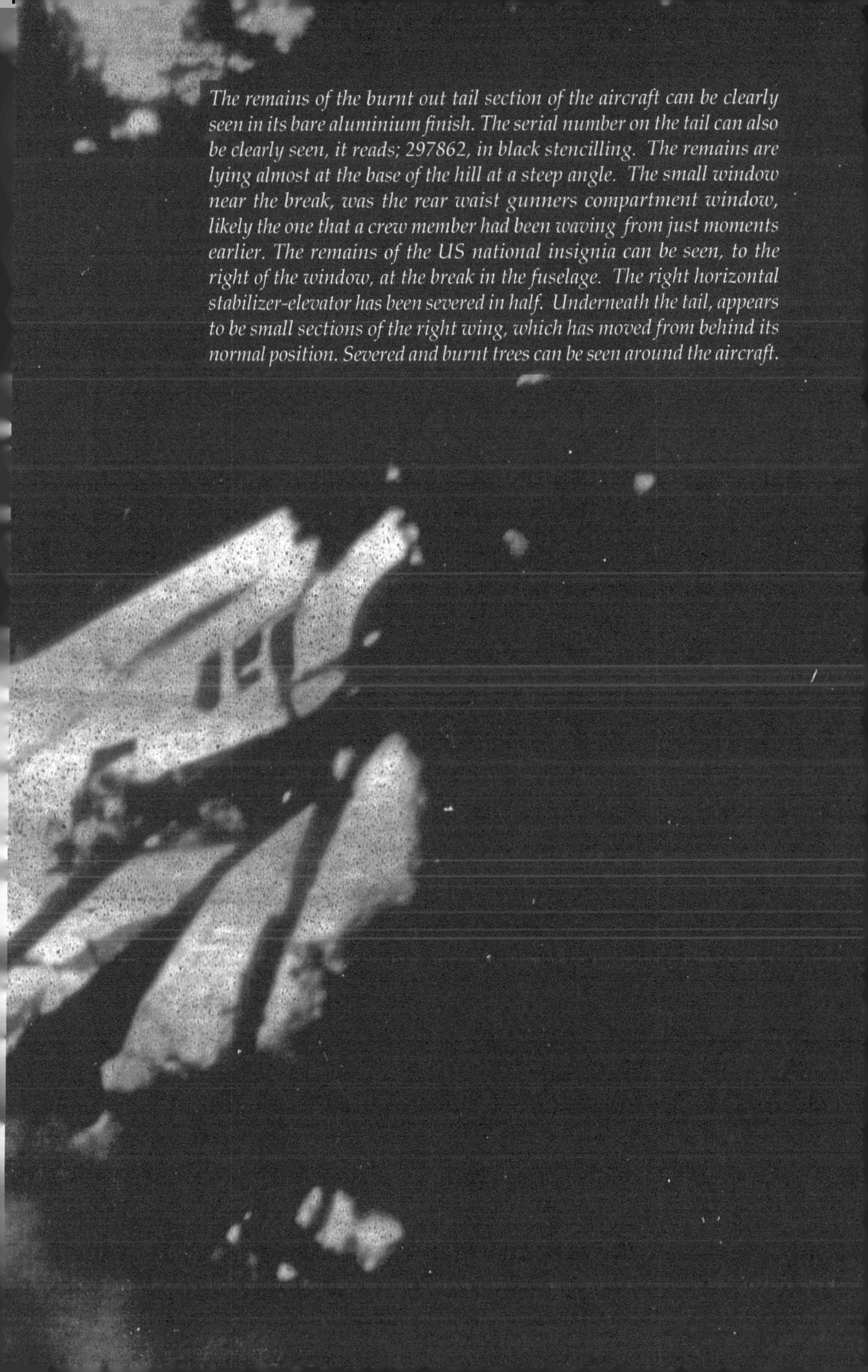

This photograph was taken around half way down the hill, at a very precarious angle, looking downwards. The main focal point of this photograph is to document the burnt out remains of the centre fuselage section and the more intact tail section to the rear. In the foreground, is the burnt out remnants of the radio room, this is likely where seven of the crew were seen by Chaplain Woosnam-Jones, as he peered into the aircraft through the break at the rear gunners compartment and likely why this photograph has been taken, to document the location. To the rear, can be seen shattered and burnt trees. To the immediate right of this photograph, appears to be the main wing spar of the aircraft's left wing, which appeared to be relatively intact and attached to the aircraft.

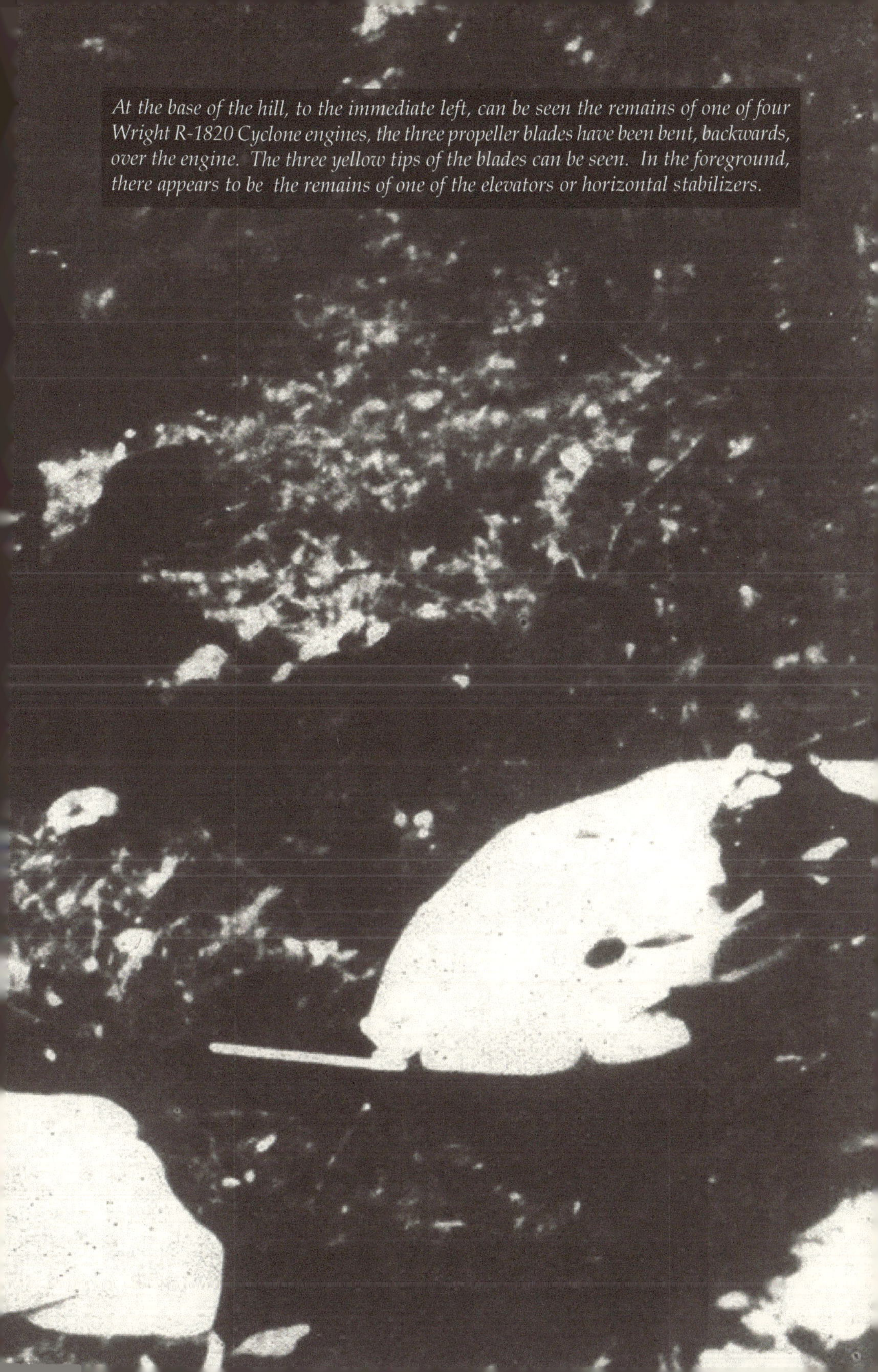

At the base of the hill, to the immediate left, can be seen the remains of one of four Wright R-1820 Cyclone engines, the three propeller blades have been bent, backwards, over the engine. The three yellow tips of the blades can be seen. In the foreground, there appears to be the remains of one of the elevators or horizontal stabilizers.

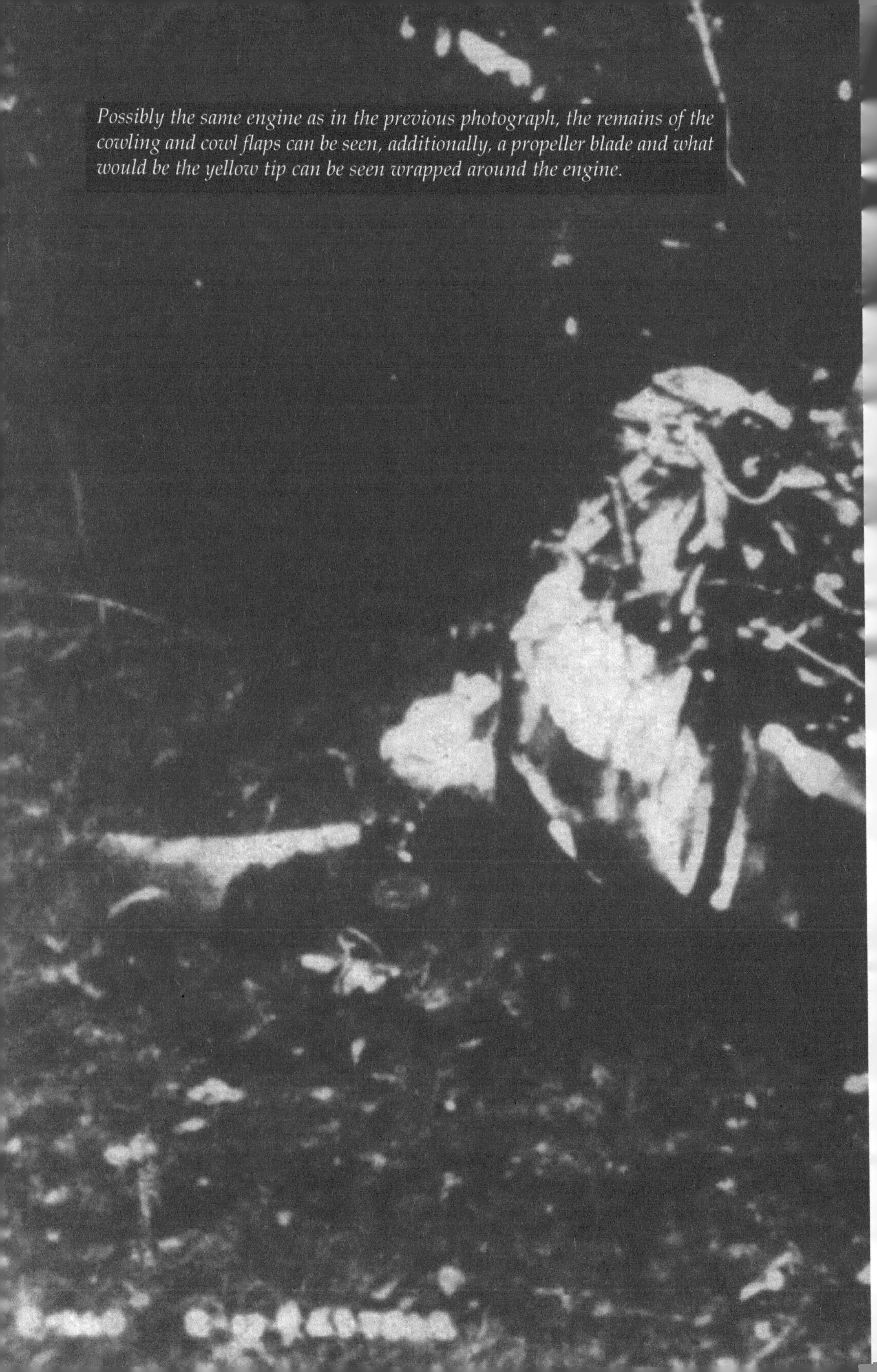

Possibly the same engine as in the previous photograph, the remains of the cowling and cowl flaps can be seen, additionally, a propeller blade and what would be the yellow tip can be seen wrapped around the engine.

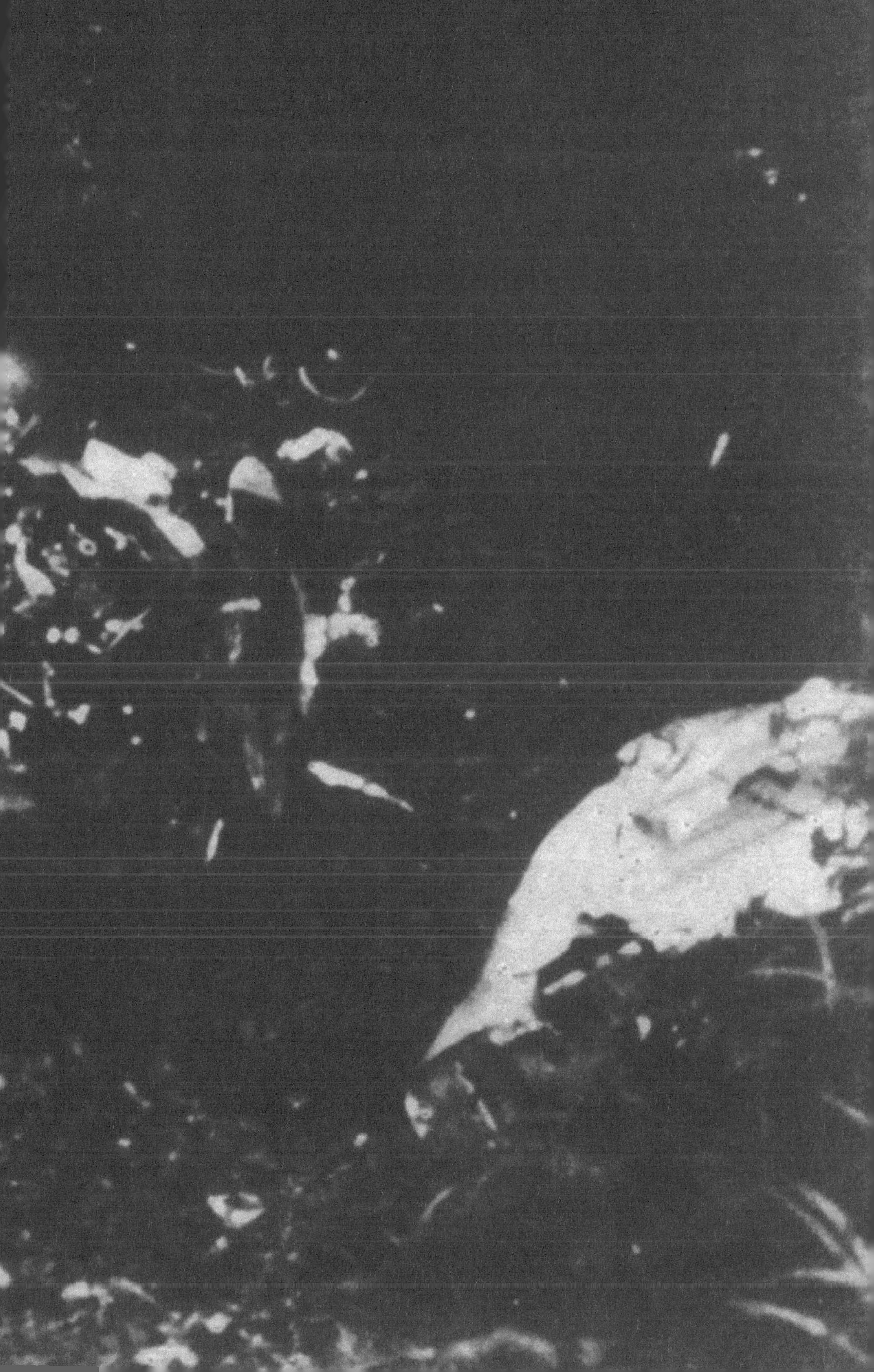

This photograph was taken at the top of the plateau, looking down on the main fuselage section, close to the gravel path. The burnt out remains of the fuselage can be clearly seen amongst a clearing the aircraft had made through trees, many of which were burnt and snapped. The fire extended to as far as the foreground. When the crash initially occurred, it would appear that most of the aircraft, from the bomb-bay backwards, would likely have been recognisable before the intense fire took hold. To the right of the photograph, the more intact left wing can be seen, with a collapsed tree close-by. An oxygen tank has wedged itself within the remnants of a tree. This is the location in which four members of the crew were removed from the site, up the hillside and likely the area in which a number of onlookers witnessed a number of horrific sites.

would have been 6ft in height was reduced to a height of around 4ft. Afterwards, he was violently sick due to the horrific experience he had just witnessed. This was the first fatal accident that he had attended and it was his introduction to life in the fire service.

A strict security cordon was immediately set up around the site by US officials and a small amount of civilian personnel were not allowed to leave under the threat of armed guard. James Doherty, an Air Raid Precaution *ARP* warden who had gave assistance to recover the crew, was now within the security cordon. Along with his colleague, they discovered a number of photographs that had been in the possession of the crew, among them, a notepad, which belonged to one of the crew, poignantly it read; *"Mother, we are now over Ireland, and will be going down in a few minutes"*. These words were followed by a long scrawl of the pen.

With his colleague, Mr. Doherty handed these items over to a US Officer, hoping they would make it back to the families of the deceased young airmen, that it might bring some comfort to the mother of the son who was thinking of her just before his life ended so tragically and so far away from home.

After the recovery of the crew that afternoon their remains were transported from the field in Jeeps, down to the roadside located at Ben Madigan Park. They were then transported to Wiltons Funeral home, which was located on the Crumlin Road, for identification and subsequent burial, which was to take place at Lisnabreeny American Military Cemetery, located in Castlereagh, on the outskirts of Belfast. Wiltons were contracted to undertake this work on behalf of the US Government for US servicemen who passed away in Northern Ireland. A small contingent of US Army Graves Registration Service personnel were stationed at Wiltons, who specialised in embalming and funeral preparations in accordance with US regulations. Their facilities allowed them to process the remains of four servicemen per day.

Meanwhile, still at the scene of the accident, Mr. Doherty and his colleague, were informed by an apologetic US Officer, that they would have to remain within the security cordon overnight, much to their dismay. Cold and hungry, they managed to locate some of the rations that had been on-board the aircraft. Amidst the chaos and destruction that had taken place, they managed to find their sense of humour, wondering how it came to be that they were stuck on the cold damp hillside, with no food or water in the middle of the night with a trigger happy MP called *"crazy guy"*. They were never given an explanation as to why they were not allowed to leave the site.

The following day, US Officers and technicians arrived on the scene. Photographs were taken of the remaining wreckage before removal and technicians began to disassemble the burnt out remnants of the rear fuselage section, presumably with oxyacetylene cutting torches and steel hawsers. A young boy, at the time, Alistair McKinley lived in Ben Madigan Park and was in school during the time of the accident. He vividly recalled that the remains of the aircraft were transported down to the road side at Ben Madigan Park, on Willys-Ford Jeeps, which had no problem climbing the steep field which was full of weeds and brambles. The remains were subsequently loaded into larger vehicles, presumably US Army GMC CCKW 6X6 Trucks or Dodge Weapons Carriers.

At Wiltons funeral home, GRS personnel were working on the identification of the crew, but due to the multiple injuries and burns incurred, 8 of the crew could not be identified through conventional means such as fingerprints, facial features, or identifying marks, additionally, their identification tags were not present. Fortunately, the pilot, Lester Brooks, was identified by his identity tag and Lawrence R. McGrane, one of the enlisted men, was identified by an identity bracelet. Tooth charts were made of the remainder of the crew by GRS personnel for future identification purposes. Their remains were each placed in a UK Casket, with a Class-A tunic overlaid on each of the remains.

Enclosed within each casket, placed within the head region, was a small bottle which contained a *"report of burial"* form to aid future identification and a *"tooth chart"*, this was known as a *"burial bottle"*.

Many locals visited the area after the crash. A young lady accessed the site with her friends through the golf course, which was close to the Floral Hall. She vividly recalled the partial remains of the burnt out aircraft lying below on the hill side and scattered debris. Amongst the scorched foliage at the top of the hill, to their horror, were the remains of a hand within a leather flying glove, the remains of which, were covered in molten aluminium. They shrieked in horror and ran away from the site.

This would not be the only time that something so horrific would be encountered by locals. A young man at the time, George McCaig and his friends were in the same area as the young lady. They quietly descended into the crash site area, from the top gravel path, so as not to be seen by the guarding police below. However, when they came across what they thought was an empty flying boot, upon lifting the boot, they were horrified that it still contained a severed foot and in their haste discarding what they had just found, the policemen below heard the scuffle and verbally chastised the boys. The three boys scurried up the hillside, onto the gravel path and ran the whole way back to Henderson Avenue, off the Cave Hill Road, which was situated at least a mile and a half distance from the crash site. *(The memories of this horrific find, remained with this boy all of his life and he only relayed the story to the authors in 2017. This can be confirmed from the official burial reports, as it was stated that one of the crew had their leg amputated).*

A young souvenir hunter, one of many at the time, had picked up a large piece of the aircraft after his adventurous visit to the site. The site had been cleared of the main wreckage, but many parts still remained. Attempting to get onto a tram, the conductor insisted that he would not be getting on-board and remarked *"do you think this is Sammy Dankers scrapyard?"*. Another group of boys located and removed an intact belt of ammunition. Subsequently, RUC Officers paid many visits to local schools, warning children that there would be terrible consequences if they had parts of the aircraft and not handed them in.

One such group the RUC were interested in, was a number of young men, one of whom worked for the golf club, situated above the crash site. They had found an intact .50 calibre machine gun from the crashed aircraft. It took four or five of them taking turns to carry it across two fields, to where they hid it, in the cupboard of a small hut that was used to store golf clubs. Days later a Belfast Corporation groundsman saw a group of boys struggling across the golf course, with a heavy object. As they got closer to the Corporation employees, in the vicinity of the Floral Hall, they realised it was a machine gun and arranged for the Police to provide a welcoming reception when the boys arrived at the tram stop on the Antrim Road.

On 4 June 1944, the funeral cortège made its way from the Crumlin Road to Lisnabreeny American Military Cemetery. At 16:00 hours a volley of three shots were fired and taps were sounded as the crew were laid to rest. After the ceremony a solemn white wooden cross was placed at the head of each grave. On 8 of the white crosses, the unidentified members of the crew were named as Unknown X-1 to Unknown X-8 respectively.

As of 2019, the main entrance and administration building of Wiltons Funeral Home, still remains. Through this arch, the remains of the crew would have arrived on the day of the accident and departed in procession on 4 June, to their resting place at Lisnabreeny American Military Cemetery.

A volley of shots are fired over the casket of a US servicemen, at Lisnabreeny American Military Cemetery. This photograph was taken prior to the accident and is representative of the same service that would have been performed for all of the crew, weeks later.

189777-S

At Lisnabreeny American Military Cemetery, mourners preside over the funeral of a U.S. airman. This is representative of what would have taken place on the day of the mass funeral for the crew.

Caledonia Sergeant Beautifies Military Center in North Ireland

Headquarters, European Theater of Operations—American troops who die while serving their country in Northern Ireland are laid to rest in Lisnabreeny American Military Cemetery, situated atop a wind-swept hill overlooking the city of Belfast.

The quiet spot is part of a wooded estate that is to be made into a national park after the war. Tall pines and rhododendrons grow about the rolling hilltops, and the green border fences bloom the entire year with bright yellow gorse.

Master Sergt. Charles C. Conner of 79 North St., Caledonia, N. Y., was among the first Yanks who landed in Ireland in January, 1942, and he, more than anyone else, has been responsible for the beautification of the military cemetery.

Sergeant Conner was a licensed mortician before entering the war and he is one of the soldier morticians of the United States Quartermaster Graves Registration Unit in North Ireland who embalm the soldiers who make the supreme sacrifice for their country. Every soldier is embalmed and clothed in a complete new uniform before interment in individual graves.

"When an American military procession passes through the streets of Belfast," said Sergeant Conner, "the people show intense reverence. The men remove their hats and stand at attention, while the women look on in grave silence."

Many of the townsfolk, including an RAF air marshal and the wife of the Chief Justice of North Ireland, have brought flowers and placed them upon the soldiers' graves.

Sergeant Conner's ancestors came from North Ireland. He has received offers to establish a business in Belfast after the war. "I'll make my mind up about that later," he remarked.

CREESLOUGH
LONDONDERRY
IRELAN
DONEGAL
OMAGH
LOUGH
ERNE
DEVENISH ISLAND
LOUGH
ALLEN
CAVAN

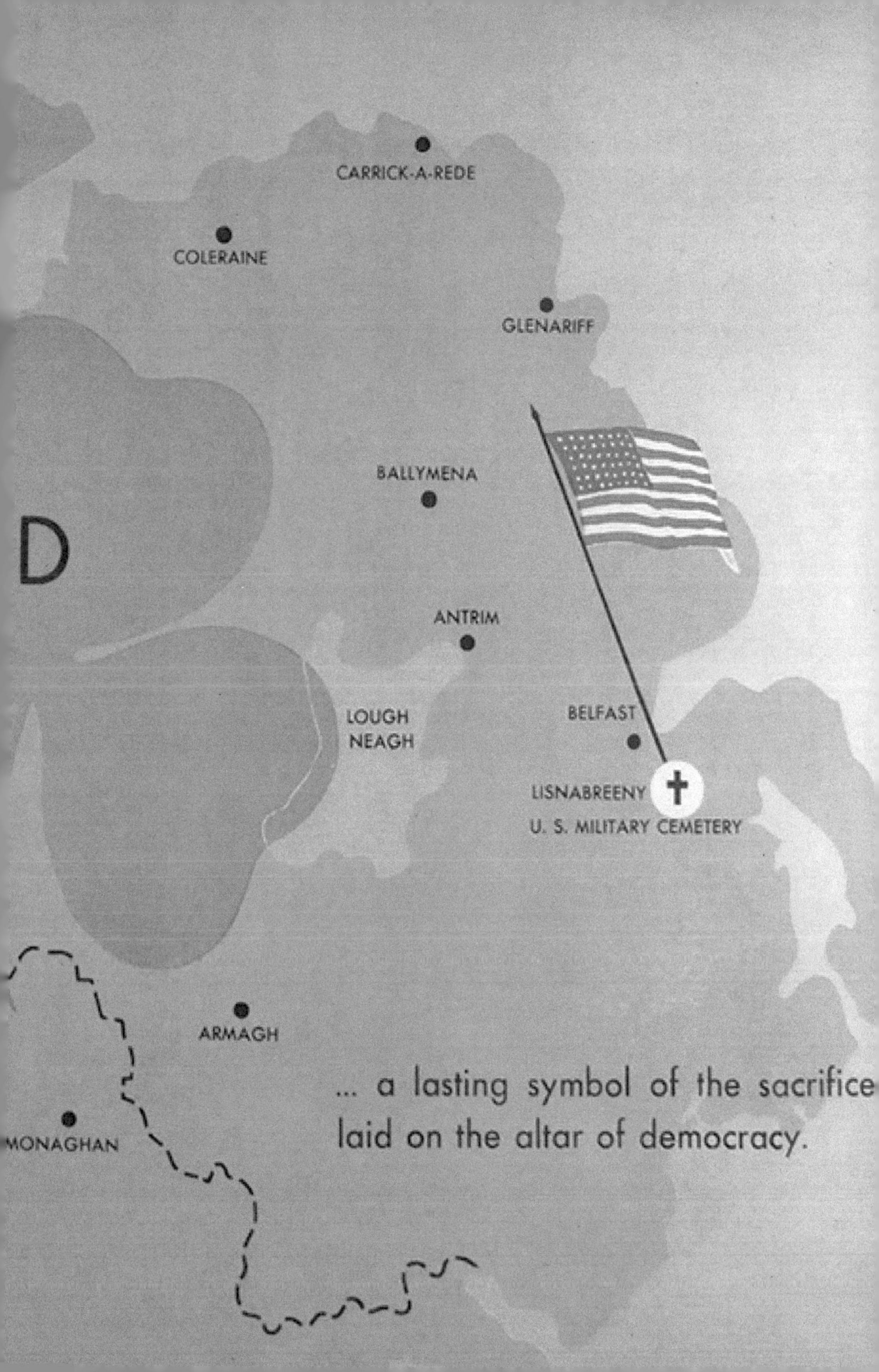

... a lasting symbol of the sacrifice laid on the altar of democracy.

Chapter Eight

Deepest sympathy

PLANE CRASH FATAL

Lieut. Lester B. Brooks

Crash of a bomber in Northern Ireland on June 1 resulted fatally for Flight Officer Lester Bryan Brooks, 22, according to information received here yesterday by his wife, Mrs. Genevieve Brooks. Lieut. Brooks, a son of Mr. and Mrs. L. G. Brooks of Union-tp, had recently reported his arrival overseas.

Born September 27, 1921 in Union-tp, Lieut. Brooks graduated from Carrollton high school in the class of 1939. He enlisted in the air corps on February 2, 1943 and received his wings on November 3, last year at George Field, Ill. He qualified as a pilot of a B-17 bomber. Before being assigned overseas he was stationed at McDill Field, Fla. His preliminary training was received at Fletcher Field, Miss., and Maxwell Field, Ala. His last furlough at home was during the week of May 11.

Lieut. Brooks was married to Miss Genevieve Rutledge, daughter of Mrs. Emma Rutledge of East Carrollton, on July 24, 1943 at Newport, Ark. Besides his wife and his parents, Lieut. Brooks is survived by a brother, Olan Brooks of Union-tp.

In the days following the crash the tragic news would soon begin to make its way to the next of kin at home, in the form of a War Department Telegram.

Ruth Dundon, the wife of Lawrence E. Dundon, received a war department telegram on 7 June, delivery had been attempted at their home but since Ruth had moved out to let the manager of her employer stay there temporarily, the two American soldiers from the War Department delivered the telegram to her mothers address. They hesitated to give her mother the telegram as it was required to be delivered in person. After some discussion, the two soldiers agreed that Ruth's mother could deliver the telegram to Ruth. At around 3pm in the afternoon, Ruth's mother called her husband and informed them both to come home immediately. Arriving home, Ruth's mother handed her the telegram, she was excited, as Larry had said he would let her know as soon as they had arrived at their destination. To say the least, it was not the message she expected;

The Secretary of War asks that I assure you of his deepest sympathy in the loss of your husband Staff Sergeant Lawrence E. Dundon.

Report received states that he was killed one June in Belfast, Northern Ireland, In a plane crash, letter follows.

The Adjutant General - June 7th, 1944

Gennie Brooks, the wife of Lester, received the telegram the same day as Ruth, as did the other next of kin of the deceased. In the case of Sgt. Robert E. Graves Jr. of Arkansas, his parents were not notified of his death until 13 June, almost two weeks after the accident.

From the east coast to the west coast of the United States, obituaries began to surface in local home town newspapers of their loved ones tragic accident. The news was met with disbelief for many of the newly widowed who believed there had been some sort of mistake on behalf of the War Department. Jeremiah Murphy's wife Norma, wrote to the War Department requesting additional information, as she could not accept the news of what had happened to her husband.

4 Kentuckians Reported Killed; 9 Hurt; 2 Missing

Four Kentuckians, including two Louisvillians, have been killed, nine have been wounded, and two are missing in action, the War and Navy Departments announced yesterday.

Staff Sgt. Lawrence E. Dundon, 32, died June 1 of injuries received when the Fortress on which he was a radio operator crashed at Belfast, North Ireland, his wife, Mrs. Ruth Taylor Dundon, 219 N. 33d, was informed by the War Department. Also surviving are his mother, Mrs. Daisy Dundon, 3222 W. Market; two half-brothers, Marine Corps Pvt. Hollie Hough, now at Camp Pendleton, Calif., and Russell Hough, South Pasadena, Calif.

El Dorado Sergeant Killed In Ireland.

El Dorado, June 9 (Spl).—Sgt. Robert L. Graves, Jr., bombardier in the Army Air Forces has been killed in an airplane accident in Ireland, the War Department notified his parents, Mr. and Mrs. R. L. Graves of El Dorado today.

Sergeant Graves, who visited his parents here a few weeks ago is believed to have arrived in Ireland very recently.

A former employe of McWilliams Hardware and Furniture Co. here, Sergeant Graves had been in the air corps about a year, also he is survived by a son.

FLYER KILLED IN IRELAND.

Jeremiah C. Murphy, 26, of 47 West Street, Albany, a flight officer, was killed in a plane crash June 1 on Cave Hill, Belfast, Ireland, it was announced Wednesday by the War Department. Survivors include his wife, the former Norma Howard of Arcadia, Fla., and a seven weeks' old daughter.

Flight Officer Leighton McKenzie Killed in Action Over Europe

● MRS. Guinevere Zaun Robinson received word last week that her son, Flight Officer Leighton McKenzie, 19, was killed in action June 1 in the western European theatre of war.

Officer McKenzie visited his mother and his grandparents, Captain and Mrs. Leighton Robinson, of Edgewood avenue, in May, reporting for duty on May 14.

He was born in Los Angeles, graduated from Old Mill school and from Tamalpais high school, where he was track high jumper, took a course in aviation mechanics at Reedley Junior college, and enlisted. He graduated from the bombardier school at Childress, Texas, in December, 1943, receiving his commission. His cartoons illustrated the class graduation book at Childress.

During his boyhood he spent much time with Captain Robinson at the San Francisco Yacht club in Belvedere, and it was there that he painted the mast of the abandoned yacht "Annie" to be used as a flagpole at the clubhouse. The "Annie" was the oldest yacht in the bay, having sailed around the Horn. It was taken out through the Golden Gate and destroyed after its mast was removed and a plaque attached. From this mast, now a flagpole, the flag hung at half staff last week in honor of Flight Officer McKenzie. Tamalpais high school flag also hung at half staff.

The young officer was the son of Malcolm McKenzie of Portland, Oregon, the grandson of Mrs. A. B. McKenzie of Martinez and the late Judge McKenzie, and the nephew of Lieutenant Colonel Shayer Robinson, USA.

S. Sgt. Brewer Dies in Crash Over Ireland

WAPELLA. — (PNS) — S. Sgt. Wilbur D. Brewer, Wapella, was killed in a plane crash early in June in Belfast, Ireland, according to word received Wednesday by his brother, Amos Brewer, Clinton, from the adjutant general's office.

He was a top turret gunner on a Flying Fortress and had been in service since October, 1942. He was on his way overseas when the crash occurred over Ireland.

He received training at Sheppard field, Tex.; Ingleside, Calif., and prior to going overseas he received his gunnery training at McDill field, Fla.

He attended high school in Wapella where he starred in athletics. He graduated in 1940.

He was born at Clinton, Oct. 29, 1922, son of Charles C. and Verna B. Brewer.

He married Miss Eileen Burns of Wapella in April, 1943. His parents and wife were killed in an auto crash near Kansas City, Mo. in May, 1943.

He is survived by five brothers, Roger F., Kansas City, Mo.; Paul A., Bloomington; Amos, Clinton; Floyd, serving with the aviation engineers in England; Charles, Clinton; his grandmother, Mrs Cliff Walker, Arcola.

Airman E. E. McGill Ireland Crash Victim

S/Sgt. Edward Ewing McGill, 29 son of Mrs. Delia McGill of Bell's Road, has been killied in an air crash in Belfast, North Ireland, the war department notified his brother, Reed S. McGill, 812 Boscobel Street, yesterday morning.

No further details of the crash were included in the short war department notification.

Sergeant McGill, a waist gunner with the army air force, first enlisted three years ago with the Canadian Royal Air Force, but was transferred to the American Air Forces two years ago in England.

He had been awarded the Air Medal with two Oak Leaf Clusters and the Distinguished Flying Cross.

Born in Nashville, Sergeant McGill was a graduate of East Nashville High School and attended Austin Peay State College at Clarksville. He was a star football player at each school.

Prior to entering the service he was employed as a shipping clerk at the Graham Paper Company here.

Arcadia, Florida
June 12, 1944

Dear Sir:

First I want to thank you for your kind letter in regards to the death of my late husband, Flight Officer Jeremiah C. Murphy. It was indeed a great shock to me, as you know, but somehow I keep hoping it is a mistake.

I am writing to you in regards to my insurance. You see I do not have any papers even though I know my husband's insurance was made out to me. People say that I will not get any insurance if I do not have papers so I would like very much to have you advise as to the matter.

Also, Sir, I would appreciate very much the return of my husband's personal belongings, if possible.

In reply, please write to this address.

Mrs. Norma Murphy
197 Madison Avenue
Albany, New York.

Yours truly,

Mrs. Norma Murphy

P.S. I am referring to

AG 201 Murphy, Jeremiah C.
PC-N 155112

197 Madison Avenue
Albany, New York
June 28, 1944

Dear Sir:

I am writing to you in regards to the letter I received from you on June 9, 1944 in which you confirmed the death of my late husband, Flight Officer Jeremiah C. Murphy, T-62092, of the Air Corps, who was reported killed in a plane crash in Belfast, Northern Ireland on June 1, 1944.

I was given no other information other than the above and I can't believe my husband is dead. My reasoning tells me that it must be true because of the telegram, but yet, something won't let me believe it. The other crew member's wives fell the same way and all my friends also. There has been so many mistakes and we have no information, so we keep hoping and praying that this is another mistake.

Please, if possibel, send me some proof that my husband is dead so I can believe it and stop this agony of not knowing.

If you could send his wallet, dog tags, or something he had with him, or else tell me if you buried him, or was he uncoverable, I would believe it. Until then I will keep praying that it isn't true.

I would appreciate it if you would get this information at once and answer for I must have some proof to ease my mind.

Yours truly,

Mrs. Norma Murphy
197 Madison Avenue
Albany, New York.

WAR DEPARTMENT

T ADJUTANT GENERAL'S FICE

WASHINGTON 25, D. C.

REPORT OF DEATH

DATE 10 June 1944
ZM/rm 4627

FULL NAME	ARMY SERIAL NUMBER	GRADE
Brewer, Wilbur D.	16 075 633	S/Sgt

HOME ADDRESS	ARM OR SERVICE	DATE OF BIRTH
Wapella, Ill.	Air Corps	29 Oct 22

PLACE OF DEATH	CAUSE OF DEATH	DATE OF DEATH
Cave Hill Belfast, North Ireland	Airplane crash	1 Jun 44

STATION OF DECEASED	DATE OF ENTRY ON CURRENT ACTIVE SERVICE	LENGTH OF SERVICE FOR PAY PURPOSES: YEARS	MONTHS	DAYS
European Area	28 Oct 42	1	7	4

EMERGENCY ADDRESSEE (NAME, RELATIONSHIP & ADDRESS)

Amos Brewer, brother, Wapella, Ill.

BENEFICIARY (NAME, RELATIONSHIP & ADDRESS)

Amos Brewer, brother, address above
Charles W. Brewer, brother, address above

INVESTIGATION MADE?		IN LINE OF DUTY		OWN MISCONDUCT		WAS DECEASED ON DUTY STATUS		AUTHORIZED ABSENCE		IN FLYING PAY STATUS		OTHER PAY STATUS (SPECIFY BELOW)	
YES	NO	YES	NO	YES	NO	YES	NO	YES	NO	YES	NO	YES	NO
	X	X			X	X				X			

ADDITIONAL DATA AND/OR STATEMENT

JUN 12 4 43 PM '44
MEMORIAL DIVISION

Non-battle

COPIES FURNISHED:		
S. G. O.	F. B. I.	F. O., U. S. A., WASH., D. C.
G. A. O.	VET. ADMIN.	ARMY EFFECTS BUREAU
Q. M. G.	OFF. FIS. DIR.	

BY ORDER OF THE SECRETARY OF WAR:

James W. Reinhart.
ADJUTANT GENERAL

WD. AGO. FORM NO. 52-1, 27 NOVEMBER 1943

No Casualty Report
9-1-44. N.C

June 28-1944
Susie Mery Efaw.
1012 E. Central.
Wichita, Kans.
87350

Effects Quartermaster:
Kansas City Mo.

Dear Sir:
I would like to know if you have received the personal effects of Howard A. Hibbler No. 37,210,378. Air Corps. who lost his life at Cave Hill, Belfast, Northern Ireland, June 1st 1944.

Sincerely Yours.
Susie Mery Efaw.

For some family members of the crew, a few personal effects were returned. Lester, prior to leaving the US, had in forethought, sent a footlocker over to England, via ship, with a small number of his personal items contained within. Unfortunately, it appeared to have been tampered with and likely a number of his personal effects had been removed by unknown persons. What remained, was a pillow, one sweater, four shirts, four socks, four pairs of trousers, handkerchiefs, three pairs of footwear, a shoe shine kit and a number of technical manuals. Sadly, he never arrived to reclaim it and it likely arrived a number of weeks after the accident. Subsequently, over a year later, these items were returned to his widow.

Lawrence McGrane, had his footlocker shipped back home from MacDill prior to his departure from the US. *His nephew, Lawrence McGrane, inherited the footlocker, as-well as a small Air Corps branch of service winged propeller pin.*

***Below and to the right**, are a number of photographs of the footlocker and the pin, as they appear today. His name and army serial number are still clearly visible stencilled in red, upon military green paint.*

A number of unspecified effects that had not succumbed to the crash and subsequent fire were recovered from the crash site. These items belonged to Joseph Nobilione and Leighton McKenzie. Presumably they would have been returned to their parents by the Army Effects Bureau as they were not married.

A personal effect belonging to Robert Graves, consisting of a Gruen wrist watch, was removed from his body at the time of burial. Unfortunately, the watch went missing and repeated attempts to locate it proved unsuccessful. A number of years after the crash, the Army Effects Bureau claimed to have located this watch and stated that they had returned it to his mother and father. The watch that they received, was a badly damaged pocket watch, of which, they claimed did not belong to him as he never carried one.

The crew carried all of their personal effects with them on the aircraft. *The officers were permitted to use the Type B-4 Flight Bag, which was a small suitcase. It could be unzipped and unfolded when not in use, doubling up as a portable wardrobe for their Class-A uniforms. The enlisted men were permitted to use the Type M-1943 Duffel Bag, additionally, some personnel, if they could acquire one, would use the AN-6505 Aviators Kit Bag.*

***Left**, an officers B-4 Flight Bag. **Below left**, Type AN-6505 Aviators Kit Bag. **Below right**, used by Enlisted Men, the Type M-1943 Duffel Bag.*

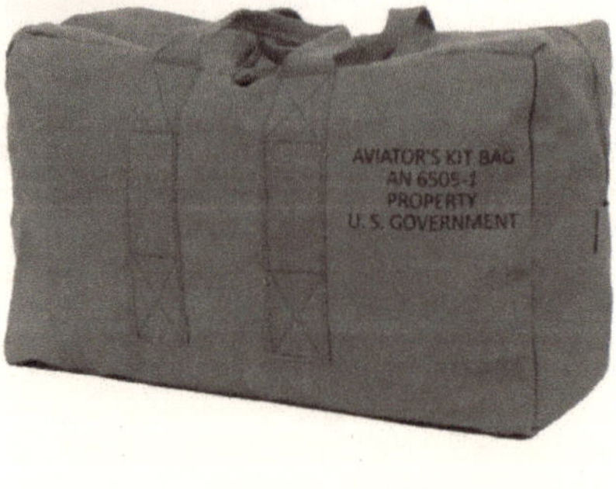

Ae
10/24

Carrollton, Ohio
Route 2
Oct. 18, 1944

Effects Quartermaster
Kansas City, Mo.

128171 IMMEDIATE ACTION

Dear Sir:—

I am writing concerning my husband, Flight Officer Lester B. Brooke, T-61593, who was reported killed in a B-17 bomber plane crash on 1 June 1944 at Belfast, North Ireland. As yet I have received very little information and none of his personal effects. It is very difficult to give up one so dear without more proof than a telegram and form letter. I would appreciate it very much if you could give me any information or tell me whether I will receive any of his personal effects and how soon. Thank you so much.

I remain
Mrs. Lester B. Brooke
Carrollton, Ohio
Route 2

file
ok

Chapter Nine

Unknown X

During the month of December 1944, Ruth Dundon, the widow of Larry, received a letter from a Belfast address. Upon opening the letter, she was greeted by a young Mr. Gordon Wade. Gordon, had obtained Ruth's address from an object he had found at the crash site. He did not mention what it was that he had found, but stated that when the war was over, he would write to her and send her the object he had uncovered.

When the war had ended, true to his word, Gordon sent the object over to Ruth. It was one of Larry's identity tags, or dog tags. Having lost a brother during the war and finding this tag at the crash site, he had realised how much it would mean to the widow of the deceased. Gordon and Ruth continued to write to each other. After he joined the Merchant Navy, she did not hear from him again. She later found out, that he passed away in 1990.

Ruth also corresponded with a lady from Northern Ireland, called Mrs. Ringland, who, upon taking a trip to the US met Gennie, the widow of Lester, in Carrollton, Ohio.

Almost a year had passed since the accident and identification of

some of the crew was still on-going. In January 1945 the remains of Unknown X-1 were tentatively identified as that of Robert L. Graves Jr. During the month of May, at the request of the Office of the Quartermaster General, It was decided that due to erroneous dental tooth charts made at the time of the accident, that three of the crew would need to be exhumed and have their tooth charts retaken. On 12 June 1945, the remains of Unknown X-2, X-7 and X-8

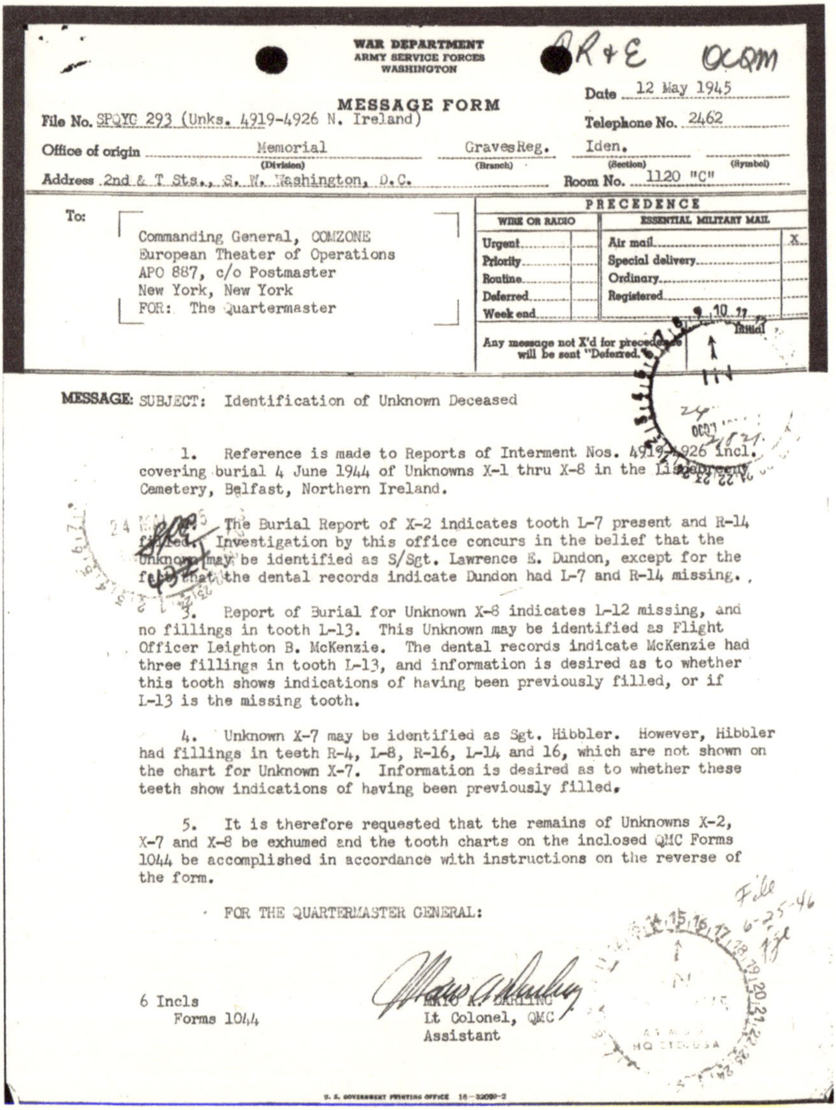

WAR DEPARTMENT
ARMY SERVICE FORCES
WASHINGTON

R+E OQM

MESSAGE FORM

Date 12 May 1945

File No. SPQYG 293 (Unks. 4919-4926 N. Ireland)

Telephone No. 2462

Office of origin Memorial (Division) GravesReg. (Branch) Iden. (Section) (Symbol)

Address 2nd & T Sts., S. W. Washington, D.C. Room No. 1120 "C"

To:

Commanding General, COMZONE
European Theater of Operations
APO 887, c/o Postmaster
New York, New York
FOR: The Quartermaster

PRECEDENCE			
WIRE OR RADIO		ESSENTIAL MILITARY MAIL	
Urgent		Air mail	X
Priority		Special delivery	
Routine		Ordinary	
Deferred		Registered	
Week end			

Any message not X'd for precedence will be sent "Deferred."

Initial

MESSAGE: SUBJECT: Identification of Unknown Deceased

1. Reference is made to Reports of Interment Nos. 4919-4926 incl. covering burial 4 June 1944 of Unknowns X-1 thru X-8 in the Lisnabreeny Cemetery, Belfast, Northern Ireland.

2. The Burial Report of X-2 indicates tooth L-7 present and R-14 filled. Investigation by this office concurs in the belief that the Unknown may be identified as S/Sgt. Lawrence E. Dundon, except for the fact that the dental records indicate Dundon had L-7 and R-14 missing.

3. Report of Burial for Unknown X-8 indicates L-12 missing, and no fillings in tooth L-13. This Unknown may be identified as Flight Officer Leighton B. McKenzie. The dental records indicate McKenzie had three fillings in tooth L-13, and information is desired as to whether this tooth shows indications of having been previously filled, or if L-13 is the missing tooth.

4. Unknown X-7 may be identified as Sgt. Hibbler. However, Hibbler had fillings in teeth R-4, L-8, R-16, L-14 and 16, which are not shown on the chart for Unknown X-7. Information is desired as to whether these teeth show indications of having been previously filled.

5. It is therefore requested that the remains of Unknowns X-2, X-7 and X-8 be exhumed and the tooth charts on the inclosed QMC Forms 1044 be accomplished in accordance with instructions on the reverse of the form.

FOR THE QUARTERMASTER GENERAL:

File 6-25-46

6 Incls
Forms 1044

MARIO A. DARLING
Lt Colonel, QMC
Assistant

U. S. GOVERNMENT PRINTING OFFICE 16-32090-2

were disinterred to establish detailed tooth charts. A most unglamorous task, the embalmer, M/Sgt. Charles J. Conner, supervised the disinterment and re-interment. M/Sgt. Conner was assigned to the American Graves Registration Service and worked on location at Wiltons Funeral Home and the American Cemetery at Lisnabreeny. It is highly likely that he was one of the embalmers who worked on the crew at the time of the accident a year earlier.

X-7

G. R.& E. DIV.
OFFICE OF THE CHIEF QUARTERMASTER
HQ. COM. ZONE, ETOUSA

TOOTH CHART

Date

UNKNOWN X-7 (LISNABREENY)

Last Name — First — Initial — Rank — Serial No.

Unit — Organization

Place of Death — Date of Death — Cause of Death

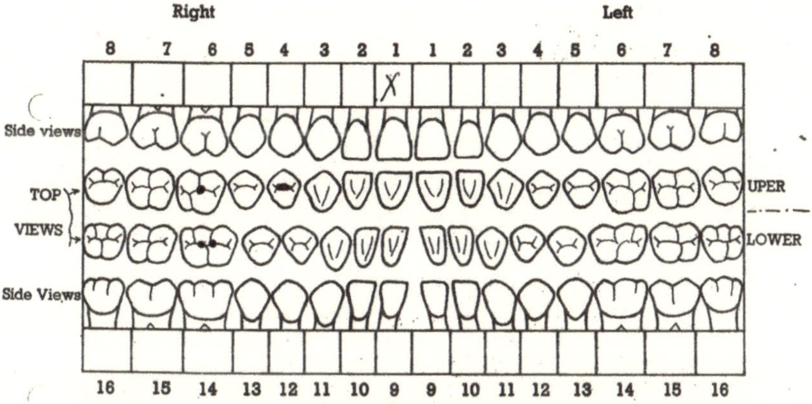

This dental chart is very important and should be filled in with great care. There are 32 teeth to be accounted for, as shown by the numbers on the chart. Beginning at the middle line in both upper and lower jaws, the teeth are arranged symmetrically on either side and classed as incisors (cutting teeth), cuspids or canines (tearing teeth), bicuspids (chewing teeth), and molars (principal chewing teeth). An examination should be made and findings charted to cover the following basic conditions : Lost teeth, crowned teeth, bridge work, fillings, caries (cavities of decay), dentures (plates), and any deformity of jaws found. See reverse side for illustrations.

L1 - missing, previous to injury. (L14 fractured and
L14- no filling. Buccal cusp buoken (unable to determine if filled on (facial)
L15- no filling. Buccal cusp broken (fractured and unable to determine if filled on facial).
L16 - filling. Buccal cusp broken (fractured and unable to determine if filled on facial).

Signature of Officer or other person who prepared Tooth chart

L8 - no occlusal filling. Lingual cusp broken. Unable to determine to if filled on lingual.

Verfied by G. R. S. Officer

R16 - no filling.
R4 - Small occlusal amalgam filling. R6-occlusal amalgam filling.
R14-occlusal and facial amalgam fillings

GRAVES REGISTRATION FORM No 1-A

OCCLUSEN Good. HEAVY BONY STRUCTURE.
R1 AND L2 show PREPARATION for 3/4 CROWNS.
REMAINS EXAMINED 12 JUNE, 1945

QMC FORM 1044
Rev. 7 Apr. 1945

RE[redacted]CTED

REPORT OF DISINTERMENT FOR IDENTIFICATION — 12 June, 1945

1. REMAINS OF (Name)		SERIAL NUMBER
~~Unknown~~ (X-7) HIBBLER, Howard A.		37210378

GRADE	ORGANIZATION
Sgt.	Station 2, European Wing Air Transport

NAME, NUMBER AND LOCATION OF CEMETERY	PLOT	ROW	GRAVE NO.
Lisnabreeny Cemetery, Belfast, Northern Ireland	"B"	4	17

2. DATE OF DISINTERMENT	DATE OF REINTERMENT
12 June, 1945	12 June, 1945

3. REPORT AS TO NATURE OF ORIGINAL BURIAL AND CONDITION OF BODY UPON DISINTERMENT.

Nature of original burial - Military.

Condition of body upon disinterment - Body was badly decomposed but Dental Charts were accomplished for additional information.

~~Ident.~~

4. WHAT IDENTIFICATION FOUND AT TIME OF DISINTERMENT: ON MARKER

Identification tag.

ON REMAINS

Dental Chart in a sealed bottle.

WHAT IDENTIFICATION USED UPON REINTERMENT: ON MARKER

Identification tag.

ON REMAINS

Dental Chart in a sealed bottle.

5. SIGNATURE OF OFFICER SUPERVISING DISINTERMENT AND REINTERMENT.

M/Sgt Charles G Conner NCO In Charge

RE[redacted]CTED

Belfast Telegraph

Decr. 18, 1945. RS/F

Mrs. Mary Broccolo,
Killingworth,
Locust Valley,
Long Island, N.Y.

Dear Madam,

In reply to your letter bearing postmark 10th inst. we have to state that an American flying fortress crashed at the side of the Cave Hill, at the rear of Hazelwood Golf Course, Belfast, about lunch-time on 14th June, 1944. The 'plane immediately took fire and all the efforts of the Belfast Fire Service were unavailing. Unfortunately, none of the occupants survived. Their deaths, however, were instantaneous. The bodies, which were recovered, were reverently interred in the plot near Belfast City specially reserved for American Servicemen. The idea at first was that the bodies would be exhumed after the war and removed for permanent burial in the United States. We understand that the opinion of relatives is being taken as to the desirability of this procedure, and it will depend on the number of requests for re-interment whether the removal will be made or not. The undertakers who carried out the internment work for the U.S.A. authorities in the North of Ireland were Messrs. Wilton & Co., Rosewood Buildings, Crumlin Road, Belfast. The name of the burial place is Lisnabreeny, Castlereagh Hills, Belfast.

May we express our sympathy with you in the tragic loss of your brother.

Yours sincerely,

R. M. Sayers.

MANAGING EDITOR.

This on-going task of trying to identify each of the crew was unknown to their family members at home. Wilbur Brewers brother Floyd, was stationed in England when he decided to take a trip to Northern Ireland before returning home, to visit his brothers resting place. Upon enquiring with cemetery personnel he was informed that there was talk of moving the cemetery to England and that there was some possibility of identifying the crew through dental work.

AMOS F. BREWER, AGENT
BASEMENT - NATIONAL BANK BUILDING
PHONE: 362
CLINTON, ILL.

January 17, 1946.

United States War Dept.
Washington, D.C.

Gentlemen:

On June 1, 1944, my brother, Staff Sgt. Wilbur D. Brewer was killed in a plane crash at Belfast, Northern Ireland. The bodies were burned beyond recognition. Another brother, Sgt. Floyd Brewer, went to Ireland before being discharged from service, and found out there was some talk of moving the cemetary from Belfast to England. He also discovered that therewas some possibility of identifiing the boys through dental work, and that this is being studied at Washington at this time.

I would appreciate it very much if you would let me know what has been done about the identification and also about moving the cemetary.

If I am contacting the wrong department, I would appreciate your notifiing me as to whom I should write.

Yours truly,

Amos F. Brewer

Amos F. Brewer.

ANGLO-AMERICAN UNDERWRITERS AGENCY
of the Liverpool and London and Globe Insurance Co. Ltd.

Upon returning home to the US Floyd informed his brother Amos, who immediately wrote a letter to the War Department. Amos received a reply, dated 15 February 1946, from the Office of the Quartermaster General - Memorial Division. It must have seemed a little disappointing to Amos, as the letter stated that all efforts to identify the crew had been exhausted and that there was contemplation of returning the crews remains to the US for interment in a National Cemetery.

SPQYG 293
Brewer, Wilbur D.
SN 16 075 633

Address Reply To
THE QUARTERMASTER GENERAL
Attention: Memorial Division

15 February 1946

Mr. Amos F. Brewer
Citizens Insurance Co.
National Bank
Clinton, Illinois

Dear Mr. Brewer:

Your letter concerning your brother, the late Staff Sergeant Wilbur D. Brewer, has been received in this office.

With deep regret I must inform you that, although the report on file in this office covering the burial of your brother discloses that his remains were properly interred in a manner befitting our honored dead, due to the manner in which he met his death, his remains as well as those of others in his crew could not be individually identified. The remains of this crew were interred as a group in the Lisnabreeny Cemetery, Belfast, Ireland.

Please be assured that the Graves Registration Services exhausts every available clue which might lead to individual identification of our deceased military personnel. If identity cannot be established, it is contemplated returning the remains of this crew to the United States for final interment in a National Cemetery.

So far as is known by this office, it is not intended that the U. S. Military Cemetery at Lisnabreeny will be evacuated until the time of repatriation of the dead.

FOR THE QUARTERMASTER GENERAL:

Sincerely yours,

JAMES L. PRENN
Major, QMC
Assistant

7

4/10/46 EMD Unks. X-1 thru X-8, N.Ireland

293 Brewer, Wilbur D.

Brewer, Wilbur D., S/Sgt., 16,075,633
Dundon, Lawrence E., S/Sgt., 35,692,675
Graves, Robert L., Jr., Sgt., 38,334,100
Hibbler, Howard A., Sgt., 37,210,378
McGill, Edward E., S/Sgt., 10,600,464
McKenzie, Leighton B., F/O., T-123650
Murphy, Jeremiah C., F/O., T-62092
Nobilione, Joseph V., 2nd Lt., 0-710299

4 June 1944.....Reports of Burial 4919-4926 submitted for Unknowns X-1 thru X-8, interred in Grs. 11 thru 18 incl., Row 4, Plot B, Lisnabreeny Cemetery, Belfast, N.Ireland. Tooth charts on each report; notation made that X-1 had bandaged right foot; Gruen wrist watch found on remains of X-1. Each Unknown is listed as one of the following:

2nd Lt. Joseph V. Nobilione, 0-710299
F/O Jeremiah C. Murphy, T-62092
F/O Leighton B. McKenzie, T-123650
S/Sgt. Edward E. McGill, 10,600,464
S/Sgt. Lawrence E. Bundon, 35,692,675
S/Sgt. Wilbur D. Brewer, 16,075,633
Sgt. Robert L. Graves, Jr., 38,334,100
Sgt. Howard A. Hibber, 37,210,378

Checked crew with Air Corps. There were ten members - the above-mentioned eight and the following two:

Brooks, Lester B. - identified and interred in Gr. 19-4-B, Lisnabreeny
McGrane, Lawrence R. - iden. and interred in Gr. 20-4-B, Lisnabreeny
(identified by identification tags)

Investigation conducted to obtain complete dental charts for the eight men.

Effort made to obtain Gruen Watch from Effects Bureau -- not received at Kansas City.

Effort also made to obtain necessary information relative to the foot injury received by Unknown X-1 -- no record.

See Dental Chart next page.

Behind the scenes further identification of the crew had been taking place for over a year. A thorough inspection of the dental charts had been made and the investigators had come to the conclusion, that they had identified some of the unknown crew members. It was now April 1946.

Belfast Adopts American Graves

Belfast—(AP)—Graves in the United States Army cemetery at Lisnabreeny, Castle Reagh, overlooking the city of Belfast, are being adopted by local residents who weekly place flowers on them.

One typical case is 18-year-old Winifred Burrows, of Loopland Park, Belfast, who places a bunch of white chrysanthemums every Sunday under the wooden cross which bears the inscription "Philip L. Jordan, T5, 74th General Hospital, April 2, 1943, of Bridgeport, Conn."

Winfred, a pretty dark-haired typist, said: "We did not know who he was or anything about him but since I started laying the wreaths his mother and I correspond regularly."

Keep Watch At Graves Of U. S. War Dead In Ireland

(Editor's note: Mrs. Cora A. Signor, Effingham, recently received a clipping from a friend in Belfast, North Ireland, taken from the April 12 issue of The Belfast Telegraph. Concerning an American military cemetery there. Several interesting extracts from the clipping follow).

"Every morning at 8 o'clock a strange ritual takes place in a field on the Castlereagh Hills. high above the smoke and noise and bustle of Belfast. It is carried out by a man in khaki American uniform.

"A few moments to eight he opens the gate of the field with his key. Then he makes his way to a grassy knoll at the farthermost edge of the field and starts hauling on the rope of a lofty flagstaff. A few seconds later a great flag is flapping and fluttering in the breeze, the flag of the United States of America.

"So another day begins at the American Military cemetery Lisnabreeny, temporary resting place of 148 American soldiers, sailors and airmen. Here they lie in serried rows of 25, each with a simple white cross at his head, with his name, rank and the date of his death briefly recorded. And behind them and high above flutters the Stars and Stripes, symbol of a great nation's loving care for her fallen sons.

"At 5 p. m. when the cemetery closes, the flag is lowered, the gates are locked, and the custodian of the cemetery sets off down the lane to get his bus back to the city. His job is finished for the day, a job which to many would be irksome and distasteful, but tomorrow will find him back at the cemetery on the stroke of eight, hauling the colors to full mast again. For him this is something more than a job. It is a sacred duty to the dead, to be carried out punctually. reverently, lovingly.

"A lonely job? 'Not at all,' he'll tell you in his drawling American. 'We've got five men working here all the time, and then there's my partner, who's an American like myself. We like it here. We like the quietness and peace, and I guess we are doing something worth while. . . .'

"They are seeing to it that that great stretch of lawn which was formerly a ten acre field — or fields — is kept velvety smooth, that the white-jacketed paths are kept free of weeds and the stone borders whitewashed, and that the ornamental trees and shrubs are pruned and healthy. . . .

"Jews, Gentiles, Protestants and Roman Catholics, white men and men of color. men with German and Dutch and Italian names — here they lie side by side with the barriers and animosities of race and creed forgotten—Americans all.

They sleep serenely in this lovely place, far from the land which gave them birth, yet not so very far — for over them flies their country's flag, symbol of a nation's love and remembrance. Faithful 'Uncle Sam' keeps vigil with his dead."

The remains interred as Unknown X-1 are undoubtedly those of Sgt. Graves. He is the only one of the eight men whose teeth were normal. The camps where he was stationed were unobtainable due to incomplete records of the AGO, and therefore could not be contacted for later dental information. The chart of Unknown X-1 states "all teeth present in good condition". It is believed that this means all were present and in good condition. Where teeth of the other Unknowns were missing posthumously, they were marked on the charts as "destroyed".

The dental chart of Unknown X-2 checks more closely with that of S/Sgt. Dundon. Missing teeth R-8,5,16, and 14; L-4,5,7,8,14,15, and 16 are identical. Teeth R-1,13, and 15 must have been filled and tooth R-2 extracted after S/Sgt. Dundon left the United States.

The remains interred as Unknown X-5 are unquestionably those of S/Sgt. McGill. S/Sgt. McGill was 29 years of age at induction--30 years 6 months at time of death. Missing teeth R-8,5,4, L-5 and 8, R-14, L-14 and 15 are identical. Fillings in R-7, L-3,6, and 12 are also identical. The filling in tooth R-1 probably dropped out, however, it was a synthetic filling and was probably overlooked. Fillings in teeth R-6, L-13 and 16 and R-15 and 16 were undoubtedly accomplished after McGill left the United States.

The tooth chart of Unknown X-7 compares favorably with that of Sgt. Hibbler. The one missing tooth (L-1) is identical with that of Hibbler. Fillings in R-6,4, and 14 are identical. Teeth L-8, 14, 15 and 16 were fractured and it could not be determined if fillings had been accomplished in these teeth. It will be noted that Hibbler is the only one of the eight men who had tooth L-1 missing.

The dental chart of Unknown X-8 is identical with that of F/O McKenzie.

The dental chart of Unknown X-3 checks closely with that of S/Sgt. Brewer. Although the tooth chart is a partial one, of the three men left unidentified, S/Sgt. Brewer is the only one with tooth R-13 missing. It will also be noted that Brewer's R-15 and L-14 were restorable carious teeth and Unknown X-3 had these teeth filled. It is believed that the recording of tooth L-7 (Unk. S-3) was erroneous. Teeth R-14 and L-15 must have been filled and tooth L-16 erupted after S/Sgt. Brewer left the United States.

This leaves Unknowns X-4 and X-6 unidentified. Murphy and Nobilione are the only remaining men killed in the crash; Nobilione has tooth R-14 missing (R-14 and 15 are the only teeth of Unknown X-6 that were not destroyed.) Unknown X-6 and Murphy have tooth R-14 filled. Unknown X-4 had teeth R-8 and R-7 filled and therefore cannot be identified as Murphy who had a complete upper denture.

In April 1947, the Memorial Division of the Office of the Quartermaster General, informed the Commanding Officer of the American Graves Registration Command, that the markings of the graves were to be changed accordingly and the Memorial Division was to be advised immediately upon completion.

In view of the fact that there were ten men killed in the crash and only two were positively identified; the dental charts submitted have been identified as follows:

Unk. X-1 -- Graves, Robert L., Jr., Sgt., 38,334,100
Unk. X-2 -- Dundon, Lawrence E., S/Sgt., 35,692,675
Unk. X-3 -- Brewer, Wilbur D., S/Sgt., 16,075,633
Unk. X-4 -- Nobilione, Joseph V., 2nd Lt., 0-710299
Unk. X-5 -- McGill, Edward E., S/Sgt., 10,600,464
Unk. X-6 -- Murphy, Jeremiah C., F/O, T-62092
Unk. X-7 -- Hibbler, Howard A., Sgt., 37,210,378
Unk. X-8 -- McKenzie, Leighton B., F/O, T-123650

All efforts to locate the Gruen watch found on the remains of X-1 have failed.

RECOMMENDATION: While the dental chart comparisons are not as accurate in each case as might be hoped for, due to the nature of the crash and condition of the bodies, the above identifications are considered adequate for individual identification. Furthermore, it is known that only these eight (8) men are concerned and, by negative comparison, this is the only possible way these dental charts can be reconciled to those submitted by the Field.

H C Ullmann
18 Apr. 1946

Arthur S. Rosengard
1st Lt. DMC

CONCURRENCE	DATE	APPROVAL	DATE
Joseph S. [illegible] Capt QMC	6 May 46	John H. Schwary Lt Col QMC	6 May '46
James L. [illegible] Maj QMC	6 May 46		

QMGMR 293 *Misc*
Unks. X-1 thru X-8
(Belfast) N. Ireland

16 April 1947

SUBJECT: Identification of Unknown Deceased

TO : Commanding Officer, American Graves Registration Command
European Area
APO 887, c/o Postmaster
New York, New York

1. The following identifications have been established from information available to this office and by comparison of dental charts of the remains interred in Lisnabreeny Cemetery, Belfast, Northern Ireland:

X-1 - GRAVES, Robert L. Jr., Sgt., 38334100, Air Corps
Plot B, Row 4, Grave 11
Killed in plane crash - 1 June 1944
Emergency Addressee - Mrs. Maggie Graves (mother)
Rt. 3, Box 72, El Dorado, Arkansas
Religious Preference - Not indicated

X-2 - DUNDON, Lawrence E. S/Sgt., 35692675, Air Corps
Plot B, Row 4, Grave 12
Killed in plane crash - 1 June 1944
Emergency addressee - Mrs. Ora Ruth Dundon (wife)
219 N. 33rd St., Louisville, Kentucky
Religious Preference - Not indicated

X-3 - BREWER, Wilbur D. S/Sgt., 16075633, Air Corps
Plot B, Row 4, Grave 13
Killed in plane crash - 1 June 1944
Emergency Addressee - Mr. Amos Brewer (brother)
Wapella, Illinois
Religious Preference - Not indicated

X-4 - MOBILIONE, Joseph V. 2nd Lt., O-710299, Air Corps
Plot B, Row 4, Grave 14
Killed in plane crash - 1 June 1944
Emergency Addressee - Mrs. Mary A. Broccolo (sister)
Tildean Lane, Bayville, New York
Religious Preference - Catholic

X-5 - McGILL, Edward E. S/Sgt., 10600464, Air Corps
Plot B, Row 4, Grave 15
Killed in Plane crash - 1 June 1944
Emergency Addressee - Mr. Reed S. McGill (brother)
812 Boscobel St., Nashville, Tenn.
Religious Preference - Not indicated

file 293 Brewer, Wilbur D. - 16075633

The crew now had their identities returned. The reason is unknown as to why it took a further year to verify their findings and the differing timespan in which the next of kin were informed. In the case of Robert L. Graves Jr., family members were informed as early as January 1945. Susie M. Efaw, the mother of Howard Hibbler, received a letter in the mail in January 1947, but it was not until May of 1947, that the family of Wilbur Brewer were informed and likely similar for other family members of the crew.

SPQYG 293
(Unknown 4919,
N. Ireland)

2 January 1945.

SUBJECT: Identification of Unknown Deceased.

TO: Chief Quartermaster, ETOUSA, APO 871, c/o Postmaster, New York, N.Y.

1. Reference is made to report of burial for Unknown American Soldier X-1, Station 2, European Wing Air Transport, interred in Grave 11, Row 4, Plot B, Lisnabreeny Cemetery, Belfast, Northern Ireland 4 June 1944.

2. The remains have been tentatively identified as Sergeant Robert L. Graves, Jr., 38,334,100, Air Corps, but in order to make a more positive identification, it is requested that this office be advised if available records show that Sergeant Graves had received and been treated for a foot injury prior to the date of the crash.

For The Quartermaster General:

H. A. BARNES,
Brig. General, Q.M.C.,
Deputy The Quartermaster General.

CCP

RPH

ed

QMGMF 293
Brewer, Wilbur D.
293 SN 16 075 633

Address Reply To
THE QUARTERMASTER GENERAL
Attention: Memorial Division

1 May 1947

Mr. Amos F. Brewer
Citizens Insurance Company
National Bank
Clinton, Illinois

Dear Mr. Brewer:

In our letter of 15 February 1946 you were informed that the remains of your brother, the late Staff Sergeant Wilbur D. Brewer, together with other members of his crew were interred as a group in the Lisnabreeny Cemetery, Belfast, Ireland.

Information has just been received which indicates that the remains of your brother have been identified and that his remains are now interred in Plot B, Row 4, Grave 13, in the United States Military Cemetery, Lisnabreeny, located within the city limits of Belfast, Ireland.

The report of burial discloses that the remains of your brother were properly identified by his tooth chart.

May I extend my sincere sympathy in the loss of your brother.

Sincerely yours,

rlc

RICHARD B. COOMBS
Major, QMC
Memorial Division

SCV

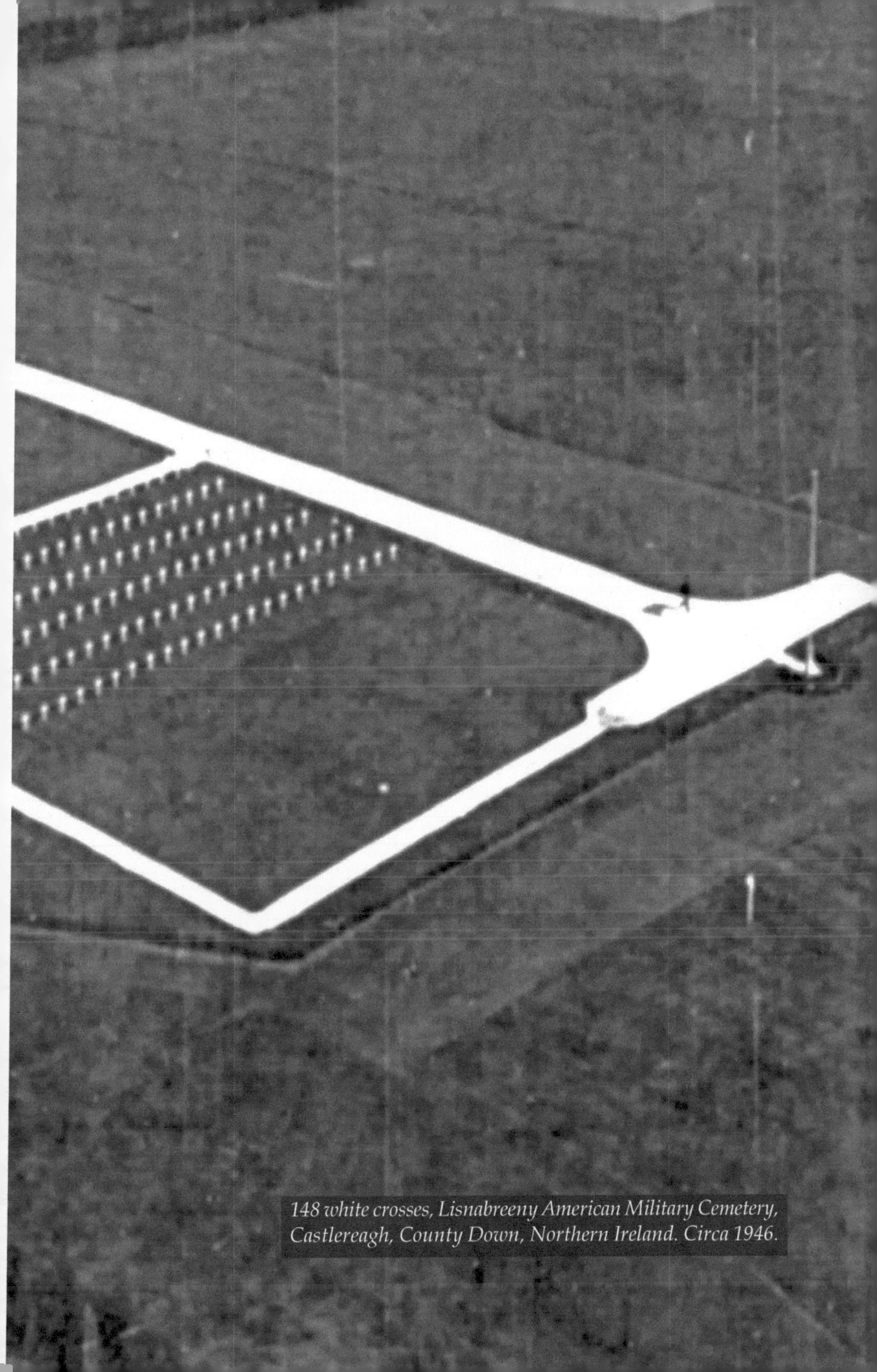

148 white crosses, Lisnabreeny American Military Cemetery, Castlereagh, County Down, Northern Ireland. Circa 1946.

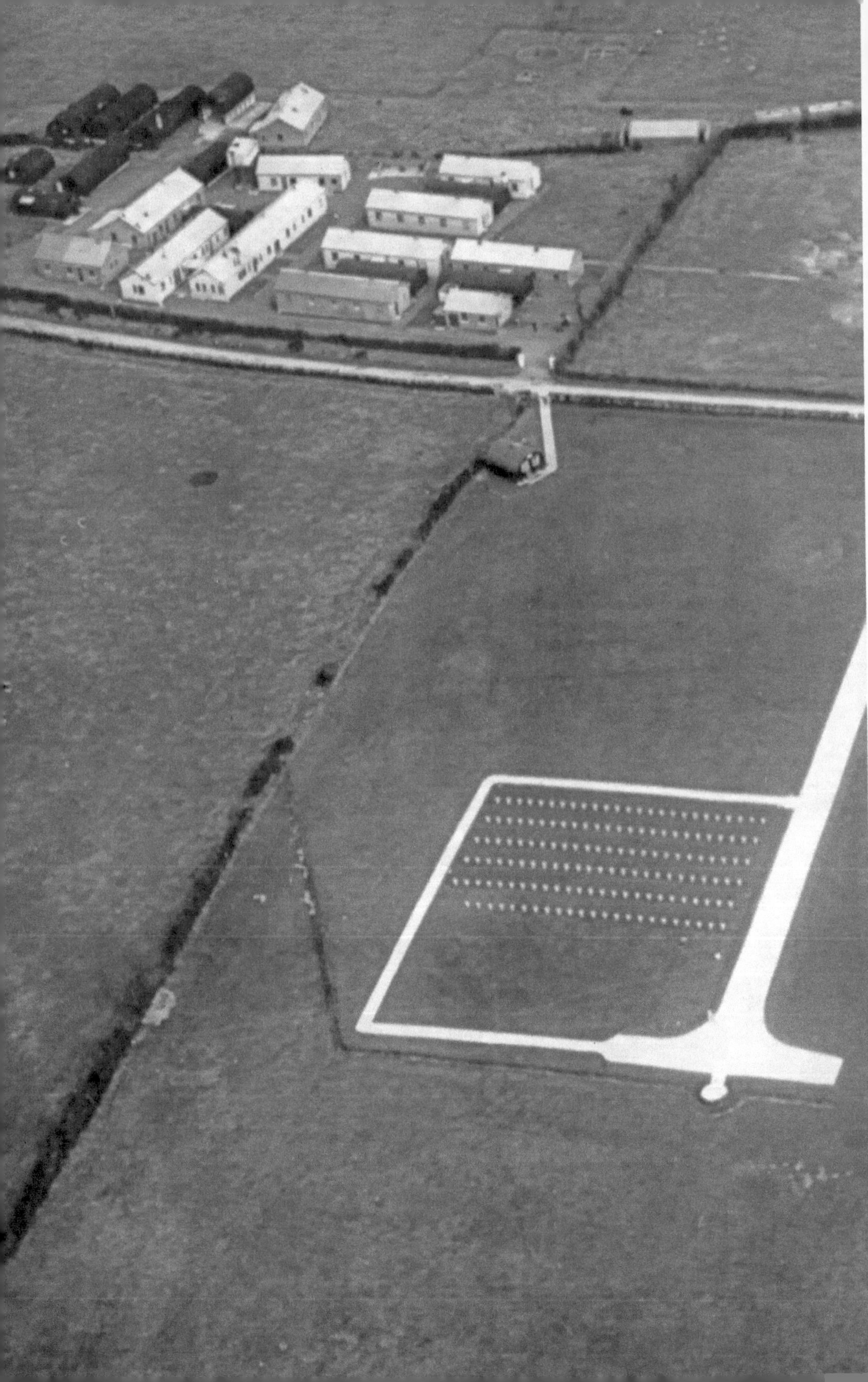

Another aerial view of Lisnabreeny American Military Cemetery. Opposite the main entrance, are the remains of the anti-aircraft artillery battery, used in the defence of Belfast. The small nissen hut in the top left hand corner of the field, was used for the storage of tools, the buildings behind, were likely used during the mass disinterments of the cemetery which began in 1947. Circa 1946.

Chapter Ten

Repatriation

With the return and mass demobilization of American servicemen completed, the US government tasked the Office of the Quartermaster General with the sacred duty of repatriating the heroic deceased of World War II, from temporary American military cemeteries, to permanent American military cemeteries. An option was provided whereby the next of kin could request that their loved ones remains where to be returned to the United States for interment at a cemetery of their choice.

From 1947 to 1948, letters were sent to the next of kin of the crew. Enclosed within each letter, were two pamphlets, *"Disposition of World War II Armed Forces Dead"* and *"American Cemeteries"*. These pamphlets explained the disposition options and services made available to the next of kin, on behalf of the US Government.

F/O Lester B. Brooks, T61 593
Plot B, Row 4, Grave 19,
Lisnabreeny Cemetery
Belfast, Ireland

21 August 1947

Mr. L. G. Bryan Brooks
Rural Delivery #3
Carrollton, Ohio

Dear Mr. Brooks:

The people of the United States, through the Congress have authorized the disinterment and final burial of the heroic dead of World War II. The Quartermaster General of the Army has been entrusted with this sacred responsibility to the honored dead. The records of the War Department indicate that you may be the nearest relative of the above-named deceased, who gave his life in the service of his country.

The enclosed pamphlets, "Disposition of World War II Armed Forces Dead," and "American Cemeteries," explain the disposition, options and services made available to you by your Government. If you are the next of kin according to the line of kinship as set forth in the enclosed pamphlet, "Disposition of World War II Armed Forces Dead," you are invited to express your wishes as to the disposition of the remains of the deceased by completing Part I of the enclosed form "Request for Disposition of Remains." Should you desire to relinquish your rights to the next in line of kinship, please complete Part II of the enclosed form. If you are not the next of kin, please complete Part III of the enclosed form.

If you should elect Option 2, it is advised that no funeral arrangements or other personal arrangements be made until you are further notified by this office.

Will you please complete the enclosed form, "Request for Disposition of Remains" and mail in the enclosed self-addressed envelope, which requires no postage, within 30 days after its receipt by you? Its prompt return will avoid unnecessary delays.

Sincerely,

Incls.

THOMAS B. LARKIN
Major General
The Quartermaster General

BUDGET BUREAU No. 49-R277.

REQUEST FOR DISPOSITION OF REMAINS

GRADE OF DECEASED, NAME, ARMY SERIAL NUMBER AND REPORTED PLACE OF BURIAL — DATE:

Cpl. Lawrence R. McGrane, 20 215 468
Plot B, Row 4, Grave 20,
Lisnabreeny Cemetery
Belfast, Ireland

20 May 1947

A		C	
B		D	

DO NOT WRITE ABOVE THIS LINE

NOTE.—The next of kin should familiarize himself with the contents of the pamphlet, "Disposition of World War II Armed Forces Dead," before filling out this form. When the proper part of this form is filled out and properly signed by the next of kin, it should be returned to the OFFICE OF THE QUARTERMASTER GENERAL, MEMORIAL DIVISION, WAR DEPARTMENT, WASHINGTON 25, D. C., in the self-addressed postage-free envelope provided for this purpose.

If you are the next of kin or authorized representative of next of kin and desire to direct the disposition of the remains, please fill in PART I of this form.

PART I

I, Thomas Edward Mc Grane (PLEASE PRINT OR TYPE NAME OF NEXT OF KIN) *(Please indicate relationship to the deceased by placing an "X" in the proper box.)*

☐ WIDOW ☐ WIDOWER ☐ SON OVER 21 YEARS OLD ☐ DAUGHTER OVER 21 YEARS OLD

☐ FATHER ☐ MOTHER ☒ BROTHER OVER 21 YEARS OLD ☐ SISTER OVER 21 YEARS OLD

☐ RELATIONSHIP OTHER THAN ABOVE (*Specify*) ______

HAVING FAMILIARIZED MYSELF WITH THE OPTIONS WHICH HAVE BEEN MADE AVAILABLE TO ME WITH RESPECT TO THE FINAL RESTING PLACE OF THE DECEASED DESIGNATED ABOVE, NOW DO DECLARE THAT IT IS MY DESIRE THAT THE REMAINS: *(Please place an "X" in the box opposite the option you have selected.)*

☐ 1. BE INTERRED IN A PERMANENT AMERICAN MILITARY CEMETERY OVERSEAS.

☐ 2. BE RETURNED TO THE UNITED STATES OR ANY POSSESSION OR TERRITORY THEREOF FOR INTERMENT BY NEXT OF KIN IN A PRIVATE CEMETERY

______ (NAME AND LOCATION OF CEMETERY)

☐ 3. BE RETURNED TO ______ (FOREIGN COUNTRY), THE HOMELAND OF THE DECEASED OR NEXT OF KIN, FOR INTERMENT BY NEXT OF KIN IN A PRIVATE CEMETERY LOCATED AT ______ (LOCATION OF CEMETERY SELECTED)

☐ 4. BE RETURNED TO THE UNITED STATES FOR FINAL INTERMENT IN A NATIONAL CEMETERY LOCATED AT Farmingdale, Long Island (LOCATION OF NATIONAL CEMETERY SELECTED)

(Please indicate if your own religious services at a location other than the selected national cemetery are desired by placing an "X" in the proper box)

☐ YES ☐ NO

THE NAME OF THE DECEASED, THE SERIAL NUMBER AND GRADE ARE CORRECT EXCEPT FOR THE FOLLOWING CHANGES: *(If no corrections are necessary, indicate this fact by inserting the word "NONE" in the space below.)*

NONE.

Approved

Coded 26 Nov. 47 ... Lt Col ...

OQMG FORM 345 MILITARY 14 NOV 1946 — 16—60411-1 — PAGE 1

PART 1 ***(Continued)***

If on Page 1 of this form you have selected Option Number 2 or 3, or Option Number 4 with your own funeral ceremonies desired at a location other than the selected national cemetery, complete one of these sections.

I, AS THE NEXT OF KIN, DO FURTHER DECLARE THAT I DESIRE THE REMAINS TO BE SENT TO THE FOLLOWING PERSON WHO HAS AGREED TO RECEIVE THEM:

LAST NAME	FIRST NAME		MIDDLE INITIAL
NUMBER AND STREET	CITY OR TOWN	COUNTY OR PROVINCE	STATE OR TERRITORY OF U. S. A., OR COUNTRY
EXPRESS OFFICE (*Nearest railroad passenger station*)	TELEGRAPH ADDRESS		TELEPHONE No.

OR

I, AS THE NEXT OF KIN, DO FURTHER DECLARE THAT I DESIRE THE REMAINS TO BE SENT TO THE FOLLOWING FUNERAL DIRECTOR WHO HAS AGREED TO RECEIVE THEM:

FULL NAME OF FUNERAL DIRECTOR			
NUMBER AND STREET	CITY OR TOWN	COUNTY OR PROVINCE	STATE OR TERRITORY OF U. S. A., OR COUNTRY
EXPRESS OFFICE (*Nearest railroad passenger station*)	TELEGRAPH ADDRESS		TELEPHONE No.

IN CASE OF EMERGENCY THE NAME AND ADDRESS OF THE PERSON NEXT IN LINE OF KINSHIP AFTER ME, AS SET FORTH IN THE PAMPHLET, "DISPOSITION OF WORLD WAR II ARMED FORCES DEAD," IS:

LAST NAME	FIRST NAME	MIDDLE INITIAL	RELATIONSHIP TO DECEASED
McGRANE	MAE		MOTHER
NUMBER AND STREET	**CITY OR TOWN**	**COUNTY OR PROVINCE**	**STATE OR TERRITORY OF U. S. A., OR COUNTRY**
CARTER'S DRIVE	STAMFORD	CONN.	CONN.

REMARKS OR ADDITIONAL INSTRUCTIONS (*For additional space use page 4.**)

AS EXPLAINED IN THE PAMPHLET, "DISPOSITION OF WORLD WAR II ARMED FORCES DEAD," I AM THE NEXT OF KIN AND THE INDIVIDUAL AUTHORIZED TO DIRECT THE DISPOSITION OF THE SAID REMAINS.

I, the undersigned, DO SOLEMNLY SWEAR (OR AFFIRM) that the statements made by me in the foregoing document are full and true to the best of my knowledge and belief.

Thomas E. McGrane (SIGNATURE OF NEXT OF KIN) — 331 HUGUENOT STREET (STREET AND NUMBER)

THOMAS E. McGRANE (NAME PRINTED OR TYPED) — NEW Rochelle, New York. (CITY AND STATE)

Subscribed and duly sworn to before me according to law by the above-named applicant this 10 day of Aug, 1947, at city (or town) of New Rochelle, county of Westchester, and State (or Territory or District) of New York.

Henry E. Colwell Jr (SIGNATURE OF OFFICER AUTHORIZED TO ADMINISTER OATHS)
HARRY E. COLWELL, Jr.
Notary Public in the State of New York
Appointed for Westchester County
(OFFICIAL TITLE)
Commission Expires March 30, 1948

*NOTE.—Page 4 is part of the notarial attestation.

PAGE 2 — 16—50411-1

PART II—RELINQUISHMENT OF DISPOSITION AUTHORITY

If you are the next of kin and you desire to relinquish your disposition authority, please fill in PART II of this form.

I, THE ______________________________ (PLEASE INSERT RELATIONSHIP) AS THE NEXT OF KIN OF THE DECEASED NAMED IN PART I OF THIS FORM, DO HEREBY RELINQUISH MY RIGHTS TO DIRECT THE FINAL DISPOSITION OF THE REMAINS OF THE DECEASED. THE NEXT EXISTING PERSON IN THE ORDER OF ELIGIBILITY OF DECEDENT'S SURVIVORS IS:

LAST NAME	FIRST NAME	MIDDLE INITIAL
RELATIONSHIP TO THE DECEASED		
NUMBER AND STREET	CITY OR TOWN	STATE OR COUNTRY

WHOM I UNDERSTAND SHALL HAVE THE RIGHT TO DIRECT FINAL DISPOSITION OF THE REMAINS OF THE DECEASED.

______________________________ (DATE)

______________________________ (SIGNATURE OF NEXT OF KIN)

______________________________ (STREET AND NUMBER)

______________________________ (NAME PRINTED OR TYPED)

______________________________ (CITY AND STATE)

PART III

If you are NOT the next of kin authorized to direct the disposition of remains, please fill in PART III of this form.

THIS IS TO NOTIFY YOU THAT I AM NOT THE NEXT OF KIN AUTHORIZED TO DIRECT THE FINAL DISPOSITION OF THE REMAINS OF THE DECEASED NAMED ON PAGE 1 OF THIS FORM. THE FOLLOWING PERSON, TO THE BEST OF MY KNOWLEDGE, IS THE NEXT OF KIN TO WHOM THIS FORM SHOULD BE DIRECTED.

LAST NAME	FIRST NAME	MIDDLE INITIAL
RELATIONSHIP TO THE DECEASED		
NUMBER AND STREET	CITY OR TOWN	STATE OR COUNTRY

______________________________ (DATE)

______________________________ (SIGNATURE)

______________________________ (STREET AND NUMBER)

______________________________ (NAME PRINTED OR TYPED)

______________________________ (CITY AND STATE)

10—80410-1

ADDITIONAL REMARKS AND INSTRUCTIONS

All remarks and information entered here will be considered as part of the Notarial Attestation.

This request for interment of my brother
Cpl Lawrence R. McGrane A.S.N. 20 215 468
was addressed to my Mother Mrs Mae McGrane,
formally of 30 White oak street, New Rochelle, N.Y.
I have filled out this form with my Mother's
knowledge and consent and without the consent
or knowledge of his wife (who has since married)
the former Dorothy O'steen of 5 East Lane
Shelbyville, Tenn.

Thomas E McGrane

PAGE 4

U. S. GOVERNMENT PRINTING OFFICE

In November 1947, the disinterment of the remains of servicemen at Lisnabreeny was on-going. On 6 and 7 November, the crews remains were disinterred from the cemetery and subsequently transported to the permanent American Military Cemetery located at Cambridge in England.

JS

1

DISINTERMENT DIRECTIVE

SECTION A — NAME AND BURIAL LOCATION OF DECEASED

DIRECTIVE NUMBER	DATE (DAY / MONTH / YEAR)
1640 00017	15 / 12 / 47

NAME	SERIAL NUMBER	RANK	ARM	DATE OF DEATH (DAY / MONTH / YEAR)
BREWER WILBUR D	16075633	S SG	1	

CEMETERY		DISPOSITION OF REMAINS (CODE / DIST. PT.)
LISNABREENY BELFAST IRELAND	1	6100 / 08

PLOT	ROW	GRAVE	COUNTRY	CAUSE OF DEATH
B	4	13	BRITISH ISLES	5

SECTION B — CONSIGNEE AND NEXT OF KIN

NAME AND ADDRESS OF CONSIGNEE	NAME AND ADDRESS OF NEXT OF KIN
REESER FUNERAL HOME 201 SOUTH CENTER STREET CLINTON, ILLINOIS	AMOS F. BREWER (BROTHER) 603½ WEST SIDE SQUARE CLINTON, ILLINOIS

SECTION C — DISINTERMENT AND IDENTIFICATION

NAME	SERIAL NUMBER	RANK	DATE OF DEATH	DATE DISTINTERRED
BREWER WILBUR D	16075633	SSG	1 JUNE 44	7 NOV 47

IDENTIFICATION TAG ON	ORGANIZATION	RELIGION	IDENTIFICATION VERIFIED BY (NAME AND TITLE)
☐ REMAINS ☒ MARKER GRS	USAAF	UNK	t/s J.F. RANDALL CAPT QMC

SECTION D — PREPARATION OF REMAINS FOR SHIPMENT

NATURE OF BURIAL	CONDITION OF REMAINS
UK CASKET. RUBBER SHEET	BODY DECOMPOSED. DISARTICULATION COMPLETE. FRACTURE OF R/L TIBIA, FIBULA, HUMERUS, FEMUR, ULNA, RADIAL.

OTHER MEANS OF IDENTIFICATION

GRS FORM NO 1 BURIED WITH REMAINS. BREWER WILBUR.D. 16075633.
ID TAG (MADE AT CEMETERY) ON MARKER. NAME PLATE ON CASKET.

MINOR DISCREPANCIES 1

NONE

REMAINS PREPARED AND PLACED IN CASKET

DATE 7 NOV 47 BY J.EARL. TUCKER

CASKET SEALED BY	EMBALMER (*Signature*)
J.EARL TUCKER	J EARL TUCKER EMB

CASKET BOXED AND MARKED	SHIPPING ADDRESS VERIFIED BY
DATE 7 NOV 47 BY ROBERT A ANDERSON CLERK RECORDER	JACK E DANIELS MAJ QMC

I hereby certify that all the foregoing operations were conducted and accomplished under my immediate supervision and that the report above is correct.

t/s DAVID L BENSHOFF CAPT INF

SIGNATURE OF GRS INSPECTOR

1 *Prepare Discrepancy Report QMC Form 1194a for major discrepancies.*

INFORMATION TRANSCRIBED FROM AGRC WORK SHEET - ATTACHED.

6131

QMC FORM REV 15 MAR 46 1194

In England, their remains were placed into *"Warehouse Storage"*, in some cases, for up to a year, before final interment at the permanent cemetery. In the case of repatriation to the US, their remains would depart in July the following year.

RECORD OF CUSTODIAL TRANSFER

1. SHIPPED			
FROM: USMC LISNABREENY		TO: CAMBRIDGE ENGLAND	
KIND OF CONVEYANCE: TRUCK-SHIP-RAIL		NAME OF CONVOYER: SAM L DAVIES MAJOR /4	
SIGNATURE OF SHIPPER: SAM L DAVIES MAJOR	DATE: 18/11/47	SIGNATURE OF RECEIVER: SAM L DAVIES MAJOR	DATE: 20/11/47
2. SHIPPED			
FROM: CAMBRIDGE (STORAGE)		TO: USMC CAMBRIDGE ENGLAND	
KIND OF CONVEYANCE: TRUCK		NAME OF CONVOYER: JACK E DANIELS MAJOR	
SIGNATURE OF SHIPPER: JACK E DANIELS MAJOR	DATE: 4/2/48	SIGNATURE OF RECEIVER: JOSEPH P CETOLA, ASST SUPT USMC	DATE: 4/2/48
3. SHIPPED			
FROM: USMC CAMBRIDGE ENGLAND		TO: CARDIFF S WALES	
KIND OF CONVEYANCE: TRUCK - RAIL		NAME OF CONVOYER:	
SIGNATURE OF SHIPPER: E.J. Komyati	DATE:	SIGNATURE OF RECEIVER:	DATE: 23 APR 1948
4. SHIPPED			
FROM: AGRC CARDIFF		TO: U S A T LAWRENCE VICTORY	
KIND OF CONVEYANCE: ZEC		NAME OF CONVOYER: S. CARROLL 1st C.	
SIGNATURE OF SHIPPER: J S TAYLOR MAJ. TC	DATE: 16 JUN 1948	SIGNATURE OF RECEIVER: Joseph J Carroll	DATE: JUN 1948
5. SHIPPED			
FROM:		TO: NY PE	
KIND OF CONVEYANCE:		NAME OF CONVOYER:	
SIGNATURE OF SHIPPER:	DATE:	SIGNATURE OF RECEIVER: McKINNON COLONEL, T.C. PORT TRANSPORTATION OFFICER	DATE: JUN 28 1948
6. SHIPPED			
FROM: NY PE		TO: D C of	
KIND OF CONVEYANCE: train		NAME OF CONVOYER: Sgt	
SIGNATURE OF SHIPPER: JAMES L. McKINNON COLONEL, T.C. PORT TRANSPORTATION OFFICER	DATE: JUN 29 1948	SIGNATURE OF RECEIVER: J. A. BENTON Captain, QMC Chief, Operations Br.	DATE: JUN 30 1948
7. SHIPPED			
FROM:		TO:	
KIND OF CONVEYANCE:		NAME OF CONVOYER:	
SIGNATURE OF SHIPPER:	DATE:	SIGNATURE OF RECEIVER:	DATE:

On 16 June 1948, in Cardiff, Wales, the remains of Flight Officer Lester B. Brooks, S.Sgt. Wilbur D. Brewer and Sgt. Lawrence R. McGrane, were loaded aboard the US Army Transport Ship, Lawrence Victory. The ship was loaded with the remains of 5,374 deceased American servicemen who had been buried in temporary cemeteries throughout Europe. Their destination was Brooklyn, New York. As the ship neared the U.S.A. messages were dispatched to the next of kin, with regards to organising the forthcoming funeral arrangements.

16 June, 1948, Cardiff, Wales, the remains of an American serviceman, is escorted on to the USAT Lawrence Victory, by British Military personnel. On this voyage, the ship would carry the remains of 5,374 deceased US servicemen, back to their homeland. British Military personnel stand to attention and a salute is made on behalf of the men, as the casket is carried on-board, whilst a crowd of civilians poignantly watch the ceremony.

MESSAGEFORM

MESSAGE CENTER NO.	TRANSMITTING MEANS	CRYPTOGRAPH OR CLEAR TEXT

CALLS	STA. SER. No.	PRECEDENCE	TRANSMISSION INSTRUCTIONS	ORIGINATOR	DATE-TIME GROUP
V	NR				

ACTION	INFORMATION	EXEMPT	OPERATING SIGNALS	GROUP COUNT
				GR

SPACE ABOVE FOR SIGNAL CENTER ONLY

FROM: (Originator)

SECURITY CLASSIFICATION: GOVT PD

PRECEDENCE FOR ACTION: ~~PRIORITY~~ DAY LETTER — INFORMATION

☐ ORIGINAL MESSAGE

REFERS TO ANOTHER MESSAGE — IDENTIFICATION — CLASSIFICATION

ACTION TO: ~~PRIORITY~~ L G BRYAN BROOKS
DLR AND REPORT ANY CHARGES
RURAL FREE DELIVERY 3 #
CARROLLTON OHIO

INFORMATION TO: FROM QMDCG 195070 BARDEN

THIS HEADQUARTERS HAS BEEN ADVISED THAT THE REMAINS OF LATE FLIGHT OFFICER LESTER B BROOKS ARE ENROUTE TO THE UNITED STATES. RECORDS OF THIS OFFICE INDICATE YOU WISH REMAINS DELIVERED TO G B ALLMON FUNERAL DIRECTOR 2ND STREET NORTHWEST CARROLLTON OHIO

PLEASE INSTRUCT FUNERAL DIRECTOR TO ACCEPT REMAINS AT RAILROAD STATION UPON ARRIVAL. WE REGRET IT IS NOT POSSIBLE AT THIS TIME TO GIVE YOU A DEFINITE DELIVERY DATE HOWEVER THREE DAYS PRIOR TO SHIPMENT FROM THIS DEPOT YOUR FUNERAL DIRECTOR WILL BE NOTIFIED BY TELEGRAM OF RAIL ROUTING AND SCHEDULED TIME REMAINS WILL ARRIVE AT RAILROAD STATION. HE WILL BE REQUESTED TO PASS THIS INFORMATION TO YOU SO THAT YOU MAY MAKE FUNERAL ARRANGEMENTS. REMAINS WILL BE ACCOMPANIED BY MILITARY ESCORT.

WITHIN 48 HOURS OF DATE OF THIS MESSAGE PLEASE CONFIRM BY TELEGRAM COLLECT TO COLUMBUS GENERAL DISTRIBUTION DEPOT COLUMBUS OHIO ABOVE DELIVERY INSTRUCTIONS OR SUBMIT NEW DELIVERY INSTRUCTIONS. PLEASE BE ADVISED THAT IT WILL NOT BE POSSIBLE TO COMPLY AT GOVERNMENT EXPENSE WITH ANY DESIRED CHANGES IN DELIVERY INSTRUCTIONS RECEIVED AFTER THE EXPIRATION OF THE 48 HOUR PERIOD. YOUR PROMPT COOPERATION WILL GREATLY ASSIST THIS OFFICE IN MAKING FINAL DELIVERY. IF YOU SHOULD DESIRE MILITARY HONORS AT FUNERAL YOU SHOULD ASK ANY LOCAL PATRIOTIC OR VETERANS ORGANIZATION TO MAKE ARRANGEMENTS. PLEASE INCLUDE FULL NAME OF DECEASED IN REPLY TELEGRAM. NOTIFY THIS OFFICE OF PATRIOTIC OR VETERANS ORGANIZATION SELECTED BY YOU TO FURNISH MILITARY HONORS.

BOWMAN CG COLUMBUS GENERAL DISTRIBUTION DEPOT COLUMBUS OHIO

MAILED JUN 2 1948 AGRS COLUMBUS GENERAL DISTRIBUTION DEPOT U. S. ARMY COLUMBUS 15, O.

SECURITY CLASSIFICATION — AUTHORIZATION

SIGNATURE

ORIGINATING AGENCY

SYMBOL	DATE-TIME GROUP	OFFICIAL TITLE
		FRANCIS FAPPIANO CAPT, QMC, Asst AGR Div

WD AGO FORM 11-168 15 JUN 1945 This form supersedes WD AGO Form 11-168, 23 Aug 44, and WD AGO Form 801, 12 Mar 43, which are obsolete. 16—45801-1 U. S. GOVERNMENT PRINTING

Model 1 Rail - Funeral Director Designated

On 28 June, amid no fanfare the USAT Lawrence Victory, quietly approached New York City and subsequently berthed at the Brooklyn Army Terminal. The remains of the 5,374 servicemen who were aboard the ship, were disembarked into the terminal and transported onto US Army Transportation Company Mortuary Rail Cars. The crew were transported to Quartermaster or Army Service Depots, known as distribution centres and would soon begin their final journey back to their families. There were 15 distribution centres across the US allocated for this purpose.

Each casket was provided with a military escort in the form of a guard, who was usually recruited from regular troop units. The military required guards of equal rank and service branch to accompany the remains. Outside of a distribution centres local area the remains travelled on local passenger trains, the military escort carrying two tickets, one for himself and a first class ticket for the deceased. Each deceased serviceman was transported to the railroad station in a flag-draped casket accompanied by their escort. Flags, draped caskets whenever they were in public view. The escort removed the flag when a casket was in the baggage rail car and re-draped the casket, upon arrival, at their final destination. He also carried a new flag for the funeral, blank ammunition, for the graveside firing party and reimbursement forms, for the family and funeral director.

MP

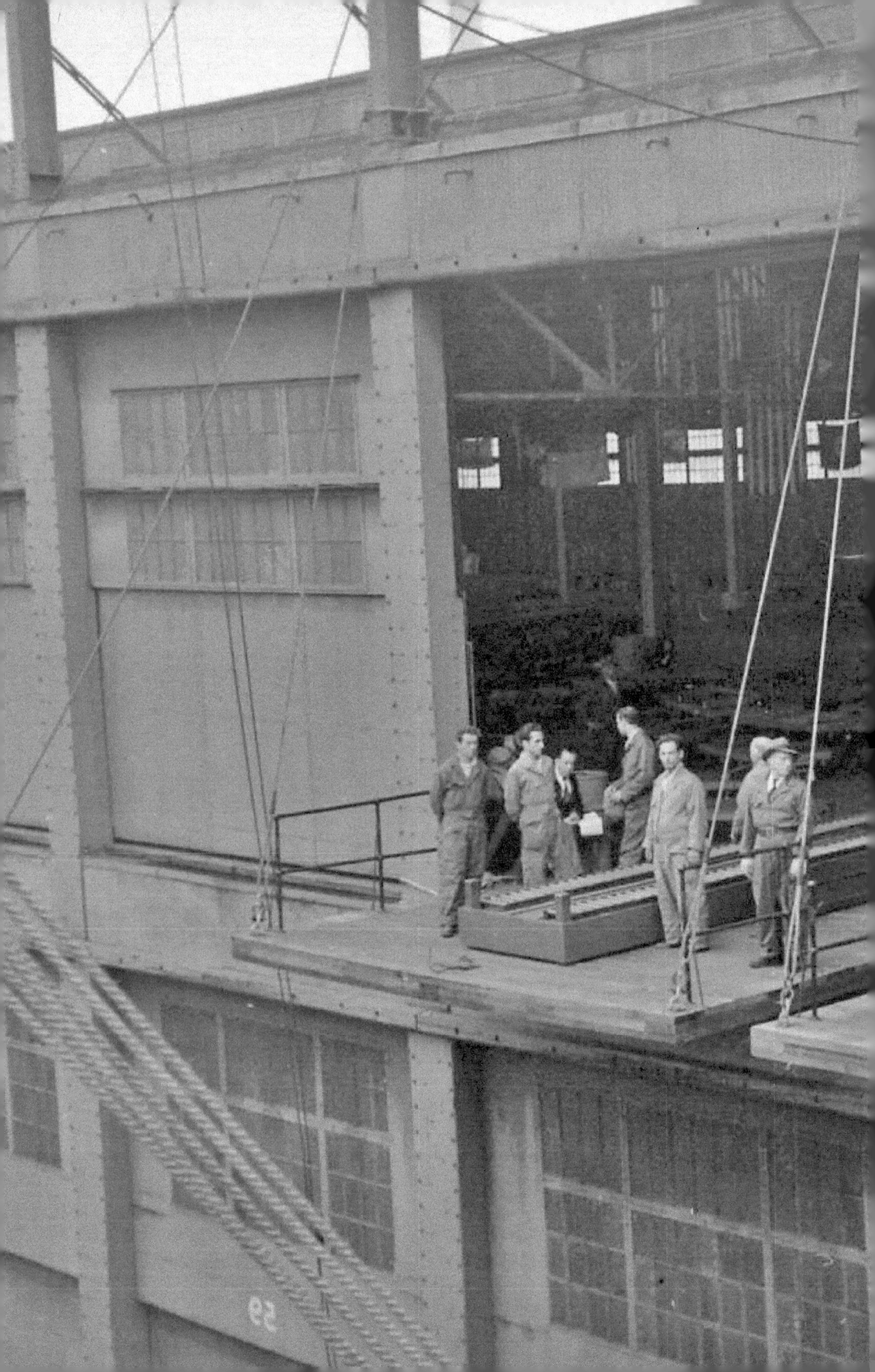

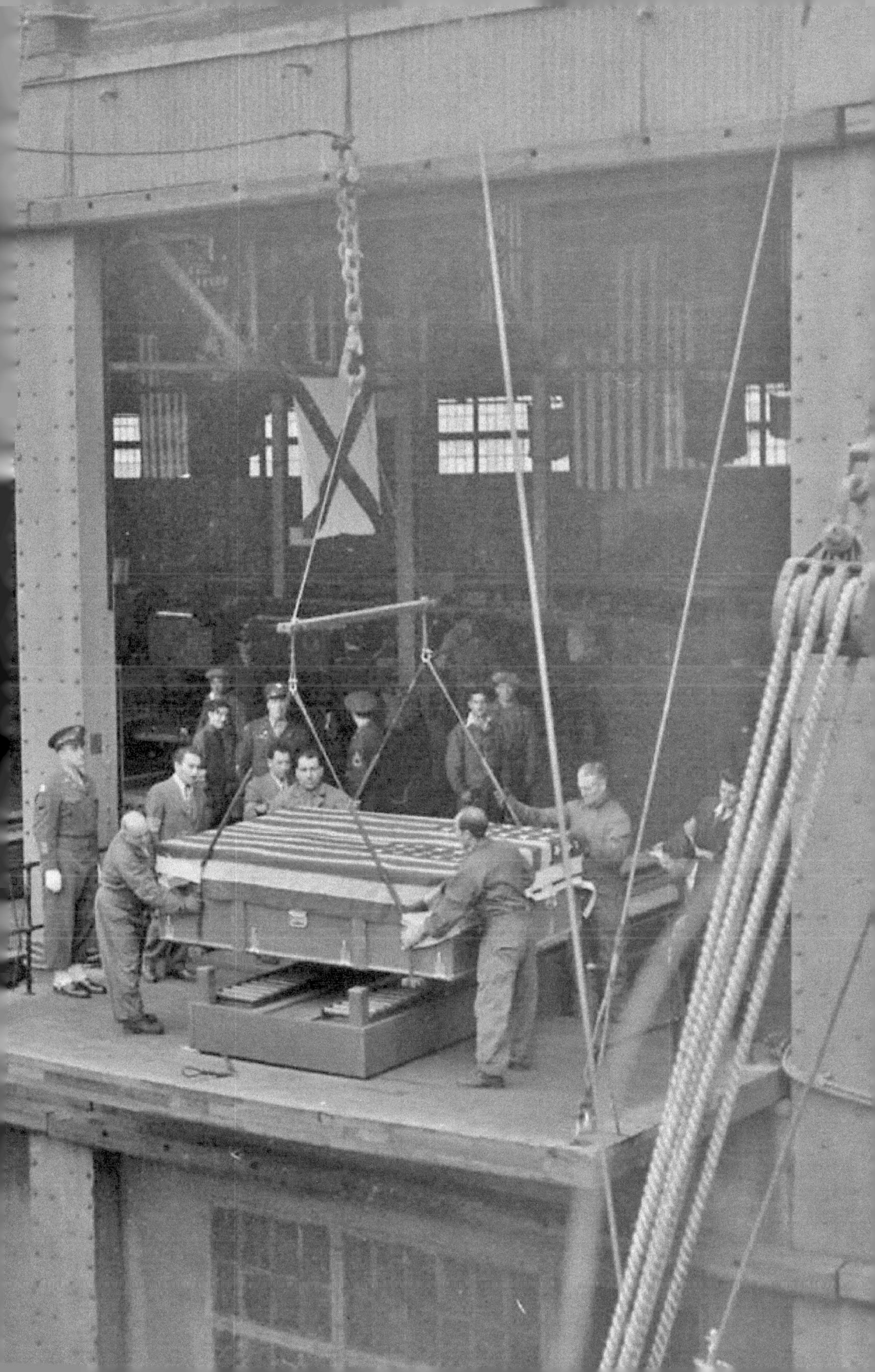

UNITED STATES ARMY

UNITED ST

ES ARMY
CORPS

2

RECEIPT OF REMAINS

DAY LETTER

DISTRIBUTION CENTER AGR DIV., CHICAGO QUARTERMASTER DEPOT
1819 W. PERSHING RD., CHICAGO, ILLINOIS

REESER FUNERAL HOME
201 S. CENTER STREET
CLINTON, ILLINOIS

ROUTINE

REMAINS CONSIGNED TO:

REMAINS OF THE LATE S/SGT. WILBUR D. BREWER

BEING SHIPPED TO YOU ACCOMPANIED BY MILITARY ESCORT. ON TRAIN NUMBER 19

I. C. RR.

LEAVING CHICAGO 11:00 AM C.S.T. FRIDAY 16 JULY 1948

AND DUE TO ARRIVE CLINTON, ILL. 1:13 PM C.S.T. FRIDAY 16 JULY 1948

REQUEST THAT YOU IMMEDIATELY INFORM THE NEXT OF KIN AND MAKE ARRANGEMENTS

TO ACCEPT REMAINS AT STATION UPON ARRIVAL. REFER TO CONTROL NUMBER 6139

CARROLL J. GRINNELL
LT. COL. Q.M.C.

I, THE UNDERSIGNED, DO HEREBY ACKNOWLEDGE RECEIPT OF THE REMAINS OF THE ABOVE-NAMED DECEASED

THIS 16 DAY OF July, 1948
DAY MONTH

S/Sgt. Jack C. DeGraw — WITNESS (Escort)

O. H. Reeser — CONSIGNEE

REV. 18B

NAT
FILE
RECORDS ANNOTATED
DATE 28 July 48
NAME [signature]
R & R BR.

DJH

QMC FORM 1193
15 NOV 46

16—58973-1 U. S. GOVERNMENT PRINTING OFFICE

On 12 July, the remains of Lester B. Brooks arrived at Dennison Railroad Station in Ohio from the Columbus AGRC Distribution Centre. With a military escort, his remains were escorted back to Carrollton, Ohio.

Graveside services were conducted in Westview Cemetery, Carrollton, Ohio, on 15 July and Lester was laid to rest, with his family and friends attending the service.

On 16 July, the remains of Wilbur D. Brewer arrived in Clinton, Illinois, from the Chicago AGRC Distribution Centre accompanied by a Military Escort.

He was laid to rest alongside his wife, Eileen, father Charles and mother, Verna, at Memorial Park Cemetery located in Clinton, DeWitt County, Illinois, on 17 July. His surviving brothers attended the service.

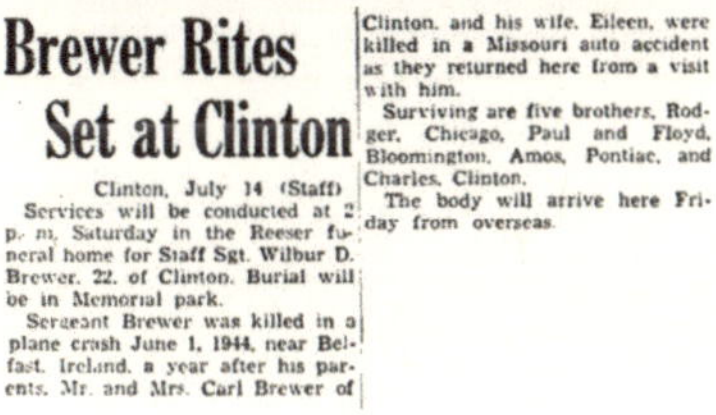

Brewer Rites Set at Clinton

Clinton, July 14 (Staff)

Services will be conducted at 2 p. m. Saturday in the Reeser funeral home for Staff Sgt. Wilbur D. Brewer, 22, of Clinton. Burial will be in Memorial park.

Sergeant Brewer was killed in a plane crash June 1, 1944, near Belfast, Ireland, a year after his parents, Mr. and Mrs. Carl Brewer of Clinton, and his wife, Eileen, were killed in a Missouri auto accident as they returned here from a visit with him.

Surviving are five brothers, Rodger, Chicago, Paul and Floyd, Bloomington, Amos, Pontiac, and Charles, Clinton.

The body will arrive here Friday from overseas.

In New York, on 23 July the remains of Lawrence R. McGrane were transported from the New York AGRC Distribution Centre, accompanied by a Military Escort consisting of; Sgt. Charles W. Beauchain. His remains were transported directly to the cemetery and laid to rest at Long Island National Cemetery, located in Farmingdale, New York. Attending the service, were his mother, wife Dorothy and a brother, Thomas McGrane.

SERVICES HELD FOR CPL. M'GRANE

JUL 23 1948

A Requiem Mass was said at 8 o'clock this morning in Blessed Sacrament Church for Corporal Lawrence R. McGrane of 331 Huguenot Street, who was killed in an airplane crash June 1, 1944, in Belfast, Northern Ireland. Interment was in Pinelawn Cemetery, Farmingdale, L. I.

Cpl. McGrane, son of Mrs. Edward McGrane of Stamford, Conn., formerly of Larchmont, and the late Mr. McGrane, had been overseas for a few weeks before his death.

He enlisted in 1940 and received his basic training at Fort McClellan, Ala. He spent 18 months in the Hawaiian Islands where he was transferred from the field artillery medical detachment to the Air Corps. The twenty-four-year-old turret gunner had his advanced training in Savannah, Ga. His last post before going overseas was MacDill Field, Fla.

Born in New York City, Cpl. McGrane was educated there and had been employed at the White Cross Laboratories in this city before entering service.

Surviving in addition to his mother are his wife, the former Dorothy Ostein of Shelbyville, Tenn., and a brother, Thomas E. McGrane of the Huguenot Street address.

LAWRENCE R. McGRANE

Funeral Tomorrow For Sgt. E. E. McGill

Funeral services for Staff Sgt. Edward Ewing McGill, 29, Nashville serviceman who was killed in Ireland June 1, 1944, will be held here at 2 o'clock tomorrow afternoon.

The Rev. Paul A. Lanius will conduct the services at Martin's funeral home, and burial will be in Mount Olivet cemetery.

Native of Nashville, he was a son of Mrs. Della McGill of 804 Boscobel st., and the late Robert McGill.

He graduated from East Nashville high school and attended Austin Peay state college in Clarksville. He was a star football player at each school.

A waist gunner with the army air forces, he first enlisted with the Royal Canadian air force in September 1941, but was transferred to the American air force in England in 1942.

He was killed in a crash of a B-17 bomber near Belfast, Ireland.

He had been awarded the air medal with two oak leaf clusters and the distinguished flying cross.

Prior to entering the service he was employed as a shipping clerk at the Graham Paper Co., here.

Sergeant McGill was a member of the Tulip Street Methodist church.

Besides his mother, he is survived by a sister, Mrs. A. R. Tidwell; and three brothers, Reid S., Robert L. and William J. McGill, all of Nashville.

In the case of Edward E. McGill, presumably, his remains were not transported back to the U.S.A. until a later date, as on 21 December, he was laid to rest at Mount Olivet Cemetery, located in Nashville, Tennessee. His mother, sister and three brothers attended the service.

Chapter Eleven

Overseas Military Cemetery

As time progressed, for some family members the thought of having their loved ones remains returned home was too painful and many thought that it was the best decision to have them interred in a permanent cemetery overseas. The mother of Howard A. Hibbler, had originally wrote to the war department expressing her thoughts on the return of her sons remains back to the US. Over time, her thoughts on the matter changed and she opted for overseas interment.

Aug 23rd 1945
Mrs. Susie E Law
855 So. Fern
Wichita, Kans.

Quartermaster General.
Washington (25) D.C.

Gentleman:

Would you please give me the location of my sons grave
Howard A. Hibbler (A.D.P.C-G 201) 37210378
who was killed at Belfast north Ireland June 1st 1944.
I would like to have his body brought back here for burial.
I have a litter from the war Dep. stating, when the war was over I could have him brought back.
I have written you before about this but have recieved no reply.
I would like to have an answer.

Yours Truly,
Mrs. Susie E Law

In the United Kingdom it was decided that there would be one permanent American Military Cemetery, for servicemen who had died during World War II. Not far from the city of London, close to Cambridge University, Cambridge American Military Cemetery was dedicated as a permanent cemetery. All cemeteries in the U.K. of a temporary nature, were to be closed, this included the small Second World War burial plot at Brookwood Cemetery and the American Cemetery in Northern Ireland, at Lisnabreeny.

BUDGET BUREAU No. 49-R277.1

REQUEST FOR DISPOSITION OF REMAINS

GRADE OF DECEASED, NAME, ARMY SERIAL NUMBER AND REPORTED PLACE OF BURIAL — DATE:

Sgt Robert L. Graves Jr., 38 334 100
Plot B, Row 4, Grave 11,
Lisnabreeny Cemetery
Belfast, Ireland
(Now at Cambridge England)

22 September 1948

A		C	
B		D	

DO NOT WRITE ABOVE THIS LINE

NOTE.—The next of kin should familiarize himself with the contents of the pamphlet, "Disposition of World War II Armed Forces Dead," before filling out this form. When the proper part of this form is filled out and properly signed by the next of kin, it should be returned to the OFFICE OF THE QUARTERMASTER GENERAL, MEMORIAL DIVISION, WAR DEPARTMENT, WASHINGTON 25, D. C., in the self-addressed postage-free envelope provided for this purpose.

If you are the next of kin or authorized representative of next of kin and desire to direct the disposition of the remains, please fill in PART I of this form.

PART I

I, (We) Mr. & Mrs. R. L. Graves
(PLEASE PRINT OR TYPE NAME OF NEXT OF KIN) *(Please indicate relationship to the deceased by placing an "X" in the proper box.)*

☐ WIDOW ☐ WIDOWER ☐ SON OVER 21 YEARS OLD ☐ DAUGHTER OVER 21 YEARS OLD

☒ FATHER ☒ MOTHER ☐ BROTHER OVER 21 YEARS OLD ☐ SISTER OVER 21 YEARS OLD

☐ RELATIONSHIP OTHER THAN ABOVE *(Specify)*

HAVING FAMILIARIZED MYSELF WITH THE OPTIONS WHICH HAVE BEEN MADE AVAILABLE TO ME WITH RESPECT TO THE FINAL RESTING PLACE OF THE DECEASED DESIGNATED ABOVE, NOW DO DECLARE THAT IT IS MY DESIRE THAT THE REMAINS: *(Please place an "X" in the box opposite the option you have selected.)*

☒ 1. BE INTERRED IN A PERMANENT AMERICAN MILITARY CEMETERY OVERSEAS

☐ 2. BE RETURNED TO THE UNITED STATES OR ANY POSSESSION OR TERRITORY THEREOF FOR INTERMENT BY NEXT OF KIN IN A PRIVATE CEMETERY

(NAME AND LOCATION OF CEMETERY)

☐ 3. BE RETURNED TO ______ (FOREIGN COUNTRY), THE HOMELAND OF THE DECEASED OR NEXT OF KIN, FOR INTERMENT BY NEXT OF KIN IN A PRIVATE CEMETERY LOCATED AT ______ (LOCATION OF CEMETERY SELECTED)

☐ 4. BE RETURNED TO THE UNITED STATES FOR FINAL INTERMENT IN A NATIONAL CEMETERY LOCATED AT ______ (LOCATION OF NATIONAL CEMETERY SELECTED)

(Please indicate if your own religious services at a location other than the selected national cemetery are desired by placing an "X" in the proper box)

☐ YES ☐ NO

THE NAME OF THE DECEASED, THE SERIAL NUMBER AND GRADE ARE CORRECT EXCEPT FOR THE FOLLOWING CHANGES: *(If no corrections are necessary, indicate this fact by inserting the word "NONE" in the space below.)*

NOV 19 1948

OQMG FORM 345 MILITARY
14 NOV 1946

PAGE 1

The next of kin of Howard A. Hibbler, Jeremiah C. Murphy, Joseph V. Nobilione, Robert L. Graves, Lawrence E. Dundon and Leighton B. McKenzie, opted for overseas burial. In November 1947, their remains were disinterred from Lisnabreeny and transported by truck, ship and rail, to Cambridge, in England. At Cambridge, their remains were placed into warehouse storage, until such time that burial could take place at the new permanent cemetery. In some cases, over a year would elapse before remains were interred, much to the dismay and distress of their families. At Cambridge, Military services were conducted at the time of the funeral and a burial flag was sent to the next of kin.

When it was officially opened, Cambridge American Military Cemetery was placed under the care and maintenance of the American Battle Monuments Commission. Each newly designated cemetery was beautified with paths, carefully trimmed lawns and in some cases large water features. Grave markers were usually a white marble cross or Star of David, depending on the religion of the deceased.

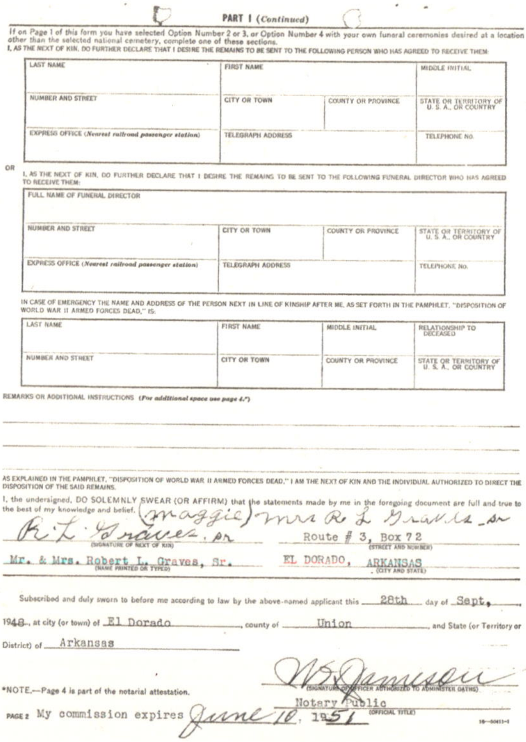

PART I (*Continued*)

If on Page 1 of this form you have selected Option Number 2 or 3, or Option Number 4 with your own funeral ceremonies desired at a location other than the selected national cemetery, complete one of these sections.

I, AS THE NEXT OF KIN, DO FURTHER DECLARE THAT I DESIRE THE REMAINS TO BE SENT TO THE FOLLOWING PERSON WHO HAS AGREED TO RECEIVE THEM:

LAST NAME	FIRST NAME		MIDDLE INITIAL
NUMBER AND STREET	CITY OR TOWN	COUNTY OR PROVINCE	STATE OR TERRITORY OF U. S. A., OR COUNTRY
EXPRESS OFFICE (*Nearest railroad passenger station*)	TELEGRAPH ADDRESS		TELEPHONE NO.

OR

I, AS THE NEXT OF KIN, DO FURTHER DECLARE THAT I DESIRE THE REMAINS TO BE SENT TO THE FOLLOWING FUNERAL DIRECTOR WHO HAS AGREED TO RECEIVE THEM:

FULL NAME OF FUNERAL DIRECTOR			
NUMBER AND STREET	CITY OR TOWN	COUNTY OR PROVINCE	STATE OR TERRITORY OF U. S. A., OR COUNTRY
EXPRESS OFFICE (*Nearest railroad passenger station*)	TELEGRAPH ADDRESS		TELEPHONE NO.

IN CASE OF EMERGENCY THE NAME AND ADDRESS OF THE PERSON NEXT IN LINE OF KINSHIP AFTER ME, AS SET FORTH IN THE PAMPHLET, "DISPOSITION OF WORLD WAR II ARMED FORCES DEAD," IS:

LAST NAME	FIRST NAME	MIDDLE INITIAL	RELATIONSHIP TO DECEASED
NUMBER AND STREET	CITY OR TOWN	COUNTY OR PROVINCE	STATE OR TERRITORY OF U. S. A., OR COUNTRY

REMARKS OR ADDITIONAL INSTRUCTIONS (*For additional space use page 4.*)

AS EXPLAINED IN THE PAMPHLET, "DISPOSITION OF WORLD WAR II ARMED FORCES DEAD," I AM THE NEXT OF KIN AND THE INDIVIDUAL AUTHORIZED TO DIRECT THE DISPOSITION OF THE SAID REMAINS.

I, the undersigned, DO SOLEMNLY SWEAR (OR AFFIRM) that the statements made by me in the foregoing document are full and true to the best of my knowledge and belief. (Maggie) Mrs R L Graves Sr

R L Graves, Sr (SIGNATURE OF NEXT OF KIN) — Route # 3, Box 72 (STREET AND NUMBER)

Mr. & Mrs. Robert L. Graves, Sr. (NAME PRINTED OR TYPED) — EL DORADO, ARKANSAS (CITY AND STATE)

Subscribed and duly sworn to before me according to law by the above-named applicant this 28th day of Sept., 1948, at city (or town) of El Dorado, county of Union, and State (or Territory or District) of Arkansas

W. B. Jamison (SIGNATURE OF OFFICER AUTHORIZED TO ADMINISTER OATHS)

*NOTE.—Page 4 is part of the notarial attestation.

Notary Public (OFFICIAL TITLE)

PAGE 2 My commission expires June 10, 1951

16—50411-1

ADDITIONAL REMARKS AND INSTRUCTIO

All remarks and information entered here will be considered as part of the Notarial Attestation.

We the parents of Sgt. Robert L. Graves, Jr., 38 334 100 believe that it is best that our son's body remain in the American Cemetery at Cambridge, England. It is our wish that he be allowed to remain there.

16—50410-1 U. S. GOVERNMENT PRINTING OFFICE

Oct 19 9 04 AM '48
O.Q.M.G.
TEL & CAB SECTION

EZZQ

EUA051

1

RR UEPOG

FM UEP 11P/36/35 U EXTRA COLLECT GOVT

ELDORAOXXX ELDORADO ARK

OCT 18 QORI 704P

CUNNINGHAM UEPOG 94A/HATT

MEMORIAL DIVISION OQMG

RETEL 18 LATE SGT ROBERT L GRAVES JR 38334100. FORMS FOR OVERSEAS BURIAL MAILED ABOUT TWO WEEKS AGO. IT IS OUR WISH THAT HE REMAIN BURIED OVERSEAS

ROBERT GRAVES SR BOX 72 RTE 3 EL DORADO ARKANSAS

845P

18 EIEERQPP 72 E.

R + R

CLASS OF SERVICE

This is a full-rate Telegram or Cablegram unless its deferred character is indicated by a suitable symbol above or preceding the address.

WESTERN UNION (08).

JOSEPH L. EGAN
PRESIDENT

1201

SYMBOLS

DL	Day Letter
NL	Night Letter
LC	Deferred Cable
NLT	Cable Night Letter
	Ship Radiogram

The filing time shown in the date line on telegrams and day letters is STANDARD TIME at point of origin. Time of receipt is STANDARD TIME at point of destination

1948 DEC 3 PM 4 15

.WZ130 21 COLLECT=ALBANY NY 3 254P=

QUARTERMASTER GENERAL, ATTENTION CAPT VOGEL=

293 F/0 T-62092 41

:I WISH MY NEPHEW JEREMIAH C MURPHY TO REMAIN BURIED IN THE AMERICAN CEMETERY IN ENGLAND THOSE ARE MY WISHES=

:JOHN J WALSH=

293 Murphy, Jeremiah C

O.Q.M.G.
L&CAB SECTION

THE COMPANY WILL APPRECIATE SUGGESTIONS FROM ITS PATRONS CONCERNING ITS SERVICE

In May 1949, the family of Robert L. Graves, received a letter from the Office of the Quartermaster General, informing them that their sons remains had been laid to rest at the permanent American Military Cemetery, in Cambridge, England. The burial flag was sent to his family on 28 February 1949.

The remaining families of the deceased who decided that their loved ones were to remain overseas, were also sent this letter, in some cases, receiving it earlier than others, informing them of their loved ones final interment. The burial flags for the deceased interred at Cambridge were dispatched on differing dates, for Lawrence E. Dundon, the flag was sent on 7 Jan 1949, for Jeremiah C. Murphy, 26 February 1949 and for Howard A. Hibbler, 15 February 1949.

At this moment in time, the dates are unknown for Joseph V. Nobilione and Leighton B. McKenzie.

2 May 1949

Sgt Robert L. Graves, Jr., ASN 38 334 100
Plot F, Row 0, Grave 26
Headstone: Cross
C mbridge (England) U. S Military Cemetery

Mr. R L. Graves, Sr.
Route #3, Box 72
El Dorado, Arkansas

Dear Mr. Graves:

This is to inform you that the remains of your loved one have been permanently interred, as recorded above, side by side with comrades who also gave their lives for their country. Customary military funeral services were conducted over the grave at the time of burial.

After the Department of the Army has completed all final interments, the cemetery will be transferred, as authorized by the Congress, to the care and supervision of the American Battle Monuments Commission. The Commission also will have the responsibility for permanent construction and beautification of the cemetery, including erection of the permanent headstone. The headstone will be inscribed with the name exactly as recorded above, the rank or rating where appropriate, organization, State, and date of death. Any inquiries relative to the type of headstone or the spelling of the name to be inscribed thereon, should be addressed to the American Battle Monuments Commission, Washington 25, D. C. Your letter should include the full name, rank, serial number, grave location, and name of the cemetery.

While interments are in progress, the cemetery will not be open to visitors. You may rest assured that this final interment was conducted with fitting dignity and solemnity and that the grave-site will be carefully and conscientiously maintained in perpetuity by the United States Government.

Sincerely yours,

H. FELDMAN
Major General
The Quartermaster General

vb

IN MEMORY OF

★★★★★

HOWARD A. HIBBLER

RANK

Sergeant, U.S. Army Air Forces

UNIT

Air Corps

DATE OF DEATH

June 1, 1944

COMMEMORATED IN PERPETUITY AT

Cambridge American Cemetery

Cambridge, United Kingdom

"Time will not dim the glory of their deeds."

— General John J. Pershing

IN MEMORY OF

★★★★★

JEREMIAH C. MURPHY

RANK

Flight Officer, U.S. Army Air Forces

UNIT

Air Corps

DATE OF DEATH

June 1, 1944

COMMEMORATED IN PERPETUITY AT

Cambridge American Cemetery

Cambridge, United Kingdom

"Time will not dim the glory of their deeds."

— General John J. Pershing

IN MEMORY OF

★★★★★

JOSEPH V. NOBILIONE

RANK

Second Lieutenant, U.S. Army Air Forces

UNIT

Air Corps

DATE OF DEATH

June 1, 1944

COMMEMORATED IN PERPETUITY AT

Cambridge American Cemetery

Cambridge, United Kingdom

"Time will not dim the glory of their deeds."

— General John J. Pershing

IN MEMORY OF

★★★★★

LAWRENCE E. DUNDON

RANK

Staff Sergeant, U.S. Army Air Forces

UNIT

Air Corps

DATE OF DEATH

June 1, 1944

COMMEMORATED IN PERPETUITY AT

Cambridge American Cemetery

Cambridge, United Kingdom

"Time will not dim the glory of their deeds."

— General John J. Pershing

IN MEMORY OF

★★★★★

LEIGHTON B. MCKENZIE

RANK

Flight Officer, U.S. Army Air Forces

UNIT

Air Corps

DATE OF DEATH

June 1, 1944

COMMEMORATED IN PERPETUITY AT

Cambridge American Cemetery

Cambridge, United Kingdom

"Time will not dim the glory of their deeds."

– General John J. Pershing

IN MEMORY OF

★★★★★

ROBERT L. GRAVES JR.

RANK

Sergeant, U.S. Army Air Forces

UNIT

Air Corps

DATE OF DEATH

June 1, 1944

COMMEMORATED IN PERPETUITY AT

Cambridge American Cemetery

Cambridge, United Kingdom

"Time will not dim the glory of their deeds."

– General John J. Pershing

In Northern Ireland, the accident remained in peoples memories for decades after the crash and it was often talked about with an air of suspicion, in regard to the strange events that took place immediately after the crash. One such person who talked about the accident and visited the crash site as a young boy with his friend, Rupert Miller, was a Mr. Alfred Montgomery Senior. Mr. Montgomery collected a few relics that remained at the crash site just days after the crash had occurred. Years later, he was married and had a family of his own, a young son, Alfred Junior. In the 1970's, he would often talk about his memories of this accident to Alfred, which would ignite a lifelong interest in the circumstances surrounding the crash.

Alfred Montgomery Junior, now takes up the story in his own words, from a young boy growing up in a trouble scarred 1970's Belfast, to flying half way across the world in pursuit of the widow of one of the crew members, the story continues.

Chapter Twelve

A young boy

As a young boy growing up in Belfast in the early 1970`s, the army on our streets was a part of everyday life. I can remember whilst sitting in class at primary school, aged around nine, the army would land helicopters on our sports pitches to drop troops, to patrol the nearby village of Ligoniel. I can recall my school teachers, on more than one occasion, scolding me, for watching them taking off and landing.

When I would return home from school in the afternoons, my cousin Craig and I, would play at "being soldiers", we would change into our *"army uniform play suits"* and patrol our local street. We were fortunate enough to have been raised in an area in North Belfast, that was not directly affected by the street violence and the troubles. The army would frequently arrive in our street, in Saracen Armoured Personnel Carriers. They would have a smoke and a coffee break, from their rations carried on-board. Craig

Alfie, immediate left, with his friends, in a Saracen APC, this photograph was taken from the front garden of his home in Springvale.

and I, would be invited to climb onto the vehicles, on more than one occasion.

My memories of growing up in Belfast in the 70`s were not all pleasant, I can remember seeing plumes of smoke, rising from the city, as bombs went off and military helicopters flew overhead. During the night, I would often wakeup to the sound of gun battles in the distance, between what would of been the army and the IRA, in the small hours of the morning.

It was nice to escape on weekends with my father to Cave Hill. He would tell me of how he and his father had watched Belfast burning, during the German air raids of 1941, the entire sky being red with the smell of burning, prevalent in the air. My father and I, would, in the summer months, collect blackberries and raspberries. In the winter months we would collect hazelnuts and beechnuts to take away with us, for novelty consumption later that day.

On our Sunday morning walks we would call in to see my grandmother, who lived at Shandarragh Park, off the Cave Hill Road. Her house was about half way between Cave Hill and my home at Springvale. My grandmother would bake apple or rhubarb pies every Sunday, so my mother, father and I, could enjoy it when we would return home later that day. As we would travel home from my grandmothers by car, we would frequently pass two vehicle army patrols and as I would always give a friendly wave, the soldiers would wave back. My father would tell me that during the war, when the American troops were here in Northern Ireland, the "yanks" would do the same to local children and were even known to give out candy bars and chewing gum.

I think that growing up in Belfast during the 1970s, which had a heavy military presence with army vehicles everywhere, awoke an interest.

Craig and Alfie, playing at being soldiers, in the back garden of Alfie's home.

Chapter Thirteen

Field trip

Sunday mornings after Sunday school were spent with my late father, walking up Cave Hill. On these outings we would talk about a lot of history and it always felt like a *"field trip"* as at that time my late father was a Museum Keeper, at the Ulster Museum in Belfast. I fondly remember on one occasion, he talked about an American plane that had crashed on Cave Hill and after the main wreckage had been removed, he had obtained some relics a day or two after the crash with a school friend. He promised that he would show me these when we got home and I was very excited.

When we got home, sitting at the table, he brought out a small cardboard box with 4 or 5 compartments.

Each compartment contained small fragments which were neatly labelled on cardboard inserts in fountain pen, in my late fathers own handwriting. One of the little bundle of fragments was a piece of khaki coloured flying jacket, with fur edging. Other fragments consisted of a small piece of plexiglass and a small piece of aluminium. The other compartments contained other World War Two era relics. One

Alfred Sr. and Alfred Jr. at Cave Hill during a field trip.

of which, was a piece of German parachute which had been used on a parachute mine bomb, dropped in Belfast during the air raids of 1941 and a piece of shrapnel from a nearby house, which received a direct hit. The shrapnel embedded itself in a broom handle in my late fathers childhood home during the air raid. The other items were my fathers ration books and my late grandfathers ARP insignia, as he was an Air Raid Warden.

My late father would have been only about sixteen years of age when he first visited the crash site and I can remember asking him what the crash site looked like. I recall him saying to me and this has stuck with me some 40 years later, that trees, soil and grass, were completely blackened and that there was a very strong smell of pine disinfectant. I have often tried to work out what the pine disinfectant smell could have been. The only thing I could think of was, as the trees had been broken and exposed, that the sap would have produced the pine fragrance.

In the background, is Alfred seniors late childhood street, after receiving a direct hit from a German Parachute Bomb. The small box to the left, is the box that Alfred senior placed on the table to show Alfred junior. The book below, "Bombs on Belfast", was an original publication published during the war, which documented in photographs, the German bombing of the city.

Some weeks later, I had pestered my late father to take me to the crash site to see where this American B-17 Flying Fortress had crashed. He agreed and I was quite disappointed to see the area, as it was not as he had described it and led me to believe. As a ten year old boy, I had not known that after a 30 year time span that the area would rejuvenate and had been returned to a wooded hillside. We walked around for some time, looking at the soil, the undergrowth and disappointingly, nothing had remained.

Some years elapsed and I often wondered what exactly had happened that this plane had crashed in this location, the ten crew members on-board, what they looked like, what they worked at, what their families were like and what their interests were. It was always at the back of my mind any time we walked on Cave Hill, or if we passed below it, on our way in and out of Belfast. As this was playing on my mind, I asked my late father if he could make enquiries through his place of employment, at the Ulster Museum in Belfast, as to where I could get records and details of what had happened. Some days later, he returned with information from

a colleague that looked after the *"Military Collection"* in the Ulster Museum, this information was an address in the United States. I immediately wrote a letter to this address and some weeks later five to six Xerox copies arrived. The pages were copies of the official aircraft accident report.

One of the pages contained a paragraph on what had happened. The other pages contained names, ranks and serial numbers of all ten crew members that had been on-board. There were a number of photographs that were of very poor quality. The report and the small 6x4 inch photographs had been photographed onto reels of 35mm microfilm during the 1960's. Upon completion of the microfilming process, the original documents were destroyed as a space saving measure, by the National Archives & Records Administration, who were the custodians of all military aircraft accident reports, dated 1918 to 1955. Another reason for archiving this material was due to poor storage of the documents, some of which, had started to erode due to damp, constant handling and decay.

Some years had gone by and I had passed my driving test. I got my own car in the early 1980`s and I was able to go to places that were of interest to me that I had never been able to persuade or coax my late parents to take me to. One of these places of course, was the crash site on Cave Hill.

Frequently after work, on summer evenings, I would drive to the car park at Belfast Castle and walk over the Cave Hill to the crash site and spend some time there. I usually had around two to three hours of daylight left to investigate the site, as the daylight usually faded at around 9.30pm. I found from the area that I had previously visited with my late father, if I went up another 60-70 ft to the steep hillside, I was unearthing and picking up small fragments of metal. These were mainly blobs of aluminium that had been burnt, melted and then solidified. I then found another area where I was getting fragments of perspex and some spent .50 cal bullet cases. These had exploded with the heat of the aircraft fire, they weren't fired from the gun in the conventional way, as the cap at the bottom did not have the firing pin mark in it and the shell was exploded-fragmented, around two-thirds from the base.

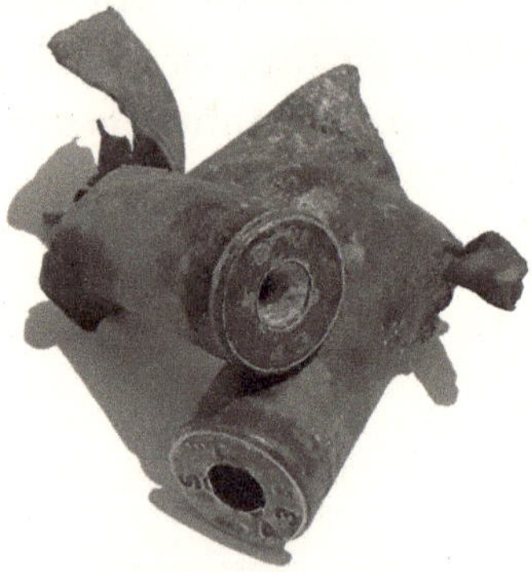

I continued to make this visit once or twice a year, until the late 1980`s and for personal reasons in the early 1990's I had more time on my hands to visit the site and I could go when I wanted to. Moving further up the hill, the fragments were becoming much more interesting. As well as finding the spent cartridge cases, I was finding bullet tips that had separated from the cases. Some were empty bullets that had been filled with magnesium, known as *"tracer bullets"*. There was one tracer bullet out of every ten in the ammunition belt of each machine gun. This tracer bullet would be seen as the magnesium burnt as it whizzed across the dark sky, giving the aerial gunner a better indication of which direction his bullets were going.

An aerial gunner in the waist gunners compartment man's a 50. calibre waist gun during a combat mission, note the spent cartridges which have accumulated on the floor of the aircraft.

I was finding small fragments of khaki uniform, a part of a headphone set and even found biscuits that had been burnt and had turned into a charcoal substance, although still intact, the word Nabisco was clearly visible.

When I returned home and did a little bit of research, included in the K-ration packs on-board a B-17 Flying Fortress, were biscuits that fitted the description of what I had unearthed earlier in the day.

The K-ration, was an individual daily combat food ration, which was introduced by the United States Army during World War II. The K-ration provided three separately boxed meal units: breakfast, dinner (lunch) and supper (dinner).

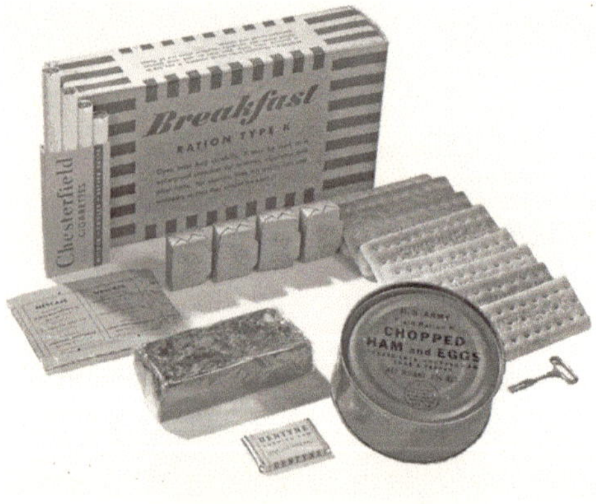

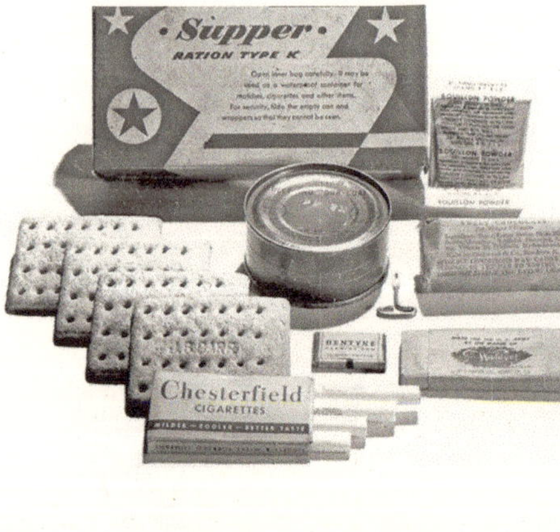

Chapter Fourteen

An overcast day

On 8 December 1993, I made a visit to the crash site. Conditions were not good to be going up the Cave Hill due to the inclement weather. The sky was overcast and a strong wind was blowing which made the trees creek and branches snap. Suddenly a heavy shower of rain came on, but there was no shelter from the trees as the foliage had fallen weeks earlier.

On that particular day I stayed for 90 minutes and found very little, my fingers were so cold as I sifted through the soil on the hillside. I only recall retrieving three items that day, which I put into my coat pocket and then came back down the hillside. Getting into my car, I went to my parents for my dinner that evening.

As I left my parents house and drove over the back of Cave Hill on a road called the Hightown Road, I looked forward to getting to my own house to clean up the relics I had found. Upon arriving home I fished the relics out of my coat pocket and starting running them under the water tap in the kitchen. The first item that I cleaned up was a small piece of Plexiglass, this particular piece was burnt, twisted and warped.

The second piece I took from my pocket was more mysterious, it felt like a washer or a hydraulic pipe olive. As I ran it under the water tap, the centre of it came away from the object, disintegrated and went down the plug hole. I instantly realised I was left holding an object that had been round but was slightly damaged from impact. I was still expecting it to come up green from a copper colour but I was surprised to see that it was getting brighter in colour and twinkling gold. I then realised that this was an item of jewellery, but not making the immediate connection that it had possibly come off the aircraft.

My late father had previously mentioned that the Floral Hall and Belfast Castle were both buildings that held dances on a Saturday night in the 1940`s and 1950's. My first thought was the possibility a couple had been to one of these venues, had a row and perhaps in temper, one or the other had thrown the item in the bushes whilst walking home.

I decided to look for a hallmark on the inside, as all gold and silver jewellery would hold this mark, that way, I could identify if it was British, American, or just an item of costume jewellery with no mark at all.

As I removed the remaining dirt and silt from the inside of the object, I was astonished to see letters and digits coming up, but at this point, I could not read or make out what they were. I dried the object off and could not believe what I was seeing, the digits read "10/21/39". Two names were present, Ruth and Larry. I recognised that the digits were in fact a date, written the American way with the month before the day and then the year.

I realised that it had come from someone on-board the aircraft. I proceeded upstairs and pulled out my file that I had received some ten years earlier. I was astonished to see that two out of the ten crew members on that aircraft were called Lawrence. I then set myself the task of finding out which Lawrence had a wife called Ruth.

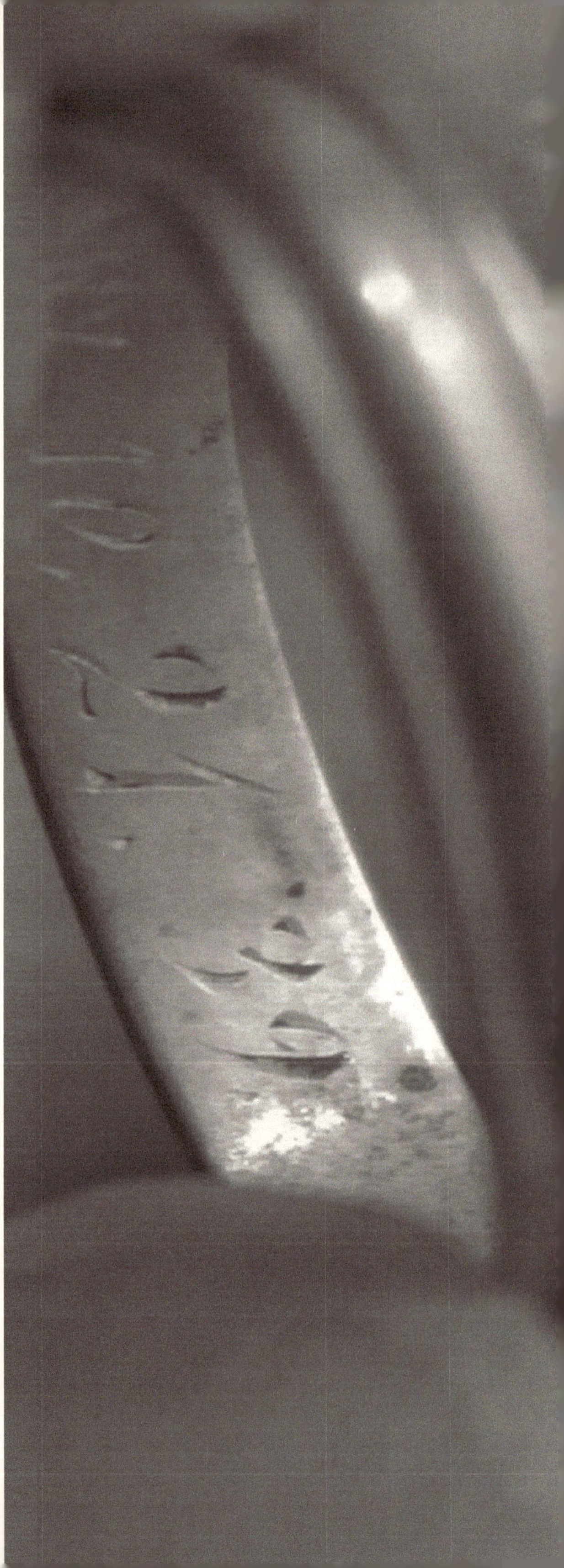

Chapter Fifteen

Finding Ruth

I found myself wondering what all the crew members looked like, what they worked at before the war and what their families had thought. This was all I could concentrate on and everything else in my life took a back seat. I knew that I would have to go through official channels to get further detailed information on the two Lawrence`s and that possibly the information may be classified.

I started this search with a letter to the American Military Cemetery, located in Cambridge, England. I received a reply within a few days stating that they had no listing of Corporal Lawrence R. McGrane, therefore his remains would have been returned to the United States at the request of his next of kin. The other Lawrence on-board, S/Sgt Lawrence E Dundon, had been from the state of Kentucky and was buried in their cemetery.

I contacted the Cabinet For Human Resources in Kentucky, which like our British Births, Deaths, and Marriages records, were responsible for holding and recording marriage details. Unfortunately they stated by return letter that they had incomplete marriage records for that era. At the same time, I had written to an agency called the "Total Army Personnel Command" in the state of Virginia, this address had been furnished to me by the American Military Cemetery, in Cambridge, England. I explained that I had found a wedding ring at the crash site of a B-17 Flying Fortress, Army Serial Number 42-97862, that had crashed in Belfast and that as the ring was inscribed with the name Larry and there were two Lawrence`s on-board, I was hoping that they could point me in the right direction. I had already drawn a blank with the Cabinet For Human Resources.

Although this letter writing and waiting for replies was ongoing, I still made frequent visits to the crash site, finding items that were identifiable fragments, such as buttons, material from uniforms, parts of handles from a .50 calibre machine gun and small fragments of clear fine glass, which could have only come from instrument dials. There was also coloured glass from the instrument warning lights and an interesting oxygen outlet control regulator disc.

Each of the crew members stations on-board the aircraft had an outlet, as when they exceeded 10,000ft altitude, supplied oxygen was needed for breathing. This disc formed part of a larger assembly that was a permanent fixture within the aircraft.

Left, *part of the Type G-1 Signal Assembly Oxygen Pressure Unit.* ***Below left***, *the sliding rule section of the navigators Type AN-5835-1 Dead Reckoning Computer.* ***Below right***, *the complete unit, with slide rule and case.*

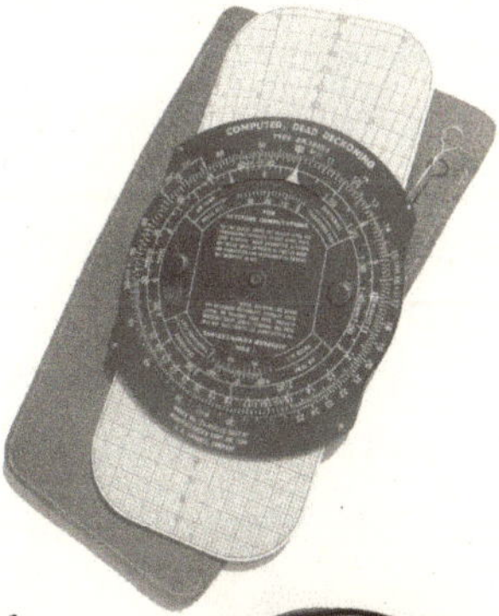

Above left, *part of a rocker cover assembly from an engine cylinder.* ***Above right***, *a piece of cooling fin from one of the engine cylinders.*

Above right, *a tunic button from a uniform belonging to one of the crew.* ***Left***, *the remains of what would have been the Demand Oxygen Regulator. An intact unit, can be seen to the far left.*

Below left, *the remains of a harness buckle, possibly from a parachute or a safety belt strap.* ***Below right***, *doping fabric, still in it's aluminium finish, this would have covered the fabric covered flight control surfaces, such as the ailerons, elevators and rudder.*

I had now established that the steep bit of the hillside I was now retrieving these relics from must have been the main centre line of the fuselage. It's quite mysterious, you could find an unburned intact item, within inches of a similar item, that has been melted or quite badly burnt. This seemed to indicate to me, that there had been a short but intense fire when it crashed. I believe had it been a prolonged fire involving a lot of fuel, everything would have been in the burnt molten state.

I unearthed some further fragments of uniform, some being a heavy felt like material, others a lighter weight material, comparable to a neck tie or shirt. To date, all of the items found had been of a military nature, however, this was the first occasion, I had unearthed any personal item, this being a silver plated soap box.

***Left**, the remains of various types of material.*

Left, the remains of a silver plated soap box.

In the previous months I had written numerous letters to various American Military Departments, whose addresses I had received from a very dear friend of mine, Mr. Ernie Cromie, from the Ulster Aviation Society and Mr. David W. Earl, Cheshire, England. Both of these gentlemen are very highly respected aviation historians.

Unfortunately none of these addresses were of any use and they would send me an acknowledgement, on receiving my letter, stating, that I could expect to hear from them in X number of weeks/months and when that date would approach, they would send another letter stating the same. At least this gave me the assurance they had not forgotten about my request, but it did not help my urgency.

On 22 September 1995, some thirteen months after sending my letter, I received a large A4 size envelope from "Total Army Personnel Command" Virginia. It was the Individual Deceased Personnel File *IDPF* for S/Sgt Lawrence E. Dundon. It contained approximately 30 pages and included official reports of burial, how each of the bodies were identified, letters to and from Lawrence`s mother, Mrs Daisy Dundon and also details of his wife, Mrs Ruth Dundon.

At this point, I learnt that only two of the ten crew members were identified by their dog tags. The remaining eight had been buried at US Military Cemetery, Lisnabreeny, Belfast, as X1 – X8 unknown.

This file also contained details of the crews dental records, these charts were disturbing for me to read, as some of the crew had been extremely burnt and some teeth were not retrievable. Fortunately Lawrence`s dental record was able to be compared with his body and with reference to teeth that had been extracted and recorded on military records, unknown X2 was labelled as S/Sgt Lawrence E Dundon.

Now that I had an emergency contact address from 1944, I took a chance and sensitively composed a letter, airmailing it to this western Louisville address in Kentucky.

Mr Alfred Montgomery
[redacted]
Co Antrim
Northern Ireland

9th October 1995

Dear Mrs Dundon,

I hope this letter is successful in finding you as I have spent many years to get this close.

I live on the outskirts of Belfast,Northern Ireland which you will recall is where your husband S/SGT.LAWERENCE E.DUNDON was tragically killed with 9 other comrades on June 1st 1944 when their B-17 aircraft crashed.I have spent many hours over the past years visiting this location and almost 3 years ago among the undergrowth and soil on this hillside I picked up along with small fragments of the aircraft a round metal object. When I returned home later that day I cleaned this and to my astonishment I found it was a wedding ring bearing an inscription "RUTH-LARRY 10/21/39"after an awful lot of correspondence with various U.S. Army Agencies I have arrived at this means of contacting you.I have vowed to myself to do everything humanly possible to return your late husband's wedding ring to you.I have also corresponded with the American Military Cemetry in Cambridge,England where your late husband is at rest and if you would prefer the wedding ring from your marriage could be placed there.

I hope this is sucessful in finding you as although I am only 30 years old I have had an interest in this tragic event for many years now and would dearly like to meet you one day. If I can be of any help whatsoever with any aspect of this great personal loss you incurred 51 years ago please do not hesitate to ask as nothing would be too much trouble for you.

I wait patiently and look forward to hearing from you

Yours Sincerely

Alfred Montgomery

Alfred Montgomery.

Chapter Sixteen

The Courier Journal

Three weeks later, my own letter was returned by the US postal service, stamped, incomplete address, return to sender. My anxiety and curiosity of this Louisville address sought me to seek a map of the area as close to 1944 as I could get. I managed to locate a 1951 map and made a comparison with the most recent map that I could obtain, which was a mid 1980's map of Louisville.

I was horrified to find that sometime between these two dates a raised six lane highway had diagonally carved up part of North 33rd Street. I could only deduce from this comparison that approximately twenty houses would have been demolished on the odd numbered side of the street. Almost all of the houses had been demolished on the even numbered side of the street. At this point I thought it was highly unlikely that I would be able to return the ring to anybody, least of all the widow of this serviceman.

I contacted the American Military Cemetery in Cambridge and discussed with them a contingency plan if my search proved unfruitful. That plan, was to place the ring within the top of S/Sgt Lawrence E. Dundon`s grave.

Cambridge American Cemetery, Cambridge, England, where the remains of six of the crew were finally laid to rest.

Over the Christmas period of 1995, the negative letters kept coming back on a weekly basis and I got the feeling that these agency departments wanted to get the matter closed by the end of that calendar year, or maybe it just seemed that way to me. The most disappointing one was from The Department of Veteran Affairs, stating that they had no record of Ruth Dundon ever claiming a pension on behalf of her late husband S/Sgt Lawrence E Dundon. This lead me to believe that she may have passed away during the war, as there was no record of any pension being drawn whatsoever. As the winter in Belfast progressed and then proceeded into the spring of 1996, I had almost put the whole project on hold, as I did not know where to go next in my search.

In July 1996, I decided that it might be a good idea to find the name of a daily newspaper in the Louisville, KY area to find out how much it would cost to put an ad in the personal column and hope that somebody may read that and come back to me.

On researching in Belfast Central Library, I found that Louisville, KY, had a newspaper called *"The Courier Journal"*. I jotted down a fax number for them and composed a short letter stating that I had found a personal object at the crash site of a World War Two American aircraft and I had traced this item to an airman, originally from Louisville, KY and wanted to know if anyone knew of S/Sgt Lawrence E Dundon, or any family he may have had.

I sent the fax and some 24 hours later when I returned home from work, there was quite a long fax waiting for me, from a Mr Bob Hill, asking for my telephone number so he could call me to discuss further. What I didn't know at the time, was that when *"The Courier Journal"* picked up my fax and read it, they decided that they would pass it to their weekly columnist, Mr Bob Hill and he was to run an article in their newspaper, on what he called *"this great find that I had made"*.

I sent my telephone number by return and within an hour, Mr. Bob Hill called me from The Courier Journals office, in Louisville, KY.

I told Bob the facts so far of my search and I felt uneasy telling the story, not because of what I had done, but because Bob seemed to be a traditional American and was addressing me as Sir. I didn't feel like I had earned this title. He came across as an older gentleman of my 31 years and I felt that he was more important than me, being a columnist of a daily American newspaper. Bob Hill reassured me that they would put an article together and that they would run it in his column within a few days. That sounded good to me and the next few days were so exciting. The rest of that week and the weekend passed by.

On Monday evening my wife Dawn (then fiancée) and I were watching television when our telephone rang at home, I answered it and it was Bob Hill, from *The Courier Journal*. Bob told me that they had run the story that day and had received several phone calls from people who knew Ruth and without him saying any more, he told me that Ruth was still alive. He asked for my permission to pass on my telephone number to Ruth herself. I told him please do and I would look forward to speaking to her.

BOB HILL

STAFF COLUMNIST

From a dead end to a possibility, place of rest sought for ring

HILL

Ever concerned, Alfred Montgomery included a photograph of the wedding ring in his most recent package from Northern Ireland. It's a bent, twisted ring with the inscription "Ruth — Larry 10/21/39."

Montgomery lives in Belfast. As a child his father had led him on walks up nearby Cave Hill, a steep, wooded place near Belfast Loch where on June 1, 1944, a U.S. Air Force B-17 Flying Fortress crashed in low clouds and burned, killing all 10 crew members.

The B-17, on its way to England, was forced to refuel in Northern Ireland. It was circling the airport when it hit the hill at about 600 feet, the pilot unaware the hill was hidden in the clouds.

Over the years, as highways and houses encrouched on its solitude, Montgomery would comb the rocky, peaty soil near the wreck site, picking up small pieces of fabric, plexiglass, even a uniform. One day in 1994 — 50 years after the crash — he bent to pick up what he thought was a steel washer. When he got it home, cleaned it up a little, he saw it was the wedding ring.

When he saw the words "Ruth — Larry," he knew this was something personal, something special, something a family might want. He began his search, writing Air Force agencies in the United States, making phone calls.

"I had a feeling it was sort of my duty to do it," he said by phone.

The search became even more complicated when the 8th U.S. Air Force records indicated there were two men named Larry on the doomed B-17. After going through the extensive personnel files, even family letters, supplied by the Air Force, Montgomery narrowed his search to Staff Sgt. Lawrence E. Dundon of Louisville.

Those records from the mid-1940s show the last known address of Dundon's mother, Daisy Dundon, to be 231 N. 26th St. The last known address of Dundon's wife, Ruth Dundon, was 219 N. 33rd St.

Dundon's body was so badly burned in the crash it could not be identified at first. Finally identified through dental records, the body was first buried near Belfast in Lisnabreney Cemetery, now a grassy field. By family request the body was later moved to a U.S. military cemetery near Cambridge, England.

The timing of all that is cloudy, the lack of information provided to loved ones during and just after that great war almost cruel. On July 20, 1945, some 13 months after the crash, Ruth Dundon wrote a letter to her late husband's superiors that read: "Dear Sirs: My husband, Staff Sgt. Lawrence Dundon, was reported killed in a crash on June 1, 1944. I would appreciate any information you could supply concerning his burial. To date I have not received any information. . . ."

Ruth Dundon also asked for a photo of her husband's grave. Two months later she received a reply. No burial information was available; no photographs were possible.

In 1947 Dundon's mother wrote seeking similar information, also asking "what is the scenery like around my son's grave?" There is no record of a reply. In 1949 she wrote to ask what service was said at her son's grave? The stiff answer came back . . . "military services at the time of burial."

A search through old Louisville city directories showed Lawrence and Ruth Dundon once lived in the 2600 block of West Market Street. Both worked for printing shops. A search of more recent city directories and the Louisville phone book did not reveal any Dundons who were related to Lawrence or Ruth.

One woman — a Dundon — did say she believed many Dundons came from Ireland, an ancestral birthplace that would have taken Lawrence E. Dundon full circle.

By phone, fax, cassette tape and mail, Alfred Montgomery has dutifully sought the Dundon family, someone who might want the wedding ring. The ring is almost sacred to him now. He left some of the original dirt on it and has it locked away for safekeeping.

"I feel that I should make every effort to try to return the ring to any family still alive. Failing that, the U.S. forces in Cambridge, England, have agreed to place it within the grave."

If you know something of Lawrence or Ruth Dundon, please write me in care of The Courier-Journal, 525 W. Broadway, P.O. Box 740031, Louisville 40201-7431. As Montgomery said in his final letter from Belfast: "I look forward to hearing from you."

Bob Hill's column appears in SCENE each Saturday, and also in the Tuesday and Thursday Metro sections of The Courier-Journal. To reach the guy, give him a call at (502) 582-4646.

***Left**, Bob Hills original article in the Courier Journal, requesting information on the Dundon family on behalf of Alfie.*

Chapter Seventeen

Is that Alfred ?

Sometime later that evening our telephone rang again and when I picked it up, on the other end was this sweet southern state American accent, of an elderly lady talking to me. She said *"Is that Alfred?"*. I confirmed it was and for a few seconds the phone went quiet, then she said *"I believe you have something that belongs to me?"*. I was able to describe the ring in great detail, she had told me that they had purchased it in a jewellers called Lemon & Son INC, in Louisville city, which is still trading today. I was able to read the engraving out to her, the phone went quiet again and she said *"that sounds very much like Larry`s ring"*. I immediately asked Mrs. Gillepsie for her address and she gave me details of an address which sounded very like the address that I had written to. This was confusing for me, but then it all started to unfold. Ruth told me that she had remarried a year or two after Larry`s death and that she had never claimed a pension on behalf of Larry. Her name had obviously changed by marriage to Ruth Gillespie. The zip code was no longer Louisville 12, it was now 40212 and ironically, she was still living in the same house that her and Larry had built together, all those years ago.

I got a shiver up my spine at that stage and I was very emotional, as my eyes filled with tears. I immediately asked Mrs Gillespie a question and she quickly corrected me to call her Ruth. From then on I felt uneasy addressing this very respectable elderly lady as Ruth, but that was the way it was to be. I told Ruth that I would get the ring dispatched to her as quickly as possible, probably by international air courier, rather than using the postal service and I made a joke about it, saying we don't want it to get lost again, she chuckled and responded by saying *"if it would not be too much trouble, could you please bring it out in person?"*. I am not often lost for words but I was at this point and I also did not want to disappoint Ruth. I felt obliged that this wedding ring should be returned to her in the safest way possible. I had pledged to myself many months before this, that it was not an item I could keep and I had to do my utmost to return it to a member of the family.

I agreed I would make enquiries and call her back within a few days. I recall spending 2 or 3 days at my desk at home, calling a lot of successful American companies that were operating in both Northern Ireland and Europe. I explained the

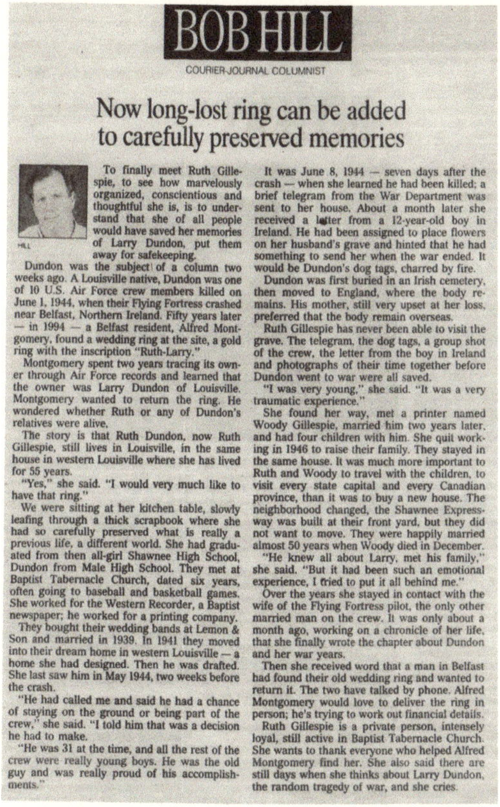

BOB HILL

COURIER-JOURNAL COLUMNIST

Now long-lost ring can be added to carefully preserved memories

HILL

To finally meet Ruth Gillespie, to see how marvelously organized, conscientious and thoughtful she is, is to understand that she of all people would have saved her memories of Larry Dundon, put them away for safekeeping.

Dundon was the subject of a column two weeks ago. A Louisville native, Dundon was one of 10 U.S. Air Force crew members killed on June 1, 1944, when their Flying Fortress crashed near Belfast, Northern Ireland. Fifty years later — in 1994 — a Belfast resident, Alfred Montgomery, found a wedding ring at the site, a gold ring with the inscription "Ruth-Larry."

Montgomery spent two years tracing its owner through Air Force records and learned that the owner was Larry Dundon of Louisville. Montgomery wanted to return the ring. He wondered whether Ruth or any of Dundon's relatives were alive.

The story is that Ruth Dundon, now Ruth Gillespie, still lives in Louisville, in the same house in western Louisville where she has lived for 55 years.

"Yes," she said. "I would very much like to have that ring."

We were sitting at her kitchen table, slowly leafing through a thick scrapbook where she had so carefully preserved what is really a previous life, a different world. She had graduated from then all-girl Shawnee High School, Dundon from Male High School. They met at Baptist Tabernacle Church, dated six years, often going to baseball and basketball games. She worked for the Western Recorder, a Baptist newspaper; he worked for a printing company.

They bought their wedding bands at Lemon & Son and married in 1939. In 1941 they moved into their dream home in western Louisville — a home she had designed. Then he was drafted. She last saw him in May 1944, two weeks before the crash.

"He had called me and said he had a chance of staying on the ground or being part of the crew," she said. "I told him that was a decision he had to make.

"He was 31 at the time, and all the rest of the crew were really young boys. He was the old guy and was really proud of his accomplishments."

It was June 8, 1944 — seven days after the crash — when she learned he had been killed; a brief telegram from the War Department was sent to her house. About a month later she received a letter from a 12-year-old boy in Ireland. He had been assigned to place flowers on her husband's grave and hinted that he had something to send her when the war ended. It would be Dundon's dog tags, charred by fire.

Dundon was first buried in an Irish cemetery, then moved to England, where the body remains. His mother, still very upset at her loss, preferred that the body remain overseas.

Ruth Gillespie has never been able to visit the grave. The telegram, the dog tags, a group shot of the crew, the letter from the boy in Ireland and photographs of their time together before Dundon went to war were all saved.

"I was very young," she said. "It was a very traumatic experience."

She found her way, met a printer named Woody Gillespie, married him two years later, and had four children with him. She quit working in 1946 to raise their family. They stayed in the same house. It was much more important to Ruth and Woody to travel with the children, to visit every state capital and every Canadian province, than it was to buy a new house. The neighborhood changed, the Shawnee Expressway was built at their front yard, but they did not want to move. They were happily married almost 50 years when Woody died in December.

"He knew all about Larry, met his family," she said. "But it had been such an emotional experience, I tried to put it all behind me."

Over the years she stayed in contact with the wife of the Flying Fortress pilot, the only other married man on the crew. It was only about a month ago, working on a chronicle of her life, that she finally wrote the chapter about Dundon and her war years.

Then she received word that a man in Belfast had found their old wedding ring and wanted to return it. The two have talked by phone. Alfred Montgomery would love to deliver the ring in person; he's trying to work out financial details.

Ruth Gillespie is a private person, intensely loyal, still active in Baptist Tabernacle Church. She wants to thank everyone who helped Alfred Montgomery find her. She also said there are still days when she thinks about Larry Dundon, the random tragedy of war, and she cries.

story and basically told them that I would require some sort of sponsorship to return this ring, in the hope that they would have aircraft couriers that take documents back and forward, to possibly ask to avail of this service as it was only a small item of jewellery.

On telling them the full story I was very disappointed that they all came back with virtually the same answer and they didn't really want to go back to the darker days of World War Two. They were now successful businesses in the new European Union. This left me feeling disappointed that they had shown little respect for the servicemen that had gave their lives here during World War Two, which now enabled them to do as they please and prosper as a business.

I then decided to try some local and national newspapers such as *"The Newsletter"* which was a long established business in Belfast, producing a morning paper. I explained the whole story to their receptionist, who seemed quite interested. Ten minutes had elapsed, when she connected me to their military correspondent, Mr. Steven Moore. Steven and I talked for some fifteen minutes, in which I told him the story from start to finish. His reaction at the end of the story was *"wow"* and he asked me to leave it with him for a day or so to see if they could help and promised that he would come back to me. True to his word, Steven did come back, with good news, that the News letter were going to fly myself and Dawn, to Louisville, KY and that Steven himself was coming along also to cover the story.

Chapter Eighteen

That's definitely my ring!

I was astonished, immediately agreeing with Steven that I would not speak to any other press. I could not wait until later that evening when I telephoned Ruth to tell her of my fortune and that a Northern Irish reporter was accompanying Dawn and I out to Louisville, KY. Steven made all of the travel arrangements for us, flying from Belfast international Airport, to Shannon in the west of Ireland, onto JFK Airport in New York and a very hurried taxi ride from JFK to La Guardia, so we could get our next flight to Baltimore, Maryland. Eventually we finally arrived in Louisville, KY.

I recall Dawn sharing her feelings with me on the amount of take-offs and landings we were having on this trip and that we were perhaps tempting fate with what we were carrying. Bearing in mind the bad luck and misfortunes, that this ring had encountered on its last airborne trip back in 1944.

When we eventually arrived at Louisville International Airport, or Standiford Field, as it was formerly known, it was around 11pm on a Saturday night. With the five hour time difference between GMT and Eastern Time, our body clock was actually 4am and we were all exhausted, having been travelling for 23 hours.

We were met at the airport by a gentleman slightly older than I and he introduced himself as

Alfie, on the balcony of their room at the Galt House Hotel, with the bouquet of flowers left by Ruth.

Bill Gillespie, this was Ruth`s eldest son. Bill's son, Taylor, gave Dawn a beautiful bunch of flowers which Ruth had sent and that struck a chord with me, that this lady was thinking that I had done something out of the ordinary.

We proceeded to the car rental desk and hired our own car. With Steven Moore in tow, we followed Bill Gillespie in convoy to Downtown Louisville, where we were staying at The Galt House Hotel. When the reservation was made with The Galt House Hotel, a standard room had been booked for us, but when we arrived at the reception desk, we were allocated a suite on the top floor. On entering our suite, a flower arrangement was situated on the table, with a little note from Ruth saying; *"thank you and I hope you enjoy your visit"*. As we prepared for bed that night, I finally realised that we were actually in Louisville and although Dawn and I had made numerous trips to the United States before to Florida, we had never been in a city like Louisville, it was so different architecturally and the people were very warm and welcoming.

On waking the next morning, 22 September 1996, after a restful night's sleep, we went down to breakfast, southern style of course, being ham and eggs. We were excited yet nervous of the plans for later that day, when I would finally get to meet Ruth and hand back Larry`s ring. I had been told before we left Northern Ireland that I would be handing Ruth the ring back in the same church *(Baptist Tabernacle)*, that Ruth and Lawrence had married in, back in 1939.

I assumed we would be handing the ring back in a hallway when the church service had finished, oh how I was so wrong.

We arrived at the church at 1.45pm and as I walked up the front steps with Dawn, Steven Moore and Bill Gillespie, I could hear the background noise of a large crowd. As we opened the exterior door of the church I could hear that the noise was coming from behind the interior door and hesitated in case the service was still ongoing. Bill Gillespie excused himself for a moment and returned with a slender, dark haired elderly lady, who without having to introduce herself, I immediately knew it was Ruth Gillespie, his mum.

There were no formal introductions, she put her arms around me, patted me on the back and said *"I'm so glad to see you Alfred "*.

We talked for a few minutes and then she beckoned me to follow her through the interior door. When it was opened, the noise of

BAPTIST TABERNACLE
BAPTIST TABERNACLE
BAPTIST TABERNACLE
MORN WORSHIP 10:45 AM
SUN EVENING 6 P M
WED PRAYER MEETING 6:15PM
DR. SAM ROBERTS PASTOR

approximately one hundred people engaged in casual conversation, diminished to a silence, as everyone turned and looked at us. When I say everyone, there must have been an age range from young children, to elderly people, filling every available space in the hall. I then realised this was not going to be a quiet affair and a little bigger than expected. Thankfully I had taken Dawn`s advice and worn a suit and not my usual attire of jeans and cowboy boots.

As I walked down the aisle of the church, Ruth walked beside Dawn and I, with Steven Moore following behind. At the top of the room there was a long table, laid out with little flags of both the British Union Jack and the American Star Spangled Banner, which were surrounding an array of cookies and cakes.

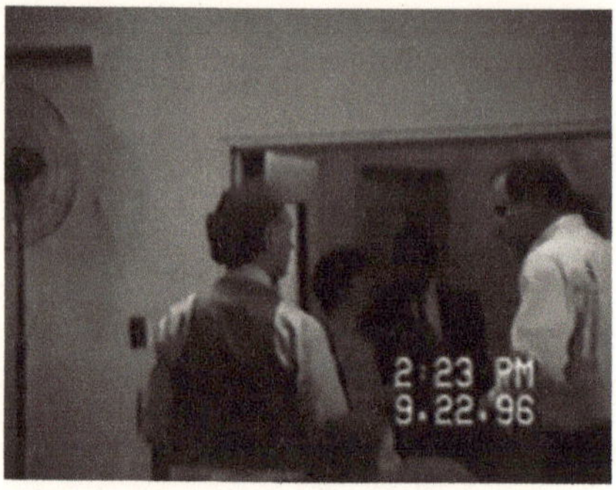

Bill Gillespie was a Professor of Communications at Georgetown University, in Georgetown, KY. He did our formal introduction to the large group of people and then to his mum, Ruth. As he finished saying why I was there and the crowd went quiet, we had travelled with the ring in a small, clear, zip lock bag and I put it in the open palm of my hand so Ruth could see, she looked at it for a few seconds, then looked at me with tears in her eyes, looked back at the ring again, then patted me on the back and said; *"That's definitely my ring, the last time I seen that was when Larry went off to war in 1944"*. This made me think that Ruth actually had a little bit of doubt that the ring was actually Larry`s, or I had got the wrong person. When I placed the ring in her hand she knew the story was true.

Ruth, had organised a reception following the handing back of the ring, which involved a lot of food, meeting her friends and family and posing for photographs for the local press.

9.22.96

Left to right, Anne Meadows, Bill Gillespie, Dawn, Alfie, Ruth, Bob Hill, Bobby Gillespie and Marc Gillespie.

Chapter Nineteen

Alfred Montgomery Day

At the reception I learnt quite a lot more about Ruth and her life. She told me how she had remarried a year or two after Larry's death, when she realised that Larry was not coming back and had met and fallen in love, with Woody Gillespie. Ruth and Woody had four children together, William (Bill), Anne, Robert (Bobby) and Marc. During their life together they travelled to almost every US state and had a very good life. Woody passed away only 6 months previous to our meeting, from Alzheimers Disease. I then realised that had my letter been successfully delivered to Ruth around that time, the outcome might have been different to what it was now, as they were going through a very difficult time and it was definitely not the time to receive a letter about a previous late husband. This gave me the strangest feeling that someone was guiding me and there was a reason behind it. I am a great believer in everything happens for a reason and I can now look back and say that all of the setbacks were for this reason.

I was then startled by a male voice tapping a spoon on a table and asking everyone to stand up and if he could have their attention. I also turned around not knowing what to expect and saw Bill Gillespie holding a blue folder, with the Louisville City Mayors Office official seal on the cover. Bill proceeded to open this and read out the proclamation the City of Louisville had made for me. They had designated September 22 1996, as *"Alfred Montgomery Day"*. I was astonished and then another certificate was lifted out, it stated that I had been made an honorary citizen of Louisville city, KY, I was lost for words!.

Bill Gillespie reads out the proclamation the city of Louisville had made for Alfie.

Office of the Mayor

Proclamation

To Whom All Those Present Shall Come, Greetings:

Whereas, *Alfred Montgomery has shown great respect and admiration for the American men and women who served in Ireland during World War II; and*

Whereas, *Alfred Montgomery was thoughtful enough to seek out the relatives of downed Louisville Airman Lawrence Dundon; and*

Whereas, *Alfred Montgomery spent two years searching Air Force records in order to return Lawrence Dundon's wedding ring to his Louisville family; and*

Whereas, *Alfred Montgomery personally returned Lawrence Dundon's wedding ring to his Louisville family on September 22, 1996; and*

Whereas, *Alfred Montgomery's kindness, spirit and generosity will forever be remembered across Louisville:*

Now Therefore, *I, Jerry E. Abramson, Mayor of Louisville, hereby proclaim September 22, 1996 as Alfred Montgomery Day and I call upon the citizens of our city to take notice of this special recognition.*

"Alfred Montgomery Day"

Done in the City of Louisville, the Commonwealth of Kentucky, this twenty-second day of September in the Year, the Nineteen Hundred and Ninety-sixth and of the City, the Two Hundred and Sixteenth.

Jerry E. Abramson, Mayor

To All to Whom These Presents Shall Come, Greeting: Know ye that

Alfred Montgomery

is hereby commissioned an

Honorary Citizen of Louisville

With all rights and privileges together with the responsibility of furthering to all the good name and tradition of warm hospitality found in the City of Louisville and Commonwealth of Kentucky.

CITY OF LOUISVILLE 1778

Done in the City of Louisville, Commonwealth of Kentucky this the 22nd day of September, 1996.

Jerry E. Abramson, Mayor

The battery of press cameras flashed again and it was published both state-side and here in Northern Ireland that I had received these certificates from the US Government. Bill started to read out a list of events that had been planned for me. Sadly we were not able to uptake all of these events, as that would have taken nearly two weeks and not the 5 days that we had planned.

Dawn and I were treated like royalty throughout this trip, even when going into restaurants people heard our accent and asked

if we were from Ireland. *Are you anything to do with the story in the papers about the ring?*, we would quietly nod or agree and then the story would have to be told once again. Over the next few days in Louisville we tried to uptake as many of the invitations as we could, we visited many places and met some wonderful people but one of the most enjoyable events was not an official one, we went to visit Ruth at her home one afternoon.

The home Larry and Ruth designed and built together. This photograph was taken in 1996.

It was just Dawn, myself and Ruth, away from all of the press and staring eyes. Steven Moore had returned to Northern Ireland. We talked to Ruth for a while and then she said that she wanted to show us an album, *"Larry`s Album"*. Ruth went off into another room to retrieve this album and I remember sitting on her settee looking

around me and looking out of her net curtains to the leaves falling from the trees like snow, as it was almost autumn and it was such a beautiful sight. I felt so at home in this house, knowing it was the home that Larry had lived in before he was tragically killed on Cave Hill, which is almost beside my home.

Alfie and Ruth look through Larry's photo album, at Ruth's home.

Alfie holds Larry's burial flag and portrait photograph, in Larry's nieces home, Bonnie Hildreth.

In this album there were photographs of Larry and his crew at various positions within a B-17 Flying Fortress, manning the overhead guns in the radio compartment and the original telegram that was sent by Union Telegram, informing Ruth about Larry`s death.

At the back of the album there were letters that had came from eyewitnesses, these must have been passed onto the US Military or Red Cross and then in turn, copies sent to Ruth. These were quite interesting, one was from a Belfast tram driver. He recalled how an aircraft passed in front of him in low cloud, so low, he thought it was going to crash into the overhead power lines that the trams got their power to operate from. Another letter was from a resident of Ben Madigan, who claimed that one of the radial engines had rolled down from the crash site through a hedge and come to rest at the gable wall of a house. Will and I, have researched that and there were only two houses that would have been adjacent to the crash site before a development in the 1960`s. Up until recently, there was still a break in that hedge!. Another letter stated that the aircraft undercarriage was lowered and that the undercarriage had struck the chimney of a house that was standing beside the Antrim Road, just below Ben Madigan. We located where that house would have been and it was almost directly in line with the crash site, however, that house was demolished in the 1970`s and we have no evidence that this did actually happen.

One of the more poignant objects Ruth showed to me was Larry's identification tag, more commonly known as a *"Dog Tag"*.

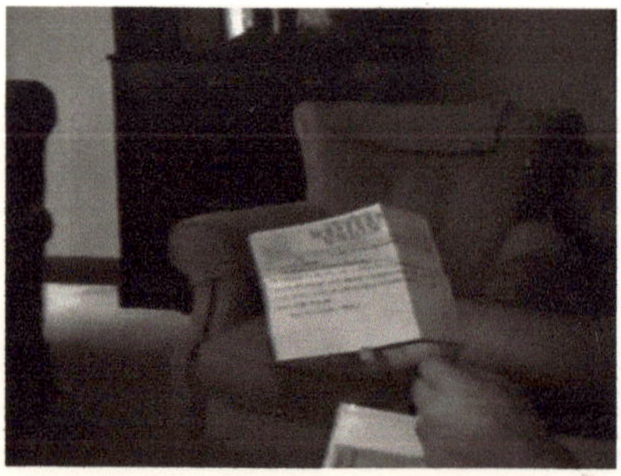

***Left**, the original telegram, informing Ruth of Larry's death.*

***Right**, Larry's dog tag, recovered by Gordon Wade.*

At the time of the accident, Larry's tag was unable to be found and consequently his remains would remain unidentified for almost three years until dental records were obtained by the US Graves Registration Service. It transpired that a number of weeks after the crash, a young schoolboy called Gordon Wade, decided to have a look around the crash site. He located Larry's tag and it was finally reunited with Ruth just after the end of World War II. Ironically, another friend of mine, Mr. Jim McKeown, found Larry's other tag while visiting the site in 2010. I was able to furnish him with the address for Larry's only living blood relative, Bonnie Hildreth, of Bowling Green, KY.

After our enjoyable afternoon with Ruth, we returned to the Galt House Hotel, where BBC Radio 5 had arranged to do a live radio interview covering *The Ring Story* as it was most aptly known.

Our trip drew to a close and the following Saturday morning, when we were due to fly out of Louisville Airport, Ruth and her entire family circle came to see us off together with Channel 9 television from Kentucky. We said our goodbyes and Ruth asked Dawn and I to be sure to call her when we got home as she was worried about us flying the distance. It only struck me then that we were travelling in the footsteps of Larry on that journey. We arrived home and immediately called Ruth as we had promised.

Ruth and Larry, during his early days of training. The lighter tan uniform was more suited to warmer climates.

Corporal Dundon and Ruth, on the steps of their home, in Louisville, Kentucky. Ruth proudly wears Larry's wings.

Staff Sergeant Dundon with his niece Bonnie. The small triangular patch on his right sleeve, denotes that he is a specialist in radio communications.

Larry poses for a quick photograph, in his class-a uniform. This photograph was presumably taken in Florida.

Chapter Twenty

Publicity

A few days later I received a telephone call from the BBC, in London. There was a producer at BBC Radio 4 who wanted to do a one hour documentary for their *"Radio 4 Document"* series, on *"this amazing story"* as they termed it. They were going to send a presenter and producer across from London and we arranged a mutually suitable time the following Sunday.

The following day, I received a call from People magazine in the US, they wanted to send a reporter and a photographer from the US to cover the story. This was arranged for the following Sunday after the BBC Radio documentary. When the presenter and producer came across from London, we did some recording at home and then proceeded up Cave Hill to the crash site. We did some investigation work and further audio recordings. It was a very successful set of recordings that were made In Northern Ireland, but they did however want to have some other material that they could use if their Editor decided to cut down on some of our field work.

They then decided that on a suitable date for Dawn and I, that we should fly across to Stansted Airport, England, where we would be collected and they would do further interviews at the RAF Museum which was located at Duxford. This is where the famous B-17 *"Sally B"* was kept. They were going to do the interviews within close proximity of the Sally B and they wanted me to bring some artefacts from 42-97862. A member of staff was going to help identify the item I had brought.

We then travelled onto the American Military Cemetery at Cambridge, where I was going to visit Larry`s grave for the first time. They were quite happy with the interviews that had been done at the crash site on Cave Hill and at our home, but they decided to not use the interviews which were recorded at the American Military Cemetery. We then flew back home again and I continued my job as a tour bus driver.

Alfie, during his time as a tour bus driver.

For the next 5 days I was looking forward to People magazine coming across on the Sunday. We talked about some of the story at our home and then proceeded to the crash site on Cave Hill to do photographs. This article appeared in the November 1996 issue of People Magazine.

Reality was starting to hit home and the Louisville trip, radio and magazine interviews were slowly fading into the distance like a pleasant dream as were the daylight hours at this time of year. It was late October, early November and it was getting dark at around 4pm. One autumnal afternoon I received a telephone call to say that Peter Woodward *(Son of Edward Woodward, who played the Equaliser, in the TV series)*, had heard my interview with the *"BBC Radio 4 Document"* programme and he wanted to write a script for a film, loosely based on *"The Ring Story "*.

Alfie pensively kneels next to the man whose wedding ring he found and returned to his widow, Staff Sergeant Lawrence E. Dundon, at Cambridge American Cemetery, England.

Chapter Twenty One

In memoriam

Ruth and I continued to be great friends, we would exchange birthday, Christmas cards and presents. We would call each other every other week and would have spoken to my late parents on many an occasions. I think my late father felt slightly responsible for all that had happened as it was him introducing me to the crash site that started this all off.

It had now become a reality that this story was not going to end, now that the ring had been handed back in Louisville. In my own mind, over the days after returning home, I thought it would be nice if a permanent memorial could be erected, possibly, or probably not on the crash site, but somewhere within the vicinity, where it would be accessible to a lot of people visiting. The two locations that fitted this bill would have been Belfast Castle or Bellevue Zoo.

During the 1990's, the zoo occupied what was the Golf Course behind Floral Hall. It was at the edge of that Golf Course in the trees, that the B-17 crashed. While the story was still fresh in everybody's mind in Northern Ireland, I composed a letter to Belfast City Council, basically outlining my idea and mailed it off to them. Within a few days I received a favourable reply and correspondence went back and forth between us, together with phone calls to the curator of the Zoo, Mr. Mark Challis. The outcome, being, that Belfast City Council, would be prepared to have a memorial placed within the Zoo complex and they would look after the maintenance of it, but did not have the monies to fund this. This left me with a small problem!. After the Christmas period in January and February, the weather was not good enough to visit the crash site on Cave Hill.

From the top of Cave Hill, the Floral Hall is to the immediate left, the aircraft crashed to the right of the small paths below the plateau. In the distance Carnmoney Hill can be seen in the background and to the immediate right, Belfast Lough.

This gave me time to compile some letters to American companies trading in Northern Ireland, to see if they would provide full or part sponsorship towards a memorial. I also thought this would be appealing to them, to have their company name or logo on the memorial as an official sponsor, however, once again, I was bitterly disappointed. All of the companies were singing from the same hymn sheet, basically, saying that they all had a successful market place in Europe nowadays and that they really did not want to go back to the darker days of the Second World War, when the United States, being an allied force, was fighting against axis occupied countries in Europe.

I took my story of requesting funding for a memorial to a local newspaper, who ran the story and my appeal for sponsorship, but once again no one came forward with the funds needed. I decided to shelve this idea in mid 1997 as it was apparent I was not going to be able to have this memorial erected without any financial sponsorship.

In mid June 1997, Dawn and I received a very official looking envelope in the post. It was an invitation to the American Consul Generals Garden Party, at his official residence in Belfast, on 4 July 1997. We attended this for a number of years consecutively and once again we were able to tell the story and talk to a number of people who were interested in the American participation in Northern Ireland, during World War Two.

Over the next few years I was frequently asked to give talks to historical groups, schools and organisations that would have speakers visit their groups on various occasions. I enjoyed doing this in the evenings, I would arrive by pre-arrangement at their venue, tell them the whole Ring Story and take a few relics of the aircraft that they could pass around and look at. Afterwards there would usually be refreshments and I would be able to answer questions.

One morning, I received a phone call from Jo Gilbert, who was the co-producer of the *"Closing the Ring"* film, along with Sir Richard Attenborough. Jo and I had met several times previously, but this particular day she was to tell me that Belfast City Council had contacted her, as they were trying unsuccessfully to find me. Jo, went on to say in our conversation that Belfast City Council were beginning a process of erecting a permanent memorial in the

Client Services Department
Parks & Amenities

Our ref:	PD182 MP/IW	Being dealt with by:	Maurice Parkinson
Your ref:		Ext:	3430
		Date:	2nd December 1997

Mr Alfred Montgomery
[redacted]

Dear Mr Montgomery

MEMORIAL TO THE U.S. AIRFORCE

You will recall over a period of time that you have been in contact with us with respect to the provision of a memorial to U.S. Airforce Personnel who lost their lives at Hazelwood during the last war.

I am aware that John Stronge, the Zoo Manager has attempted to contact you on a number of occasions and I understand there has been no response.

I would really like to have this matter tidied up with respect to determining what the Council should be doing and in that respect I will be proposing a suitable course of action to members of the Parks & Amenities Sub-Committee.

Whilst I understand these matters do take time to resolve, I trust you understand that I require to report to the Parks & Amenities Sub-Committee in the near future. I propose therefore that unless I hear from you within three weeks from the date of this letter that I will be reporting to the Sub-Committee accordingly.

I trust I will be hearing from you in the near future.

With best wishes.

Yours sincerely

MAURICE PARKINSON
HEAD OF PARKS & AMENITIES

Maurice G. Parkinson *M.Hort. (RHS), D.H.E.(Hons)*
HEAD OF PARKS & AMENITIES

BELFAST CITY COUNCIL
THE CECIL WARD BUILDING • 4-10 LINENHALL STREET • BELFAST BT2 8BP
TELEPHONE: 01232 320202 • FAX: 01232 237070

Client Services Department
Parks & Amenities

Our ref: PD182MP/IW

Your ref:

Being dealt with by: Maurice Parkinson

Ext: 3430

Date: 20 December 1996

Mr Alfred Montgomery
[redacted]

Dear Mr Montgomery

MEMORIAL TO THOSE WHO DIED IN THE US AIRFORCE CRASH

You will recall that you wrote to me some time ago concerning the possible placing of a memorial to those who died in a US Airforce crash during the last war.

In turn I asked that you would make direct contact with Mr John Stronge, the Zoo Manager. I understand from Mr Stronge that he has not heard from you.

At a recent Parks & Amenities Sub-Committee a number of members of the Committee expressed their support and desire to proceed with some form of memorial and therefore it would be very useful to know in detail of your proposal. It would be most useful, therefore, if I knew of your intentions at this time, so that I could update the Sub-Committee members and in this regard I would be most grateful if you would make contact with Mr Stronge.

I look forward to hearing from you.

Yours sincerely

MAURICE G PARKINSON
HEAD OF PARKS & AMENITIES SECTION

Maurice G. Parkinson *M.Hort. (RHS), D.H.E.(Hons)*
HEAD OF PARKS & AMENITIES

BELFAST CITY COUNCIL
THE CECIL WARD BUILDING • 4-10 LINENHALL STREET • BELFAST BT2 8BP
TELEPHONE: 01232 320202 • FAX: 01232 237070

War bomber memorial is hit by sponsor shortage

By Staff Reporter

A MEMORIAL plan for 10 US airmen killed when their bomber crashed into Cavehill during World War II is under threat because of a lack of sponsorship.

Earlier this month Belfast City Council agreed to a request from Carnmoney man Alfred Montgomery for a monument marking the tragedy.

The proposal was for a memorial to be put up in Belfast Zoo, close to the spot where the B17 Flying Fortress came down.

However Mr Montgomery has admitted he is having difficulty raising the estimated £500-£600 cost of the memorial.

Initial inquiries to American companies in Northern Ireland have so far been fruitless.

But Mr Montgomery is optimistic a trip to Washington DC this weekend will prove more successful.

He is going to America to carry out research into the Second World War US airbase at Langford Lodge, near Nutts Corner.

That was where the B17 was headed for a refuelling stop on the fateful day of June 1 1944 when it crashed in bad weather.

While in Washington he intends raising the matter of the memorial with American ex-service organisations in the hope they may be interested in helping.

For although the council has indicated it will maintain the monument, it is unlikely public money would be available to build it.

zoo complex, on Cave Hill. I Immediately phoned Belfast Zoo, introduced myself and within minutes I received a telephone call from the Curator. They invited Dawn and I to meet with them, which we did, during the following days. When we arrived at the Zoo we were made more than welcome. At this point, they had not decided on a format or design for the memorial, this then enabled me to put forward my suggestion of what I had mentally designed in the years previous. My suggestion was a slightly smaller copy of the memorial that stands to this day in the grounds of Belfast City Hall, which was unveiled during the Second World War by Dwight D. Eisenhower, in memory of all American military personnel lost in Northern Ireland and its surrounding waters.

As our meeting progressed, I suggested that rather than a graphic information board, a granite or marble stone engraved with all of the ten crew members names and their home states, together with a brief description of how they were killed and the type of aircraft involved, might be more dignant and appealing as a lasting memorial to these men. I further suggested that a silhouette of the aircraft would be a nice addition to this memorial-information stone.

The final debate we had that day, was exactly where to locate the memorial in the Zoo complex. After a lengthy discussion, we concurred that the most logical location, was to have it at the highest point of the Zoological Gardens, which overlooks the crash site and it would be less than 100 metres from the impact point. This would be an ideal location as the Zoo have a small cafe in the vicinity. The representatives from Belfast City Council agreed with my suggestions and construction of the memorial would soon start to take shape.

As 1 June 2006 approached, that being the planned unveiling of the memorial, I was in contact several times with Mark Challis to supply him with information and photographs for the big day.

Exactly two weeks prior to the unveiling, I was unexpectedly and out of the blue, hit with the sudden death of my mother. Dawn and I had taken her on a shopping trip to Ballymena followed by dinner at our house. I dropped my mum home to her Belfast residence late in the evening, however, the next morning, I received a phone call from my Auntie Ruby *(mum`s sister)*, who lived in the same street and the news being relayed to me did not sound good. She could not reach my mum by telephone and by knocking on the house door, there was no reply. Dawn and I jumped into the car and drove frantically to mum`s house. Upon arrival an ambulance, and the police were already there. I was told that my mum had died in her sleep. I vividly remember when the paramedic told me this, I got a feeling like somebody pouring cold water on the top of my head, which in the following seconds, filtered down through my body to my feet. My next memory was of Dawn putting her arm around me. As I sat with the police and paramedics in mums living room, I got almost detached from reality and could almost hear my mums voice saying; *"I wish you wouldn't go up Cave Hill to that crash site - your luck always changes for the worst "*.

I only realised afterwards that the police and paramedics had taken me into this room to ask me what seemed to be senseless questions about mum, so I did not see the funeral directors removing her body from the upstairs bedroom out of the house of which I had grown up in. Within the following days the cause of mums death was relayed to me, she had died of natural causes, having suffered for many years with hypertension. I found this unbelievable, that two weeks before one of my biggest connections with this plane crash, that my mum passed away. The following days were a torture, with all the legal paperwork one has to deal with, being an only child when their parent dies, however, the planning and upcoming event distracted my sorrows and looking back now, helped me immensely deal with my pain.

Chapter Twenty Two

A day of remembrance

The first of June 2006, was a beautiful day, scattered cloud at around 8000ft, a light wind out of the south west and intermittent sunshine on the ground. Dawn and I arrived at Belfast Zoo at around 10am in our World War Two Jeep, which is called *The Dawn Patrol*. The Jeep was to be parked and used as a static backdrop during the unveiling. I was introduced to many politicians and dignitaries before the

unveiling ceremony commenced. The American Consul General, Dean Pitman, spoke initially and I recall how he spoke from the bottom of his heart, how appreciative and thankful he was, not only to me, but to the people and City Council of Belfast in the erection of this memorial. He was followed by speakers from both the Catholic and Anglican churches.

1 June 2006, the ceremony to dedicate the memorial, which is located in the Belfast Zoo Complex.

Afterwards we all waited with our eyes focused eastwards over Belfast Lough, for the appearance of the B17 Flying Fortress, called *"Sally B"*, which was flying from Duxford, England, to make several fly-pasts over the memorial and the crash site. I was standing close to a contact on the ground, who told me she had hit headwinds over the Isle of Man, in the Irish Sea and this would delay her by four to six minutes, but air traffic control had given her priority and were holding civilian flights on the ground. Aircraft that were already in the air, were in a holding pattern, just off the approach to both Belfast International Airport and Belfast City Airport. Suddenly I could see a dot approaching from the mouth of Belfast Lough, at a lower level than I am used to seeing aircraft, but knowing all other air movements at this time were on hold, it had to be her. The aircraft approached from the east, flying over Belfast Lough and as it got closer, I could undoubtedly see it was a B-17 Flying Fortress, flying directly towards us and very strangely, the cemetery where my late parents are buried. Being about a mile and a quarter from our location, the B-17 flew straight over their grave.

Upon arrival at the memorial, the B-17 flew directly over our heads at a height I would estimate of around 600ft higher than we were *(bearing in mind we are already around 600ft above sea level)*. The aircraft with its four Wright-Cyclone engines has a very distinctive sound and it sent a shiver throughout my body as it passed exactly over us and the crash site, not once, not twice, but three times. On the third circuit she came in lower than us, we were actually looking down on the aircraft in the direction of Belfast Lough. I could see the insignia markings on the top surface of the wings, just through the tears that were in my eyes. As the droning of the engines faded, the US Military attaché bugled *"Taps"*. The Royal British Legion with heads bowed, lowered the flag of the United States and the United Kingdom.

I was immediately surrounded by press for further interviews on my finding of the ring, the film that was currently in production and the City Councils erection of the memorial, probably none of which, would have happened had I not been on the bleak, dull, Cave Hill, that cold December afternoon back in December 1993.

1 June 2006, B-17 Sally-B approaching the memorial on Cave Hill, as it made one of many flypast's that day, Carnmoney Hill can be seen in the background.

I must and feel the need to say at this point, that my finding and returning of the ring, did not warrant the attention that it did, I was and am not by any means a hero, but those ten young men who perished in the crash, were not only in my opinion, war hero's, but at that time aviation pioneers, as transatlantic crossings were still in their infancy.

After the unveiling of the memorial, we then moved to a reception lunch, hosted by Belfast City Council at Belfast Castle. Driving my Jeep, I was accompanied by Dawn and a uniformed US Army officer, who had presented his men at the memorial. The memorial is visible to thousands of people per year who visit Belfast Zoo, together with the display and information board, located in the visitors centre of nearby Belfast Castle and has become a main focal point for us when any relatives of the aircraft crew members visit Belfast.

The Memorial Stone and Information Marker, as it stands today.

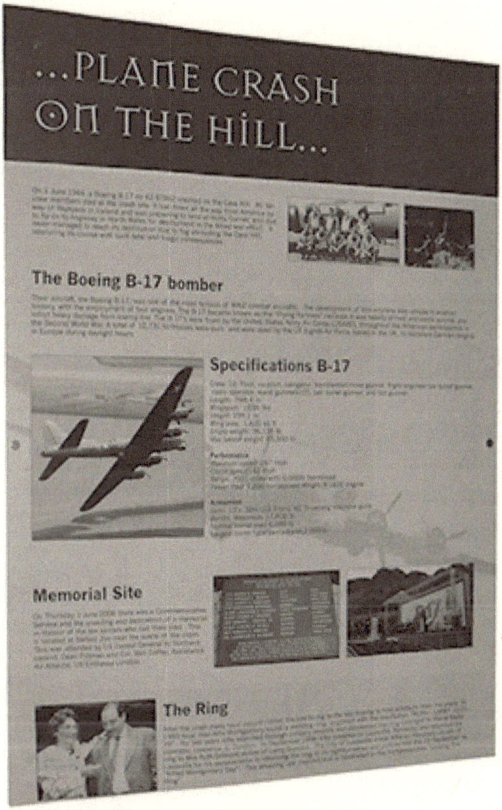

***Left**, a photograph of the information display board, located in Belfast castle. **Below**, a number of items which are on display at Belfast Castle, they consist of a Cigarette Case, a set of Bombardiers Wings and the remains of the Ball Turret. These items were recovered by Jim McKeown.*

Chapter Twenty Three

In retrospect

Over the years and after several annual vacations to Kentucky later, which had been spent visiting members of both Ruth and Larry`s family, I had the pleasure of welcoming to Belfast, Hollie, Scott and Charlie Cummings. Hollie is the great niece of Radio Operator Lawrence Dundon. We visited the crash site and the permanent memorial in Belfast Zoo. My friends at Ulster Television sent along a news crew to record a feature for the six o`clock news that evening.

Some months later, Mr. Frank Fiordalisi of New York, made his first visit to the crash site and the memorial. Frank is the nephew of the Navigator who was on-board the aircraft, 2nd Lieutenant Joseph V. Nobilione. He was astonished at what the city of Belfast had erected in relation to the memorial near the crash site at Belfast Zoo. This visit once again made the UTV six o`clock news. Frank and I have remained good friends and share a lot in common. I worked for many years as a truck driver here in Ireland and Frank had a similar career as a truck driver, serving with the US Army here in Europe, this still gives us a lot to talk about.

Through my contact with Ruth, I also made contact with Lester Brooks wife, Gennie Peterson. Gennie and Ruth had stayed close friends since before the accident and often visited one another. Gennie was very pleased and grateful for what I had done. Upon finding a set of pilots wings at the site, I returned these to Gennie, as they belonged to Lester, or his co-pilot Jeremiah, whom Gennie knew very well.

The nephew of the navigator, Mr. Frank Fiordalisi stands next to the memorial monument and marker, just above the crash site where his uncle perished, many years earlier.

In early 2013, I received an e-mail from a local WWII aviation researcher and author called Will Lindsay. Will was looking for information that I already had about the crash and the crew. We exchanged information we both had on the Cave Hill crash and kept in touch regularly. Will, being a local of the Crumlin area, had for many years been documenting the history of the former WWII American airfields located at Langford Lodge and Nutts Corner, which are close to his home. Over the years he has amassed a growing collection of USAAF WWII memorabilia relating to Langford Lodge and the US Army Air Forces, which consists of thousands of wartime photographs, official declassified documents, crash site artefacts, aircraft parts and an un-restored WWII Jeep. He has been hard at work contacting families in the US since autumn 2001. In that time, like I, returning artefacts from aircraft crash

sites in which their loved ones had perished in.

We had lead two completely different lives, but we had, essentially, been undertaking the same type of work. Will, recalled that he already knew about my story from his days as a teenager when he spent Saturday afternoons at Langford Lodge, when the Ulster Aviation Society was based there. Many members of the society would frequently talk about my association with the crash and the recovery of the ring.

His first association with the crash came in autumn 2002 when our mutual friend Ernie Cromie, who at that time was the chairman of the Ulster Aviation Society, asked Will if he could obtain the official crash report from his source in the Air Force Historical Research Association, in the US. AFHRA had custody of all American aircraft accident reports which had been archived onto microfilm.

Taken in the early 2000's the Ulster Aviation Society Heritage Centre, which was located in the former parachute packing building, at Langford Lodge. To the immediate left, is Ernie Cromie, who at the time, was the chairman of the Ulster Aviation Society.

ICON

In the summer of 2004, Will, to the left, visits the site with Robin Long, below. In his hand are the small fragments he recovered that day.

Will had made good friends with a number of the archivists at AFHRA, of which, they observed the good work he was endeavouring to undertake in documenting their fallen servicemen. The archivists frequently supplied him with hundreds of documents relating to aircraft accidents in Northern Ireland, in some cases, documents would be arriving on a weekly basis. Will would share this new information he was discovering with his friends at Langford Lodge. In many cases the accident reports arriving were related to Langford Lodge. He recalls excitedly making copies of the reports before

Early 2004, in the UAS heritage building, at Langford Lodge, to the immediate left, the late Eric Grey, Will, Leonard, Andy, Neville and to the immediate right, Ernie, in detailed discussion

heading on down to the museum to share them with the gang, namely Ernie, Big Al, Andy, Robin, and Jim McSweeney. Jim as a young boy visited the crashed B-17 on Cave Hill a day after the accident. At times, Will would head out onto the airfield and try to locate where some of the crashes they were reading about in these old documents occurred. Like the solace I found on Cave Hill, Will, as a 17 year old teenager, found the same solace at Langford Lodge, almost feeling like he had more in common with the war heroes he was researching, than some of the people

he had been acquainted with in previous years. At Langford he found a dedicated group of people with like minded interests who were welcoming, encouraging, helpful and had a passion for their interest in aviation activities relating to Northern Ireland. His time with the UAS at Langford and the friendships he made he recalls were more than character building or inspiring, it lead to a life long passion, determination and interest in researching USAAF activities in Northern Ireland during the Second World War, that continues to this day.

In the mid to late 1990's, I, like Will, frequently attended the U.A.S. museum located at Langford Lodge, making some very good friendships, some of which have stood the test of time. At one time I was captivated by this old airfield, it was like no other I have visited before or since. The old runways, the control tower and the hospital, had a strange hold on me and still do to this day. I can understand why Will could almost get lost in thought at this

location, one could easily imagine the roar of a B-17 or a P-38 flying overhead when standing on the old runways.

Due to our generational gap and differing interests at that time, our paths would not cross for over 15 years later, but strangely enough, our paths likely crossed on the many occasions the Ulster Aviation Society held their yearly open days at Langford Lodge.

In the summer of 1995, one pivotal event, that ignited Will's initial interest in Langford Lodge and USAAF activities, was an open air day hosted by the UAS, at Langford Lodge. This was the day the B-17*"Sally-B"*arrived. It's sheer size and the low buzzing flyby's of the airfield it performed that day were awe inspiring to a then, eleven year old boy. In 2003, one of the society members who frequently attended the museum every Saturday afternoon was Robin Long. In 2004, Robin kindly took Will to visit the crash site of the Cave Hill B-17. This was his first visit to the site which he can vividly remember. He was sworn to secrecy as to the location

Taken in the early 2000's another interior view of the Ulster Aviation Society Heritage Centre, which was located in the former parachute packing building, at Langford Lodge. The small canteen and gift shop is visible to the immediate left, many a weekend Will would frequently ask Ernie for; "A tin of Coke and a Mars bar please Ernie"

of the site by Robin, as Robin was fearful of attracting too much unwanted attention to the area. Will came away with a few fragments of the aircraft from the hillside that day, like I, years before with my late father, he still has them in the original box he placed them in.

Before Will and I had ever made contact with each other, I was well acquainted with Will's work as I had purchased one of his previously published books pertaining to American aircraft accidents at Langford Lodge. We both agree and often talk about how the strangest of things can happen in this hobby. It would seem that things have an unexplained way of occurring, when you have all

but given up on finding a family member of a serviceman, an old document, photograph, or a lead to new information, it seemingly turns up when it is least expected. There are many people in this line of research that we are sure will agree with us and have likely experienced such strange phenomenon, during their research into crash sites and the crews who manned these aircraft. It would appear more than mere chance that when you start researching, the synchronisation of events that begin to unfold would lead one to believe that there is more going on behind the scenes than what we can comprehend.

The Ulster Aviation Society Heritage Building at Langford Lodge. This photograph was taken on the weekend of the society's open day and fly-in, in 2002.

In 2015, Will and Louise had come over to our house for a bite to eat and a look through my finds at the crash site over the years. We got chatting and the topic of conversation moved towards writing a book. In mutual agreement, we thought it would be a good idea to document the complete story from start to finish, in chronological order. Our work began shortly thereafter, blowing the dust off my dicta-phone I took myself off to a quiet part of the house and began to recollect about days gone by with my late father, the crash site, the ring story, Larry, Ruth and how my mother always told me not to go up there and to; *"stay at home - don`t go there as your luck always seems to change for the worst when you go there"*.

In the weeks following my verbal dicta-phone recordings my wife Dawn, transcribed my memories into written format to send on to Will. In the meantime, Will was hard at work on the wartime document and eye-witness account side of things, including analysis of the reports and the circumstances of the last minutes of that fateful flight. In the early 2000's Will had completed a number of flying hours during his flying training to become a Private Pilot at nearby RAF Aldergrove airfield. He acquired a good first hand knowledge of what it was like to fly an aircraft above the skies of Ulster and over the airfield he had been researching for so long, Langford Lodge. He has applied his 18 years of experience into understanding the circumstances behind the crash and the events that ensued thereafter.

In mid 2016, our book was all but ready to be published and to go-to press, but to my dismay, Will decided it was a good idea to hold off until we had acquired new information that was pending from many varying sources, such as official departments in the US, local eye-witness statements and additional material furnished by newspaper reports and family members of the crew. In hindsight we both agree that it was for the best as we can now tell the full story in as much detail as possible.

Whilst waiting for documents to arrive we thought it would be a good idea to contact Frank Mitchell at U105, a local radio station. Frank had conducted several television interviews with me back in 2007 in relation to *"The Closing the Ring film"* and *"the true ring story"* to see if I could do another radio interview, requesting if any listeners had any stories to tell about the accident.

This proved most valuable, as we made contact with a number of people who either witnessed the crash or were related to someone who remembered the accident. Through this interview we made contact with Gerard Brannigan, of the Cave Hill Conservation Campaign. Gerard has been most helpful in providing contact details of eye-witnesses who saw the crash all of those years ago and we offer him our sincere thanks.

As of December 2018, since we took our hiatus to allow new documents and stories to come to light, we have acquired a number of very detailed eye-witness statements, several official records pertaining to seven out of the ten crew members, four flight log records, outlining the pilot, co-pilot, navigator and bombardiers flight time, the official history of their training units in the US and many original photographs of the crew during their training. We have also gained a further understanding of where the aircraft impacted the rock face and came to rest, after the crash.

On 23 December 2018, Will, Dawn and I, visited the crash site with a strict plan in mind. Our plan that day was to establish and either prove or disprove a number of theories that we had talked about on many occasions. The first, being the exact flight path of the aircraft, the second, at what altitude did the aircraft strike the rock face and thirdly, how was the wreckage removed from the site, was it pulled up towards the golf course, or removed down the hillside toward the houses at Ben Madigan Park.

74 years later, in 2018, this is the location in which one of the official photographs were taken in 1944, the tail section would have been located in the centre of the photograph, many of the original trees still bear scars from the fire and impact.

Alfie and Will examine the remains of a commutator, likely from a generator or starter motor unit from the aircraft.

Due to the time of year, the foliage on the trees was sparse, being mid-winter and some weeks after the fall had ended, this allowed us to establish the exact location of the impact point. We were surprised at how very little the area and the surrounding trees, damaged at the time of the crash had not changed in the past 74 years. Many of the trees that were damaged during the crash still remain with their top's cut off. Due to this, many of them are now rotten and subsequently have fallen down the hillside. However, many still remain and we were able to identify a number of them that appeared in one of the original photographs taken at the time of the accident. With our newly acquired information and photographs the daylight had started to fade, so we began our descent down the hillside to our vehicles, in preparation for the forthcoming Christmas holidays that were to follow in the days ahead.

Will and Alfie discuss the flight path of the aircraft. Their spades were useful walking and climbing aids due to the dense foliage and slippery terrain which is prevalent in the area during the winter months.

This trip made me feel warm inside as I recalled my childhood days on this part of Cave Hill with my now late father. During the past forty years my numerous visits to this site have caused me to realise how much we all cherish memories. In the mid 1970`s, when I would pick up a fragment of aircraft I would proudly hold it up to show to my father, who was standing on the hillside, some sixty feet below me. I was so excited to have found a fragment, as then, a young boy. Now, as a middle aged man, that moment on the Cave Hill is one of my most cherished memories between my father and I.

There are times in the past when I have visited the site as an escape from everyday problems that inevitably come up in ones life, having a tear in my eye on more than one occasion. Finding Larry's wedding ring at one of the lowest points in my life was a turning point that changed my outlook. With the media attention, returning the ring and making many new friends in the United States, as the 1990`s progressed my fiancé Dawn and I, were planning to marry on the upcoming millennium which we did in March 2000.

I often find myself thinking, of the descendants of the perished crew members, whom we still speak to on a regular basis, not to mention the ten US Army personnel whose young lives quite literally ended in an instant. As we say in Britain, "They shall not grow old, and at the going down of the sun, and in the morning, we will remember them".

The Army Air Corps Song

Off we go into the wild blue yonder
Climbing high into the sun;
Here they come zooming to meet our thunder,
At'em boys, giv'er the gun!
Down we dive spouting our flames from under,
Off with one hell-uv-a roar!
We live in fame or go down in flame,
Nothing'll stop the Army Air Corps!

Minds of men fashioned a crate of thunder
Sent it high into the blue
Hands of men blasted the world asunder,
How they live God only knew!
Souls of men dreaming of skies to conquer
Gave us wings ever to soar,
With scouts before and bombers galore,
Nothing can stop the Army Air Corps!

Here's a toast to the host of those
Who love the vastness of the sky,
To a friend we send the message
Of his brother men who fly.
We drink to those who gave their all of old,
Then down we roar
to score the rainbow's pot of gold.
A toast to the host of men we boast the Army Air Corps.

Off we go into the wild sky yonder,
Keep the wings level and true!
If you'd live to be a gray haired wonder,
Keep your nose out of the blue!
Flying men guarding our nation's borders,
We'll be there followed by more,
In echelon we carry on!

Nothing'll stop the Army Air Corps!

APPENDIX I

B-17 Flying Fortress interior diagrams

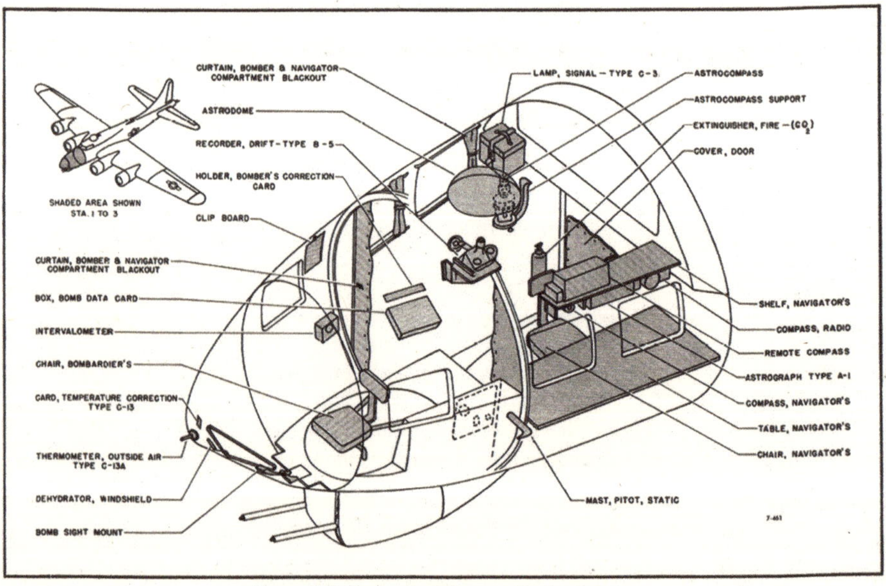

Figure 331—Equipment Diagram—Station 1 to 3

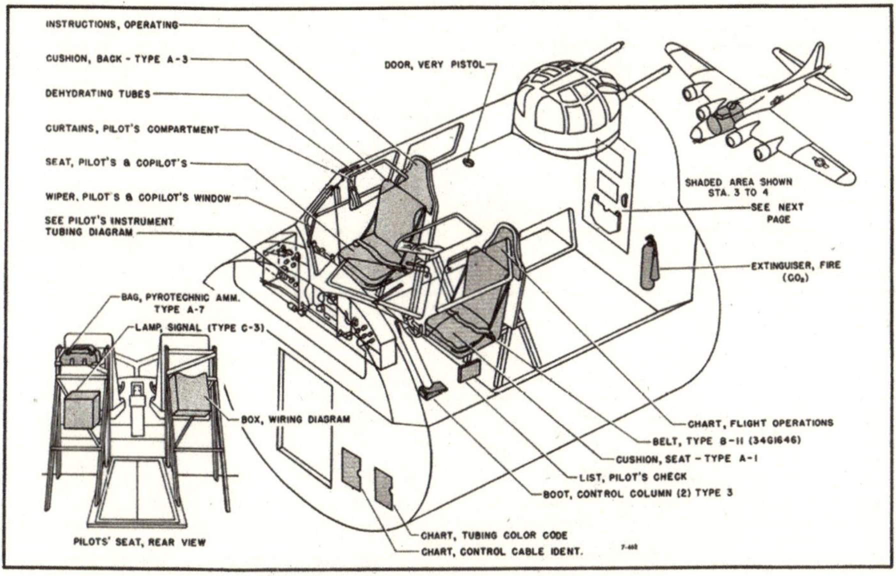

Figure 332—Equipment Diagram—Station 3 to 4

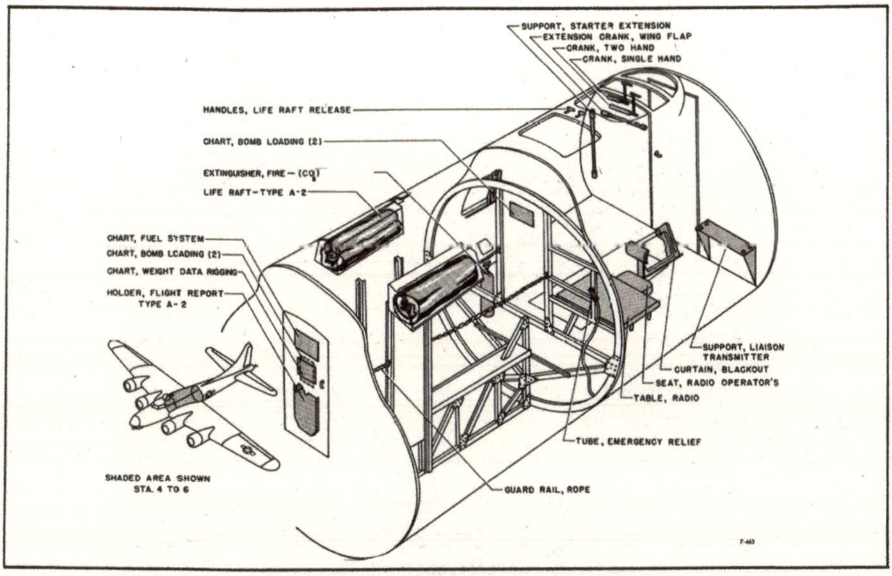

Figure 333—Equipment Diagram—Station 4 to 6

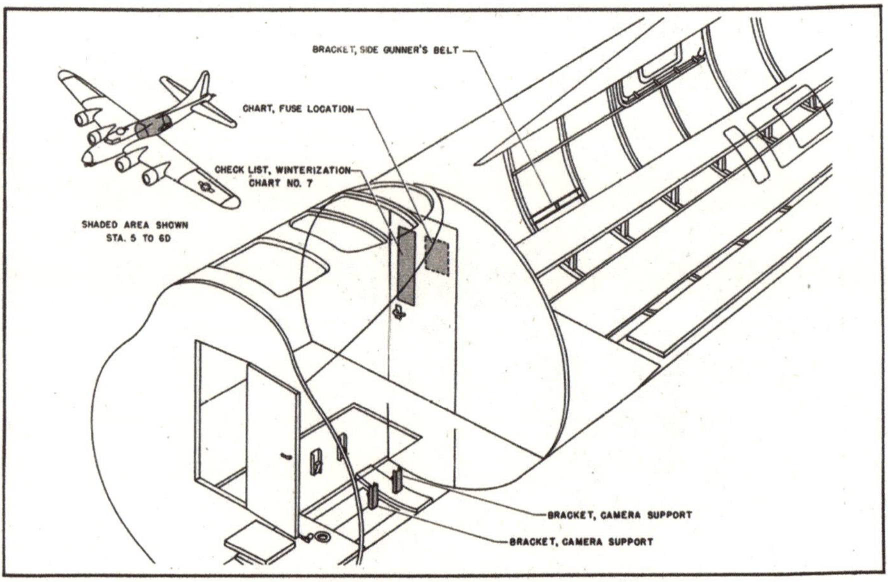

Figure 334—Equipment Diagram—Station 5 to 6D

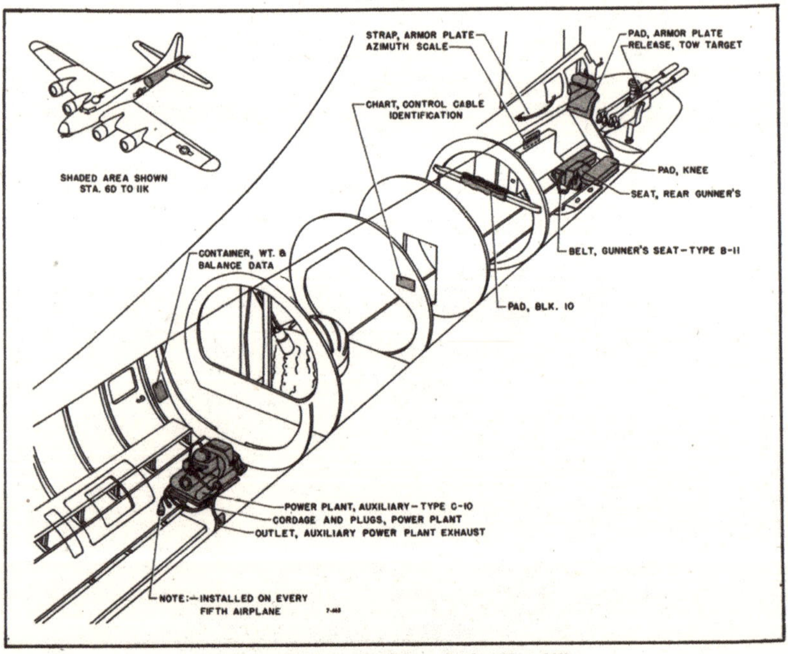

Figure 335—Equipment Diagram Station 6D to 11K

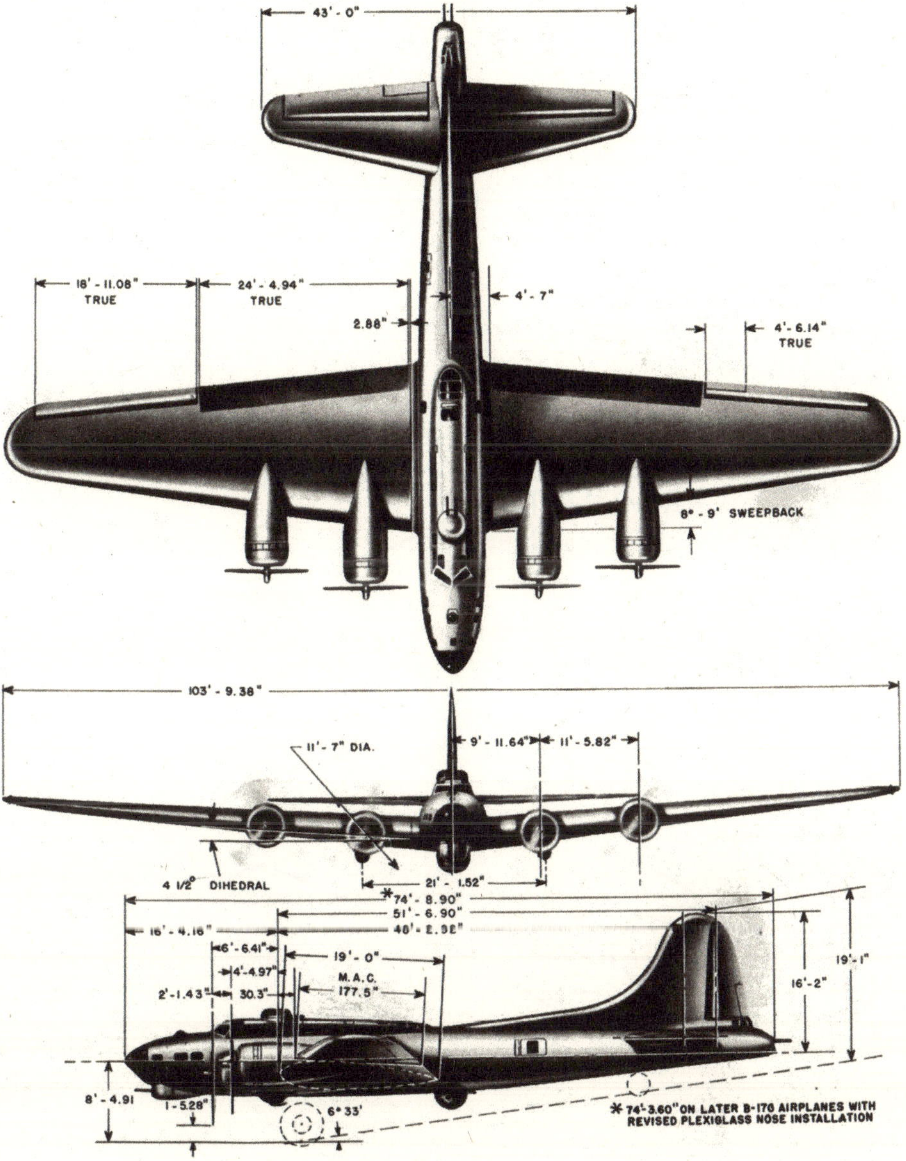

Figure 1—General Arrangement

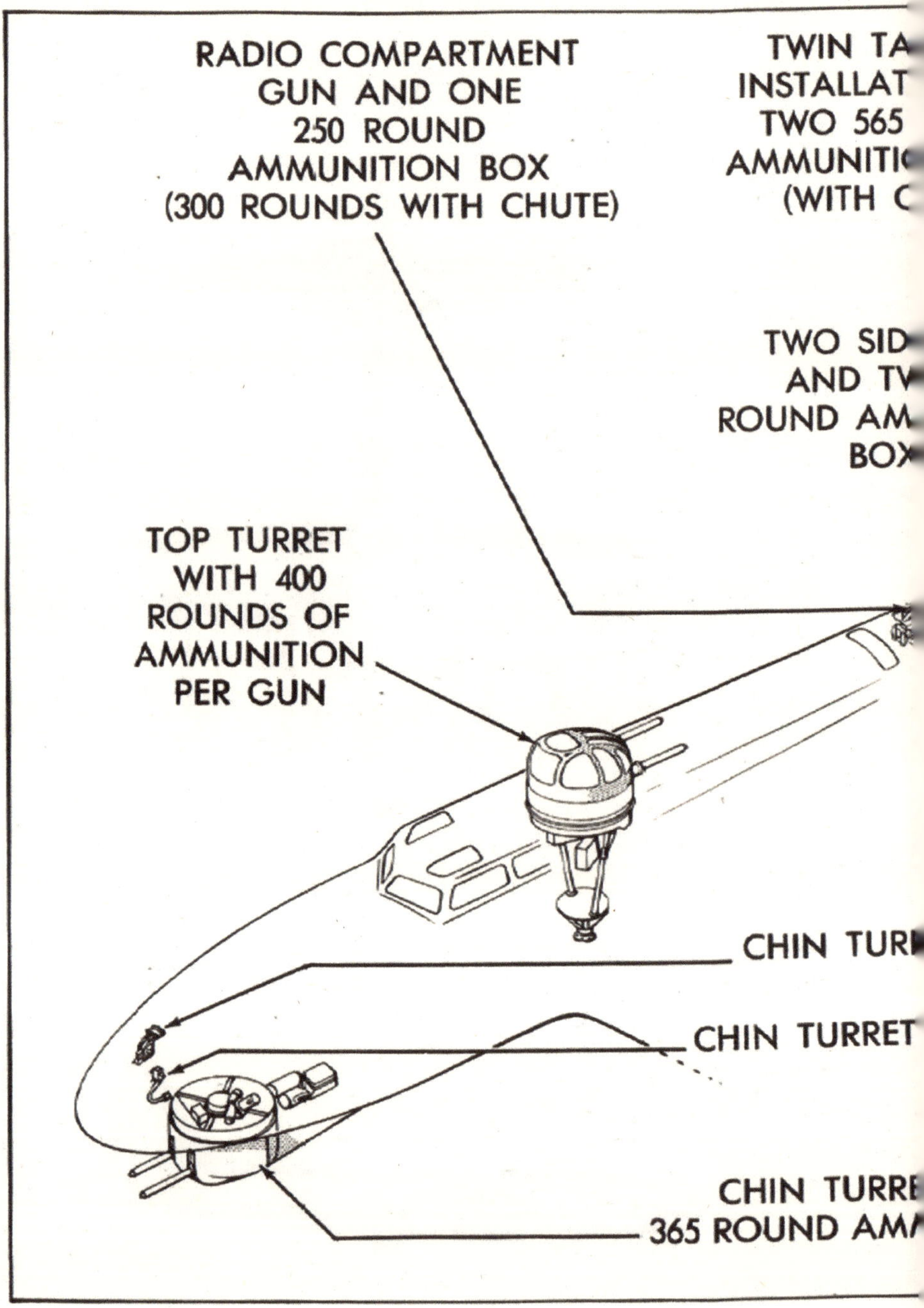

Figure 382—Gu

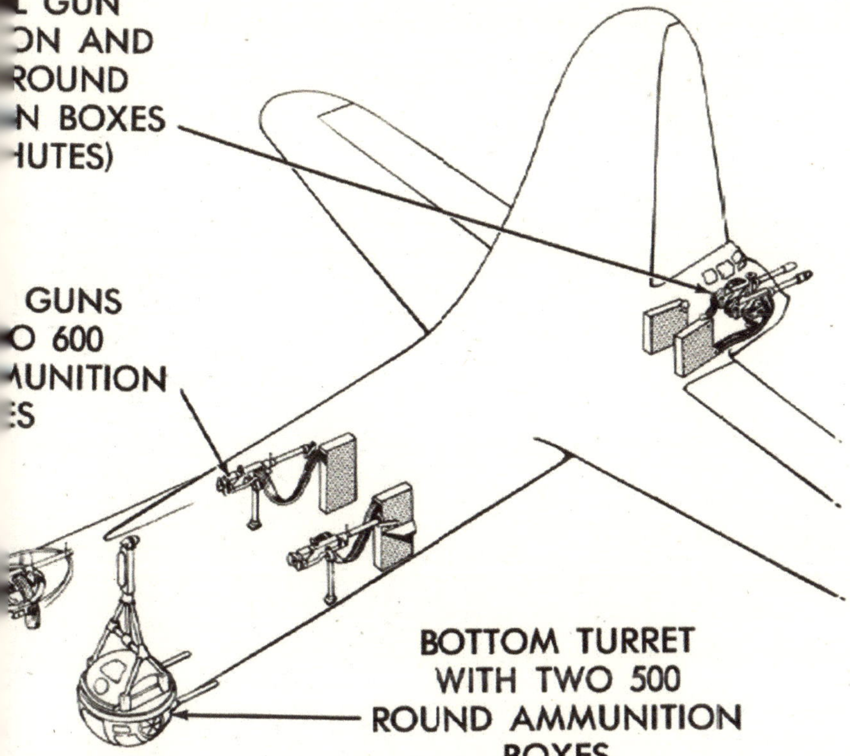

ery Equipment

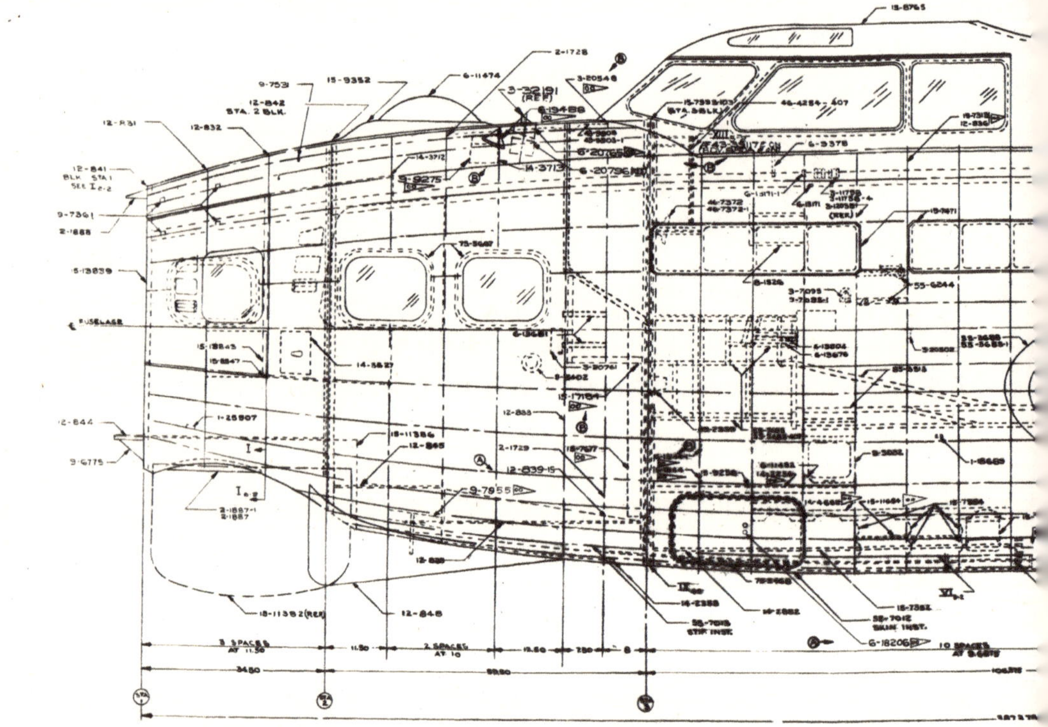

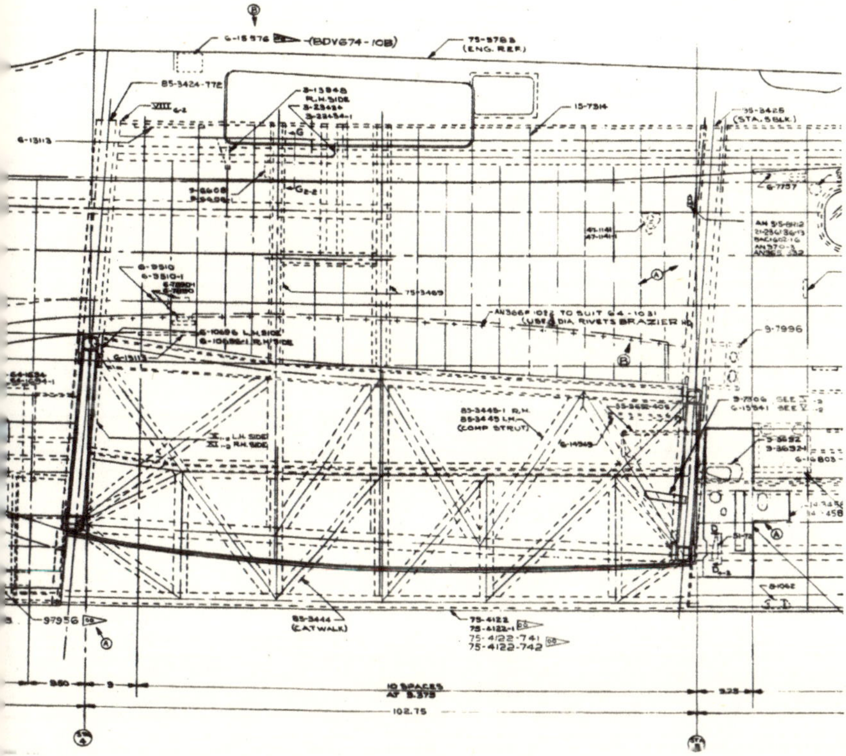
(BDV674-10B)
75-5788
(ENG. REF.)
85-3424-772
15-7314
9-7996
85-3444
(CATWALK)
75-4122
75-4122-1
75-4122-741
75-4122-742
10 SPACES
AT 9.375
102.75

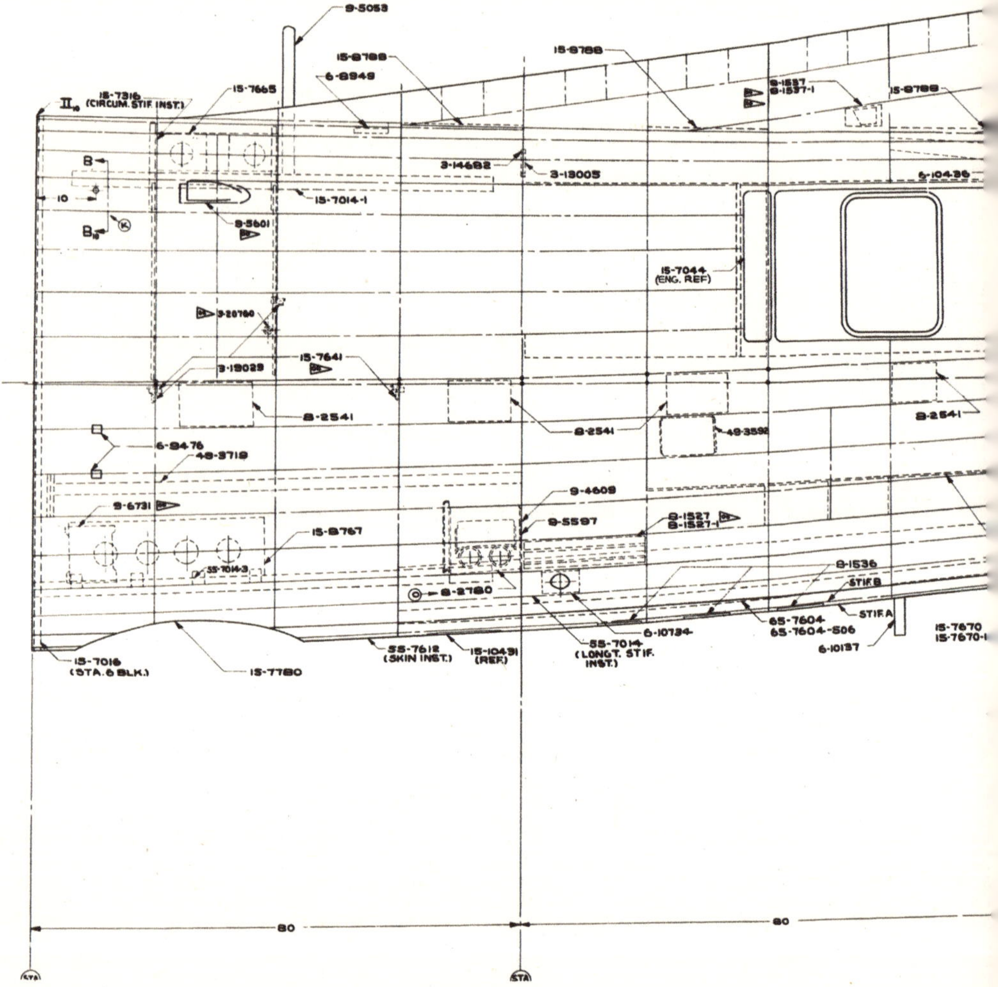
9-5053
15-8788
6-8949
15-7316
(CIRCUM. STIF. INST.)
15-7665
3-14682
3-13005
15-7014-1
9-5601
15-7044
(ENG. REF)
6-10436
3-19029
15-7641
8-2541
49-3592
6-9476
48-3719
9-6731
15-8767
9-4609
9-5597
8-1527
8-1527-1
8-1536
8-2780
6-10734
65-7604
65-7604-506
6-10137
15-7016
(STA. 6 BLK.)
15-7780
55-7612
(SKIN INST.)
15-10431
(REF.)
55-7014
(LONGT. STIF. INST.)
80

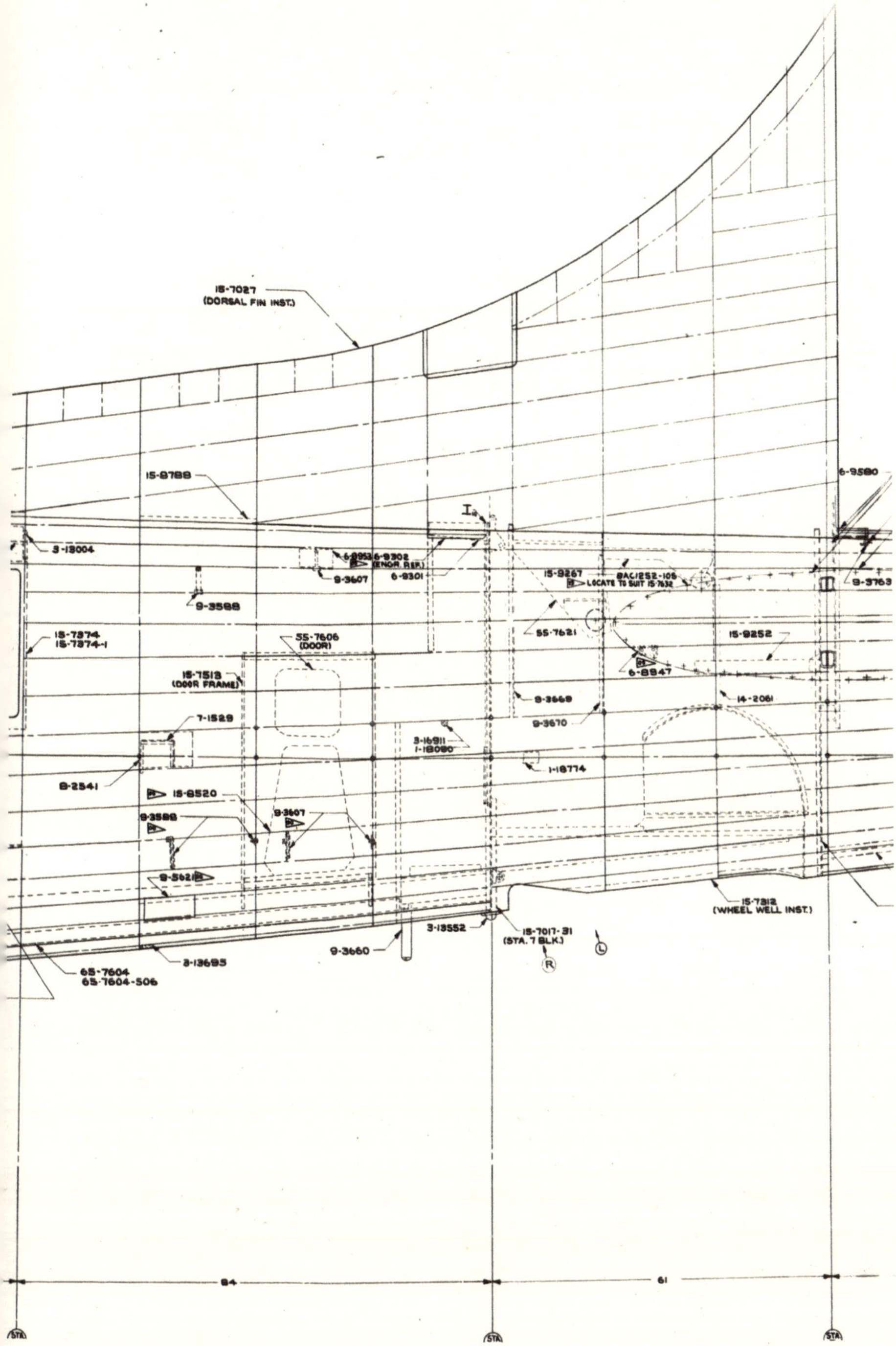
15-7027
(DORSAL FIN INST.)
15-8788
6-9580
3-13004
6-9302
(ENGR. REF.)
9-3607
6-9301
9-3588
15-9267
LOCATE TO SUIT 15-7632
BAC1252-105
9-3763
15-7374
15-7374-1
55-7606
(DOOR)
55-7621
15-9252
15-7513
(DOOR FRAME)
6-8947
9-3669
14-2061
7-1529
9-3670
3-16911
1-18080
1-18774
8-2541
15-8520
9-3588
9-3607
9-5621
3-13552
15-7017-31
(STA. 7 BLK.)
15-7312
(WHEEL WELL INST.)
9-3660
3-13695
65-7604
65-7604-506
84
61
STA
STA
STA

APPENDIX II

B-17 Flying Fortress Cockpit diagrams

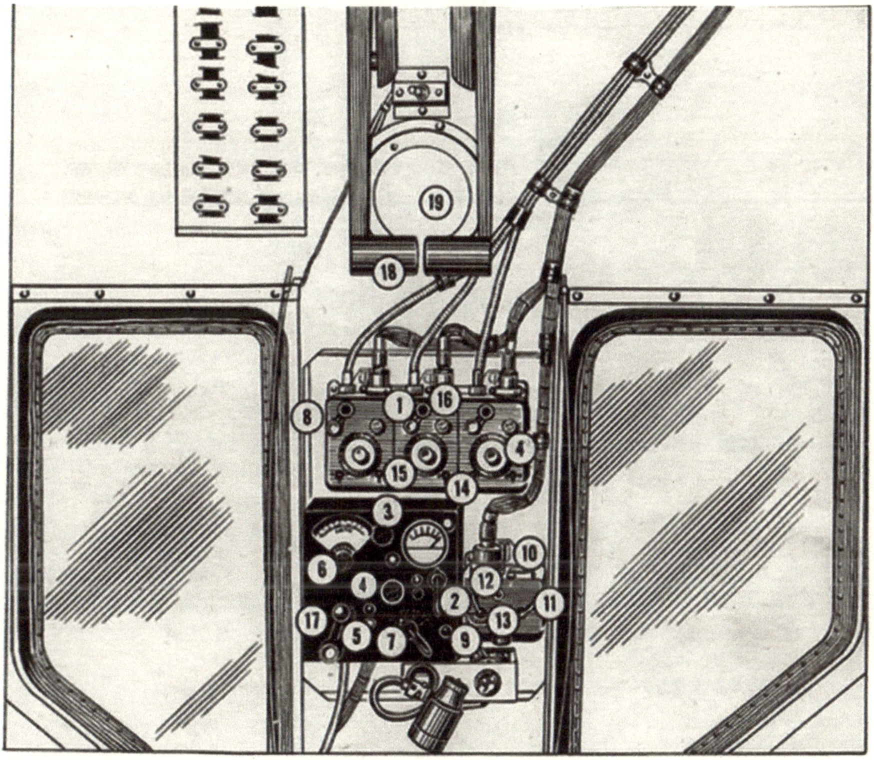

PILOT'S COMPARTMENT CEILING

1. Command receiver control unit
2. Loop control switch
3. Light control switch
4. Volume control
5. Control indicator lamp
6. Band selector knob
7. Power switch
8. Tuning crank
9. Control push button
10. Transmitting key
11. Transmission selector switch (Tone-CW-Voice)
12. Transmitter power switch
13. Channel selector switch
14. A-B channel switch
15. Signal selector switch
16. Volume control
17. Tuning crank
18. Emergency hand brake
19. Dome light

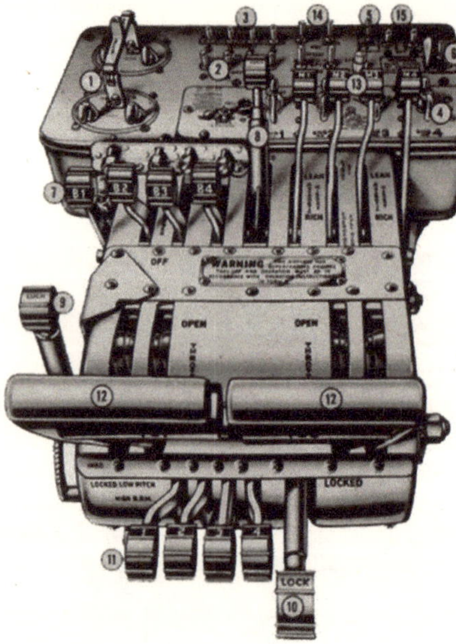

CONTROL PANEL AND PEDESTAL

1. Ignition switches
2. Fuel boost pump switches
3. Fuel shut-off valve switches
4. Cowl flap control valves
5. Landing gear switch
6. Wing flap switch
7. Turbo-supercharger controls (B-17F)
8. Turbo and mixture control lock
9. Throttle control lock
10. Propeller control lock
11. Propeller controls
12. Throttle controls
13. Mixture controls
14. Recognition light switches
15. Landing light switches

LOWER CONTROL PEDESTAL

1. Elevator trim tab control
2. Automatic flight control panel
3. Rudder tab control
4. Elevator and rudder lock
5. Tailwheel lock

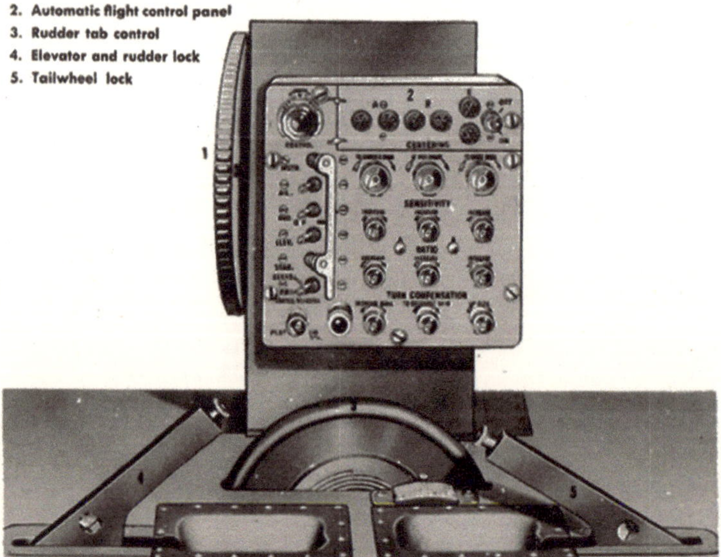

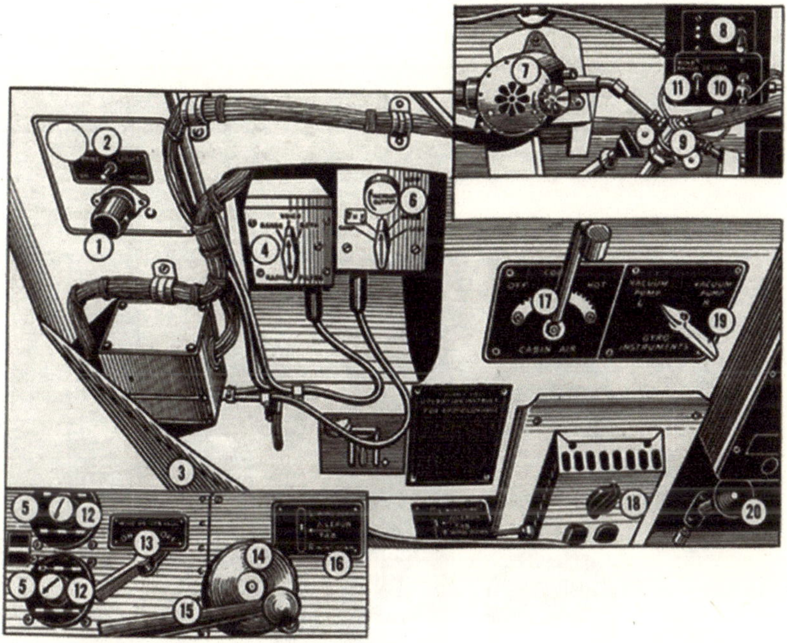

CONTROLS AT PILOT'S LEFT

1. Panel light
2. Panel light switch
3. Pilot's seat
4. Filter selector switch
5. Propeller anti-icer switch
6. Interphone jackbox
7. Oxygen regulator
8. Windshield wiper controls
9. Portable oxygen unit recharger
10. Windshield anti-icer switch
11. Windshield anti-icer flow control
12. Propeller anti-icer rheostats
13. Surface de-icer control
14. Aileron trim tab control
15. Pilot's seat adjustment lever
16. Aileron trim tab indicator
17. Cabin air control
18. Suit heater outlet
19. Vacuum selector valve
20. Emergency bomb release

PILOT'S CONTROL PANEL

1. Passing light switch
2. Running lights switch
3. Ammeters
4. Generator switches
5. Voltmeter
6. Battery switches
7. Alarm bell switch
8. Hydraulic pump servicing switch
9. Landing gear warning horn switch
10. Position lights switch
11. Voltmeter selector switch
12. Panel lights
13. Panel lights switch
14. Pitot heater switch
15. Interphone call light switch
16. Bomber call light switch
17. Inverter switch

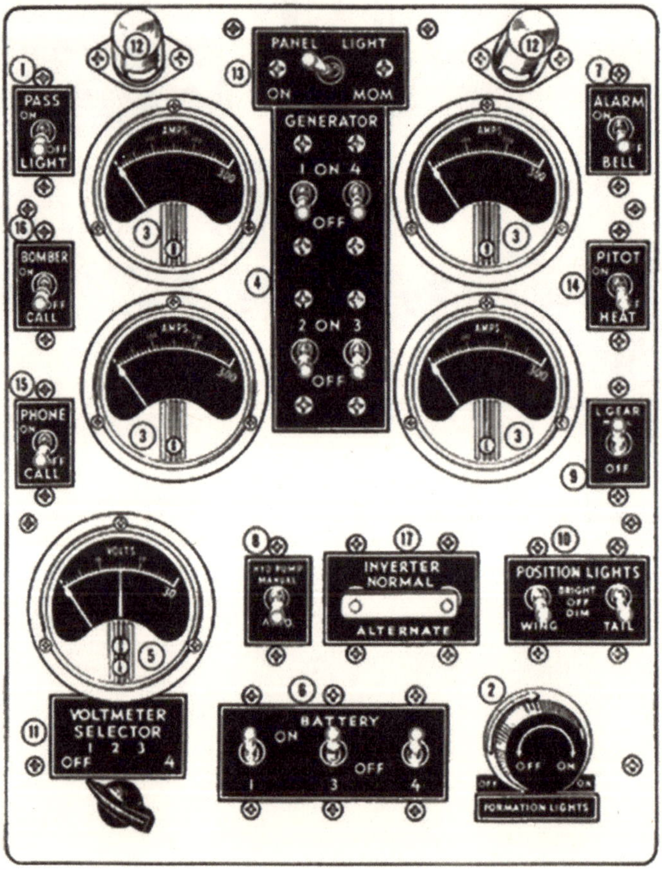

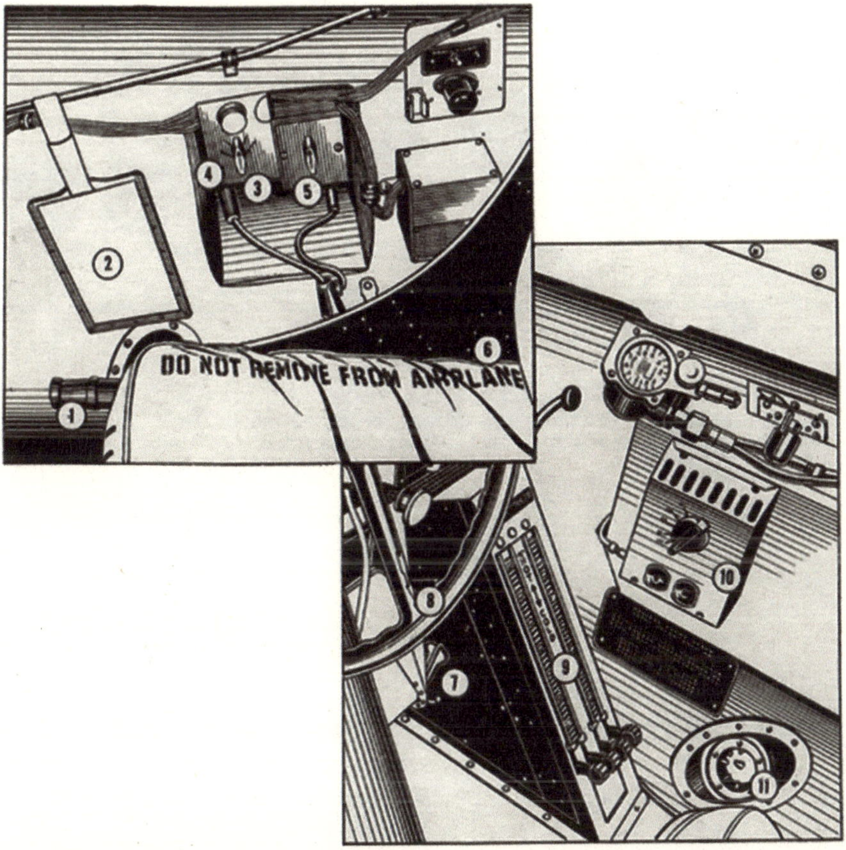

CONTROLS AT COPILOT'S RIGHT

1. Hydraulic hand pump
2. Checklist
3. Interphone selector switch
4. Interphone jackbox
5. Filter selector switch
6. Copilot's seat
7. Rudder pedal adjustment
8. Copilot's control wheel
9. Intercooler controls
10. Suit heater outlet
11. Engine primer

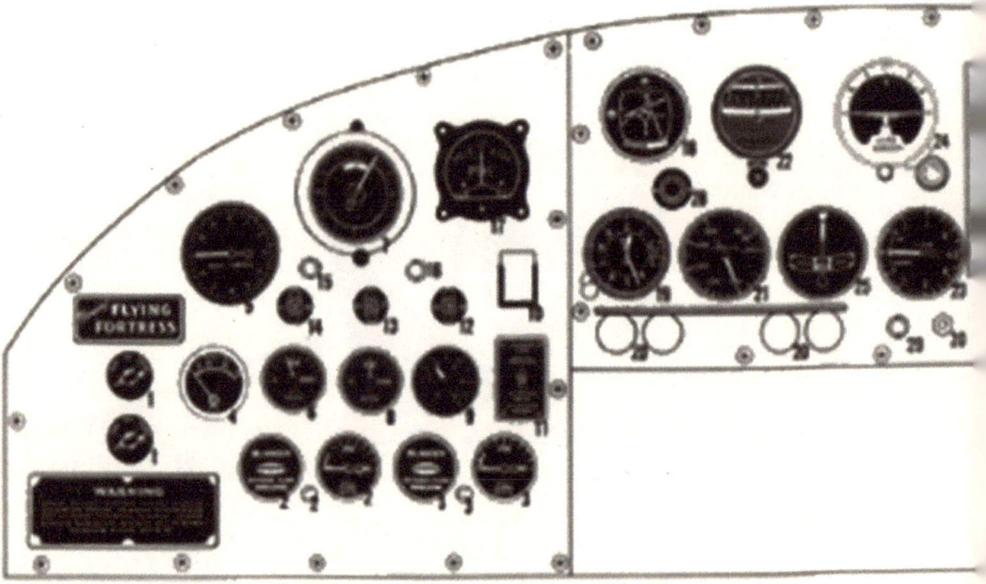

1. Fluorescent light switches
2. Pilot's oxygen flow indicator, warning light and pressure gage
3. Copilot's oxygen flow indicator, warning light and pressure gage
4. Voltmeter (AC)
5. Radio compass
6. Emergency oil pressure gage (Not on G)
7. Flux gate compass
8. Hydraulic oil pressure gage
9. Suction gage
10. Altimeter correction card
11. Airspeed alternate source switch
12. Vacuum warning light
13. Main system hydraulic oil warning light
14. Emergency system hydraulic oil warning light (Not on G)
15. Bomb door position light (Not on G)
16. Bomb release light
17. Pilot's directional indicator
18. Pilot's localizer indicator
19. Altimeter
20. Propeller feathering switches
21. Airspeed indicator

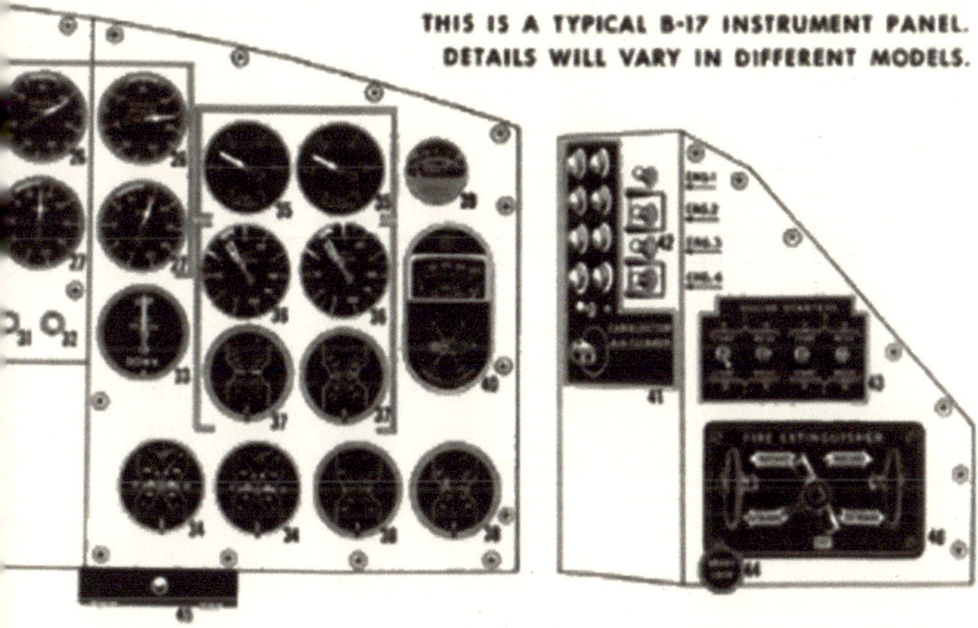

THIS IS A TYPICAL B-17 INSTRUMENT PANEL. DETAILS WILL VARY IN DIFFERENT MODELS.

22. Directional gyro
23. Rate-of-climb indicator
24. Flight indicator
25. Turn-and-bank indicator
26. Manifold pressure gages
27. Tachometers
28. Marker beacon light
29. Globe test button
30. Bomber call light
31. Landing gear warning light
32. Tailwheel lock light
33. Flap position indicator
34. Cylinder-head temperature gages
35. Fuel pressure gages
36. Oil pressure gages
37. Oil temperature gages
38. Carburetor air temperature gages
39. Free air temperature gage
40. Fuel quantity gage
41. Carburetor air filter switch
42. Oil dilution switches
43. Starting switches
44. Parking brake control
45. Spare fuse box
46. Engine fire extinguisher controls (on some airplanes)

RESTRICTED

APPENDIX III

B-17 Flying Fortress crew duties

DUTIES AND RESPONSIBILITIES OF

THE AIRPLANE COMMANDER

Your assignment to the B-17 airplane means that you are no longer just a pilot. You are now an airplane commander, charged with all the duties and responsibilities of a command post.

You are now flying a 10-man weapon. It is your airplane, and your crew. You are responsible for the safety and efficiency of the crew at all times—not just when you are flying and fighting, but for the full 24 hours of every day while you are in command.

Your crew is made up of specialists. Each man—whether he is the navigator, bombardier, engineer, radio operator, or one of the gunners—is an expert in his line. But how well he does his job, and how efficiently he plays his part as a member of your combat team, will depend to a great extent on how well you play your own part as the airplane commander.

Get to know each member of your crew as an individual. Know his personal idiosyncrasies, his capabilities, his shortcomings. Take a personal interest in his problems, his ambitions, his need for specific training.

See that your men are properly quartered, clothed, and fed. There will be many times, when your airplane and crew are away from the home base, when you may even have to carry your interest to the extent of financing them yourself. Remember always that you are the commanding officer of a miniature army—a specialized army; and that morale is one of the biggest problems for the commander of any army, large or small.

Crew Discipline

Your success as the airplane commander will depend in a large measure on the respect, confidence, and trust which the crew feels for you. It will depend also on how well you maintain crew discipline.

Your position commands obedience and respect. This does not mean that you have to be stiff-necked, overbearing, or aloof. Such characteristics most certainly will defeat your purpose.

Be friendly, understanding, but firm. Know your job; and, by the way you perform your duties daily, impress upon the crew that you do know your job. Keep close to your men, and let them realize that their interests are uppermost in your mind. Make fair decisions, after due consideration of all the facts involved; but make them in such a way as to impress upon your crew that your decisions are to stick.

Crew discipline is vitally important, but it need not be as difficult a problem as it sounds. Good discipline in an air crew breeds comradeship and high morale, and the combination is unbeatable.

You can be a good CO, and still be a regular guy. You can command respect from your men, and still be one of them.

"To associate discipline with informality, comradeship, a leveling of rank, and at times a shift in actual command away from the leader, may seem paradoxical," says a brigadier general, formerly a Group commander in the VIII Bomber Command. "Certainly, it isn't down the military groove. But it is discipline just the same—and the kind of discipline that brings success in the air."

Crew Training

Train your crew as a team. Keep abreast of their training. It won't be possible for you to follow each man's courses of instruction, but you can keep a close check on his record and progress.

Get to know each man's duties and problems. Know his job, and try to devise ways and means of helping him to perform it more efficiently.

Each crew member naturally feels great pride in the importance of his particular specialty. You can help him to develop his pride to include the manner in which he performs that duty. To do that you must possess and maintain a thorough knowledge of each man's job and the problems he has to deal with in the performance of his duties.

THE COPILOT

The copilot is the executive officer—your chief assistant, understudy, and strong right arm. He must be familiar enough with every one of your duties—both as pilot and as airplane commander—to be able to take over and act in your place at any time.

He must be able to fly the airplane under all conditions as well as you would fly it yourself.

He must be extremely proficient in engine operation, and know instinctively what to do to keep the airplane flying smoothly even though he is not handling the controls.

He must have a thorough knowledge of cruising control data, and know how to apply it at the proper time.

He is also the engineering officer aboard the airplane, and maintains a complete log of performance data.

He must be a qualified instrument pilot.

He must be able to fly good formation in any assigned position, day or night.

He must be qualified to navigate by day or at night by pilotage, dead reckoning, and by use of radio aids.

He must be proficient in the operation of all radio equipment located in the pilot's compartment.

In formation flying, he must be able to make engine adjustments almost automatically.

He must be prepared to take over on instruments when the formation is climbing through an overcast, thus enabling you to watch the rest of the formation.

Always remember that the copilot is a fully trained, rated pilot just like yourself. He is subordinate to you only by virtue of your position as the airplane commander. The B-17 is a lot of airplane; more airplane than any one pilot can handle alone over a long period of time. Therefore, you have been provided with a second pilot who will share the duties of flight operation.

Treat your copilot as a brother pilot. Remember that the more proficient he is **as a pilot**, the more efficiently he will be able to perform the duties of the vital post he holds as your second in command.

Be sure that he is allowed to do his share of the flying, in the pilot's seat, on takeoffs, landings, and on instruments.

The importance of the copilot is eloquently testified by airplane commanders overseas. There have been many cases in which the pilot has been disabled or killed in flight and the copilot has taken full command of both airplane and crew, completed the mission, and returned safely to the home base. Usually, the copilots who have distinguished themselves under such conditions have been copilots who have been respected and trained by the airplane commander **as pilots.**

Bear in mind that the pilot in the right-hand seat of your airplane is preparing himself for an airplane commander's post too. Allow him every chance to develop his ability and to profit by your experience.

THE NAVIGATOR

The navigator's job is to direct your flight from departure to destination and return. He must know the exact position of the airplane at all times.

Navigation is the art of determining geographic positions by means of (a) pilotage, (b) dead reckoning, (c) radio, or (d) celestial navigation, or any combination of these 4 methods. By any one or combination of methods the navigator determines the position of the airplane in relation to the earth.

Pilotage

Pilotage is the method of determining the airplane's position by visual reference to the ground. The importance of accurate pilotage cannot be over-emphasized. In combat navigation, all bombing targets are approached by pilotage, and in many theaters the route is maintained by pilotage. This requires not merely the vicinity type, but **pin-point pilotage.** The exact position of the airplane must be known not within 5 miles but within ¼ of a mile.

The navigator does this by constant reference to groundspeeds and ETA's established for points ahead, the ground, and to his maps and charts. During the mission, so long as he can maintain visual contact with the ground, the navigator can establish these pin-point positions so that the exact track of the airplane will be known when the mission is completed.

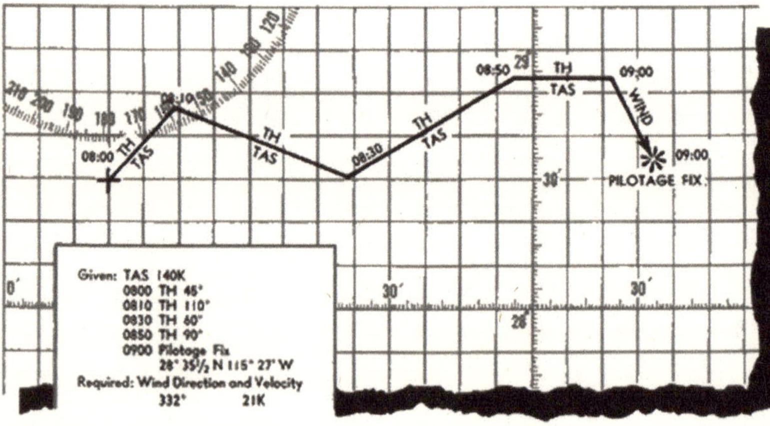

Dead Reckoning

Dead reckoning is the basis of all other types of navigation. For instance, if the navigator is doing pilotage and computes ETA's for points ahead, he is using dead reckoning.

Dead reckoning determines the position of the airplane at any given time by keeping an account of the track and distance flown over the earth's surface from the point of departure or the last known position.

Dead reckoning can be subdivided into two classes:

1. **Dead reckoning as a result of a series of known positions obtained by some other means of navigation.** For example, you, as pilot, start on a mission from London to Berlin at 25,000 feet. For the first hour your navigator keeps track by pilotage; at the same time recording the heading and airspeed which you are holding. According to plan, at the end of the first hour the airplane goes above the clouds, thus losing contact with the ground. By means of dead reckoning from his last pilotage point, the navigator is able to tell the position of the aircraft at any time. The first hour's travel has given him the wind prevalent at altitude, and the track and groundspeed being made. By computing track and distance from the last pilotage point, he can always tell the position of the airplane. When your airplane comes out of the clouds near Berlin, the navigator will have a very close approximation of his exact position, and will be able to pick up pilotage points quickly.

2. **Dead reckoning as a result of visual references other than pilotage.** When flying over water, desert, or barren land, where no reliable pilotage points are available, accurate DR navigation still can be performed. By means of the drift meter the navigator is able to determine drift, the angle between the heading of the airplane and its track over the ground. The true heading of the airplane is obtained by application of compass error to the compass reading. The true heading plus or minus the drift (as read on the drift meter) gives the track of the airplane. At a constant airspeed, drift on 2 or more headings will give the navigator information necessary to obtain the wind by use of his computer. Groundspeed is computed easily once the wind, heading, and airspeed are known. So, by constant recording of true heading, true airspeed, drift, and groundspeed, the navigator is able to determine accurately the position of the airplane at any given time. For greatest accuracy, the pilot must maintain constant courses and airspeeds. If course or airspeed is changed, notify the navigator so he can record these changes.

Radio

Radio navigation makes use of various radio aids to determine position. The development of many new radio devices has increased the use of radio in combat zones. However, the ease with which radio aids can be jammed, or bent, limits the use of radio to that of a check on DR and pilotage. The navigator, in conjunction with the radio man, is responsible for all radio procedures, approaches, etc., that are in effect in the theater.

Celestial

Celestial navigation is the science of determining position by reference to 2 or more celestial bodies. The navigator uses a sextant, accurate time, and many tables to obtain what he calls a line of position. Actually this line is part of a circle on which the altitude of the particular body is constant for that instant of time. An intersection of 2 or more of these lines gives the navigator a fix. These fixes can be relied on as being accurate within approximately 10 miles. One reason for inaccuracy is the instability of the airplane as it moves through space, causing acceleration of the sextant bubble (a level denoting the horizontal). Because of this acceleration, the navigator takes observations over a period of time so that the acceleration error will cancel out to some extent. If the navigator tells the pilot when he wishes to take an observation, extremely careful flying on the part of the pilot during the few minutes it takes to make the observation will result in much greater accuracy. Generally speaking, the only celestial navigation used by a combat crew is during the delivering flight to the theater. But in all cases celestial navigation is used as a check on dead reckoning and pilotage except where celestial is the only method available, such as on long over-water flights, etc.

Instrument Calibration

Instrument calibration is an important duty of the navigator. All navigation depends directly on the accuracy of his instruments. Correct calibration requires close cooperation and extremely careful flying by the pilot. Instruments to be calibrated include the altimeter, all compasses, airspeed indicators, alignment of the astrocompass, astrograph, and drift meter, and check on the navigator's sextant and watch.

Pilot-Navigator Preflight Planning

1. Pilot and navigator must study flight plan of the route to be flown and select alternate airfields.
2. Study the weather with the navigator. Know what weather you are likely to encounter. Decide what action is to be taken. Know the weather conditions at the alternate airfields.
3. Inform your navigator at what airspeed and altitude you wish to fly so that he can prepare his flight plan.
4. Learn what type of navigation the navigator intends to use: pilotage, dead reckoning, radio, celestial, or a combination of all methods.
5. Determine check points; plan to make radio fixes.
6. Work out an effective communication method with your navigator to be used in flight.
7. Synchronize your watch with your navigator's.

Pilot-Navigator in Flight

1. **Constant course**—For accurate navigation, the pilot—you—must fly a constant course. The navigator has many computations and entries to make in his log. Constantly changing course makes his job more difficult. A good navigator is supposed to be able to follow the pilot, but he cannot be taking compass readings all the time.
2. **Constant airspeed** must be held as nearly as possible. This is as important to the navigator as is a constant course in determining position.
3. **Precision flying** by the pilot greatly affects the accuracy of the navigator's instrument readings, particularly celestial readings. A slight error in celestial reading can cause considerable error in determining positions. You can help the navigator by providing as steady a platform as possible from which he can take readings. The navigator should notify you when he intends to take readings so that the airplane can be leveled off and flown as smoothly as possible, preferably by using the automatic pilot.

Do not allow your navigator to be disturbed while he is taking celestial readings.

4. **Notify the navigator of any change in flight,** such as change in altitude, course, or airspeed. If change in flight plan is to be made, consult the navigator. Talk over the proposed change so that he can plan the flight and advise you about it.

5. If there is doubt about the position of the airplane, pilot and navigator should get together, refer to the navigator's flight log, talk the problem over and decide together the best course of action to take.

6. Check your compasses at intervals with those of the navigator, noting any deviation.

7. Require your navigator to give position reports at intervals.

8. You are ultimately responsible for getting the airplane to its destination. Therefore, it is your duty to know your position at all times.

9. Encourage your navigator to use as many navigation methods as possible as a means of double-checking.

Post-flight Critique

After every flight, get together with the navigator and discuss the flight and compare notes. Go over the navigator's log. If there have been serious navigational errors, discuss them with the navigator and determine their cause. If the navigator has been at fault, caution him that it is his job to see that the same mistake does not occur again. If the error has been caused by faulty instruments, see that they are corrected before another navigation mission is attempted. If your flying has contributed to inaccuracy in navigation, try to fly a better course next time.

Miscellaneous Duties

The navigator's primary duty is navigating your airplane with a high degree of accuracy. But as a member of the team, he must also have a general knowledge of the entire operation of the airplane.

He has a .50-cal. machine gun at his station, and he must be able to use it skillfully and to service it in emergencies.

He must be familiar with the oxygen system, know how to operate the turrets, radio equipment, and fuel transfer system.

He must know the location of all fuses and spare fuses, lights and spare lights, affecting navigation.

He must be familiar with emergency procedures, such as the manual operation of landing gear, bomb bay doors, and flaps, and the proper procedures for crash landings, ditching, bailout, etc.

THE BOMBARDIER

Accurate and effective bombing is the ultimate purpose of your entire airplane and crew. Every other function is preparatory to hitting and destroying the target.

That's your bombardier's job. The success or failure of the mission depends upon what he accomplishes in that short interval of the bombing run.

When the bombardier takes over the airplane for the run on the target, he is in absolute command. He will tell you what he wants done, and until he tells you "Bombs away," his word is law.

A great deal, therefore, depends on the understanding between bombardier and pilot. You expect your bombardier to know his job when he takes over. He expects you to understand the problems involved in his job, and to give him full cooperation. Teamwork between pilot and bombardier is essential.

Under any given set of conditions—groundspeed, altitude, direction, etc.—there is only one point in space where a bomb may be released from the airplane to hit a predetermined object on the ground.

There are many things with which a bombardier must be thoroughly familiar in order to release his bombs at the right point to hit this predetermined target.

He must know and understand his bombsight, what it does, and how it does it.

He must thoroughly understand the operation and upkeep of his bombing instruments and equipment.

He must know that his racks, switches, controls, releases, doors, linkage, etc., are in first-class operating condition.

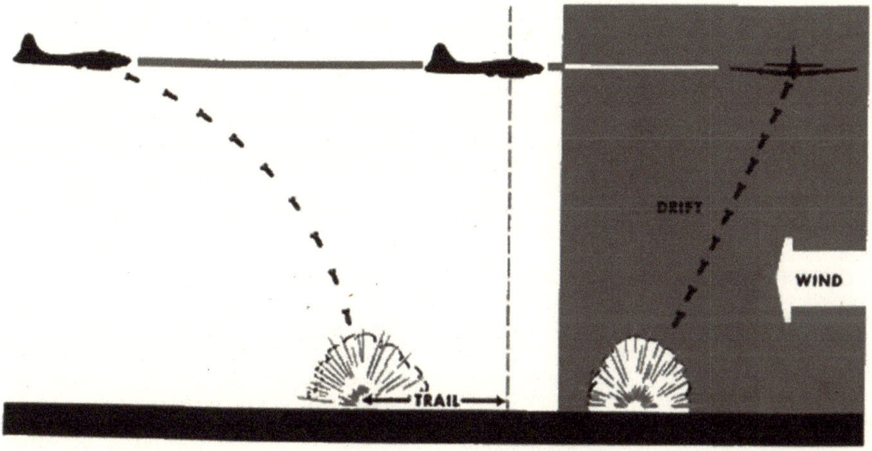

He must understand the automatic pilot as it pertains to bombing.

He must know how to set it up, make any adjustments and minor repairs while in flight.

He must know how to operate all gun positions in the airplane.

He must know how to load and clear simple stoppages and jams of machine guns while in flight.

He must be able to load and fuse his own bombs.

He must understand the destructive power of bombs and must know the vulnerable spots on various types of targets.

He must understand the bombing problem, bombing probabilities, bombing errors, etc.

He must be thoroughly versed in target identification and in aircraft identification.

The bombardier should be familiar with the duties of all members of the crew and should be able to assist the navigator in case the navigator becomes incapacitated.

For the bombardier to be able to do his job, the pilot of the aircraft must place the aircraft in the proper position to arrive at a point on a circle about the target from which the bombs can be released to hit the target.

Consider the following conditions which affect the bomb dropped from an airplane:–

1. **ALTITUDE:** Controlled by the pilot. Determines the length of time the bomb is sustained in flight and affected by atmospheric conditions, thus affecting the range (forward travel of the bomb) and deflection (distance the bomb drifts in a crosswind with respect to airplane's ground track).

2. **TRUE AIRSPEED:** Controlled by the pilot. The measure of the speed of the airplane through the air. It is this speed which is imparted to the bomb and which gives the bomb its initial forward velocity and, therefore, affects the trail of the bomb, or the distance the bomb lags behind the airplane at the instant of impact.

3. **BOMB BALLISTICS:** Size, shape and density of the bomb, which determines its air resistance. Bombardier uses bomb ballistics tables to account for type of bomb.

4. **TRAIL:** Horizontal distance the bomb is behind the airplane at the instant of impact. This value, obtained from bombing tables, is set in the sight by the bombardier. Trail is affected by altitude, airspeed, bomb ballistics and air density, the first 2 factors being controlled by the pilot.

5. **ACTUAL TIME OF FALL:** Length of time the bomb is sustained in air from instant of release to instant of impact. Affected by alti-

tude, type of bomb and air density. Pilot controls altitude to obtain a definite actual time of fall.

6. **GROUNDSPEED:** The speed of the airplane in relation to the earth's surface. Groundspeed affects the range of the bomb and varies with the airspeed, controlled by the pilot.

Bombardier enters groundspeed in the bombsight through synchronization on the target. During this process the pilot must maintain the correct altitude and constant airspeed.

7. **DRIFT:** Determined by the direction and velocity of the wind, which determines the distance the bomb will travel downwind from the airplane from the instant the bomb is released to its instant of impact. Drift is set on the bombsight by the bombardier during the process of synchronization and setting up course.

The above conditions indicate that the pilot plays an important part in determining the proper point of release of the bomb. Moreover, throughout the course of the run, as explained below, there are certain preliminaries and techniques which the pilot must understand to insure accuracy and minimum loss of time.

Prior to takeoff the pilot must ascertain that the airplane's flight instruments have been checked and found accurate. These are the altimeter, airspeed indicator, free air temperature gauge and all gyro instruments. These instruments must be used to determine accurately the airplane's attitude.

The Pilot's Preliminaries

The autopilot and PDI should be checked for proper operation. It is very important that PDI and autopilot function perfectly in the air; otherwise it will be impossible for the bombardier to set up an accurate course on the bombing run. The pilot should thoroughly familiarize himself with the function of both the C-1 autopilot and PDI.

If the run is to be made on the autopilot, the pilot must carefully adjust the autopilot before reaching the target area. The autopilot must be adjusted under the same conditions that will exist on the bombing run over the target. For this reason the following factors should be taken into consideration and duplicated for initial adjustment.

1. Speed, altitude and power settings at which run is to be made.

2. Airplane trimmed at this speed to fly hands off with bomb bay doors opened.

The same condition will exist during the actual run, except that changes in load will occur before reaching the target area because of gas consumption. The pilot will continue making adjustments to correct for this by disengaging the autopilot elevator control and re-trimming the airplane, then re-engaging and adjusting the autopilot trim of the elevator.

Setting Up the Autopilot

One of the most important items in setting up the autopilot (see pp. 185-188) for bomb approach is to adjust the turn compensation knobs so that a turn made by the bombardier will be coordinated and at constant altitude. Failure to make this adjustment will involve difficulty and delay for the bombardier in establishing an accurate course during the run—with the possibility that the bombardier may not be able to establish a proper course in time, the result being considerably large deflection errors in point of impact.

Uncoordinated turns by the autopilot on the run cause erratic lateral motion of the course hair of the bombsight when sighting on target. The bombardier in setting up course must eliminate any lateral motion of the fore-and-aft hair in relation to the target before he has the proper course set up. Therefore, any erratic motion of the course hair requires an additional correction by the bombardier, which would not be necessary if autopilot was adjusted to make coordinated turns.

USE OF THE PDI: The same is true if PDI is used on the bomb run. Again, coordinated smooth turns by the pilot become an essential part of the bomb run. In addition to added course corrections necessitated by uncoordinated turns, skidding and slipping introduce small changes in airspeed affecting synchronization of the bombsight on the target. To help the pilot flying the run on PDI, the airplane should be trimmed to fly practically hands off.

Assume that you are approaching the target area with autopilot properly adjusted. Before reaching the initial point (beginning of bomb run) there is evasive action to be considered. Many different types of evasive tactics are employed, but from experience it has been recommended that the method of evasive action be left up to the bombardier, since the entire antiaircraft pattern is fully visible to the bombardier in the nose.

EVASIVE ACTION: Changes in altitude necessary for evasive action can be coordinated with the bombardier's changes in direction at specific intervals. This procedure is helpful to the bombardier since he must select the initial point at which he will direct the airplane onto the briefed heading for the beginning of the bomb run.

Should the pilot be flying the evasive action on PDI (at the direction of the bombardier) he must know the exact position of the initial point for beginning the run, so that he can fly the airplane to that point and be on the briefed heading. Otherwise, there is a possibility of beginning to run too soon, which increases the airplane's vulnerability, or beginning the run too late, which will affect the accuracy of the bombing. For best results the approach should be planned so the airplane arrives at the initial point on the briefed heading, and at the assigned bombing altitude and airspeed.

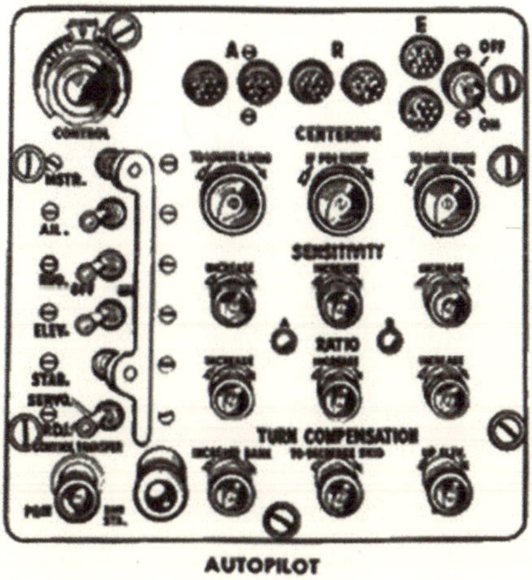

AUTOPILOT

PDI

At this point the bombardier and pilot as a team should exert an extra effort to solve the problem at hand. It is now the bombardier's responsibility to take over the direction of flight, and give directions to the pilot for the operations to follow. The pilot must be able to follow the bombardier's directions with accuracy and minimum loss of time, since the longest possible bomb run seldom exceeds 3 minutes. Wavering and indecision at this moment are disastrous to the success of any mission, and during the crucial portion of the run, flak and fighter opposition must be ignored if bombs are to hit the target. The pilot and bombardier should keep each other informed of anything which may affect the successful completion of the run.

HOLDING A LEVEL: Either before or during the run, the bombardier will ask the pilot for a level. This means that the pilot must accurately level his airplane with his instruments (ignoring the PDI). There should be no acceleration of the airplane in any direction, such as an increase or decrease in airspeed, skidding or slipping, gaining or losing altitude.

For the level the pilot should keep a close check on his instruments, not by feel or watching the horizon. Any acceleration of the airplane during this moment will affect the bubbles (through centrifugal force) on the bombsight gyro, and the bombardier will not be able to establish an accurate level.

For example, assume that an acceleration occurred during the moment the bombardier was accomplishing a level on the gyro. A small increase in airspeed or a small skid, hardly perceptible, is sufficient to shift the gyro bubble liquid 1° or more. An erroneous tilt of 1° on the gyro will cause an error of approximately 440 feet in the point of impact of a bomb dropped from 20,000 feet, the direction of error depending on direction of tilt of gyro caused by the erroneous bubble reading.

HOLDING ALTITUDE AND AIRSPEED: As the bombardier proceeds to set up his course (synchronize), it is absolutely essential that the pilot maintain the selected altitude and airspeed within the closest possible limits. For every additional 100 feet above the assumed 20,000-foot bombing altitude, the bombing error will increase approximately 30 feet, the direction of error being over. For erroneous airspeed, which creates difficulty in synchronization on the target, the bombing error will be approximately 170 feet for a 10 mph change in airspeed. Assuming the airspeed was 10 mph in excess, from 20,000 feet, the bomb impact would be short 170 feet.

The pilot's responsibility to provide a level and to maintain a selected altitude and airspeed within the closest limits cannot be over-emphasized.

If the pilot is using PDI (at the direction of the bombardier) instead of autopilot, he must be thoroughly familiar with the corrections demanded by the bombardier. Too large a correction or too small a correction, too soon or too late, is as bad as no correction at all. Only through prodigious practice flying with the PDI can the pilot become proficient to a point where he can actually perform a coordinated turn, the amount and speed necessary to balance the bombardier's signal from the bombsight.

Erratic airspeeds, varying altitudes, and poorly coordinated turns make the job of establishing course and synchronizing doubly difficult for both pilot and bombardier, because of the necessary added corrections required. The resulting bomb impact will be far from satisfactory.

After releasing the bombs, the pilot or bombardier may continue evasive action—usually the pilot, so that the bombardier may man his guns.

The pilot using the turn control may continue to fly the airplane on autopilot, or fly it manually, with the autopilot in a position to be engaged by merely flipping the lock switches. This would provide potential control of the airplane in case of emergency.

REDUCING CIRCULAR ERROR: One of the greatest assets towards reducing the circular error of a bombing squadron lies in the pilot's ability to adjust the autopilot properly, fly the PDI, and maintain the designated altitude and airspeeds during the bombing run. Reducing the circular error of a bombing squadron reduces the total number of aircraft required to destroy a particular target. For this reason both pilot and bombardier should work together until they have developed a complete understanding and confidence in each other.

THE ENGINEER

Size up the man who is to be your engineer. This man is supposed to know more about the airplane you are to fly than any other member of the crew.

He has been trained in the Air Forces' highly specialized technical schools. Probably he has served some time as a crew chief. Nevertheless, there may be some inevitable blank spots in his training which you, as a pilot and airplane commander, may be able to fill in.

Think back on your own training. In many courses of instruction, you had a lot of things thrown at you from right and left. You had to concentrate on how to fly; and where your equipment was concerned you learned to rely more and more on the enlisted personnel, particularly the crew chief and the engineer, to advise you about things that were not taught to you because of lack of time and the arrangement of the training program.

Both pilot and engineer have a responsibility to work closely together to supplement and fill in the blank spots in each other's education.

To be a qualified combat engineer a man must know his airplane, his engines, and his armament equipment thoroughly. This is a big responsibility: the lives of the entire crew, the safety of the equipment, the success of the mission depend upon it squarely.

He must work closely with the copilot, checking engine operation, fuel consumption, and the operation of all equipment.

He must be able to work with the bombardier, and know how to cock, lock, and load the bomb racks. It is up to you, the airplane commander, to see that he is familiar with these duties, and, if he is hazy concerning them, to have the bombardier give him special help and instruction.

He must be thoroughly familiar with the armament equipment, and know how to strip, clean, and re-assemble the guns.

He should have a general knowledge of radio equipment, and be able to assist in tuning transmitters and receivers.

Your engineer should be your chief source of information concerning the airplane. He should know more about the equipment than any other crew member—yourself included.

You, in turn, are his source of information concerning flying. Bear this in mind in all your discussions with the engineer. The more complete you can make his knowledge of the reasons behind every function of the equipment, the more valuable he will be as a member of the crew. Who knows? Someday that little bit of extra knowledge in the engineer's mind may save the day in some emergency.

Generally, in emergencies, the engineer will be the man to whom you turn first. Build up his pride, his confidence, his knowledge. Know him personally; check on the extent of his knowledge. Make him a man upon whom you can rely.

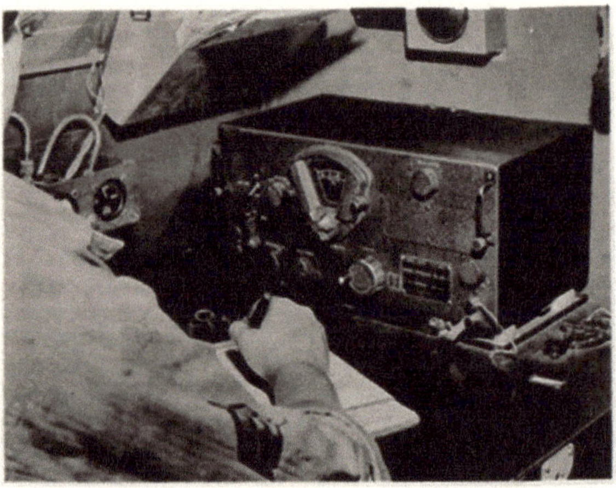

THE RADIO OPERATOR

There is a lot of radio equipment in today's B-17's. There is one man in particular who is supposed to know all there is to know about this equipment. Sometimes he does, but often he doesn't. And when the radio operator's deficiencies do not become apparent until the crew is in the combat zone, it is then too late. Too often the lives of pilots and crew are lost because the radio operator has accepted his responsibility indifferently.

Radio is a subject that cannot be learned in a day. It cannot be mastered in 6 weeks, but sufficient knowledge can be imparted to the radio man during his period of training in the United States if he is willing to study. It is imperative that you check your radio operator's ability to handle his job before taking him overseas as part of your crew. To do this you may have to check the various departments to find any weakness in the radio operator's training and proficiency and to aid the instructors in overcoming such weaknesses.

Training in the various phases of the heavy bomber program is designed to fit each member of the crew for the handling of his jobs. The radio operator will be required to:

1. Render position reports every 30 minutes.
2. Assist the navigator in taking fixes.
3. Keep the liaison and command sets properly tuned and in good operating order.
4. Understand from an operational point of view:
    (a) Instrument landing
    (b) IFF
    (c) VHF

and other navigational aids equipment in the airplane.

5. Maintain a log.

In addition to being a radio operator, the radio man is also a gunner. During periods of combat he will be required to leave his watch at the radio and take up his guns. He is often required to learn photography. Some of the best pictures taken in the Southwest Pacific were taken by radio operators. The radio operator who cannot perform his job properly may be the weakest member of your crew—and the crew is no stronger than its weakest member.

THE GUNNERS

The B-17 is a most effective gun platform, but its effectiveness can be either applied or defeated by the way the gunners in your crew perform their duties in action.

Your gunners belong to one of two distinct categories: turret gunners and flexible gunners.

The power turret gunners require many mental and physical qualities similar to what we know as inherent flying ability, since the operation of the power turret and gunsight are much like that of airplane flight operation.

While the flexible gunners do not require the same delicate touch as the turret gunner, they must have a fine sense of timing and be familiar with the rudiments of exterior ballistics.

All gunners should be familiar with the coverage area of all gun positions, and be prepared to bring the proper gun to bear as the conditions may warrant.

They should be experts in aircraft identification. Where the Sperry turret is used, failure to set the target dimension dial properly on the K-type sight will result in miscalculation of range.

They must be thoroughly familiar with the Browning aircraft machine gun. They should know how to maintain the guns, how to clear jams and stoppages, and how to harmonize the sights with the guns.

While participating in training flights, the gunners should be operating their turrets constantly, tracking with the flexible guns even when actual firing is not practical. Other airplanes flying in the vicinity offer excellent tracking targets, as do automobiles, houses, and other ground objects during low altitude flights.

The importance of teamwork cannot be overemphasized. One poorly trained gunner, or one man not on the alert, can be the weak link as a result of which the entire crew may be lost.

Keep the interest of your gunners alive at all times. Any form of competition among the gunners themselves should stimulate interest to a high degree.

Finally, each gunner should fire the guns at each station to familiarize himself with the other man's position and to insure knowledge of operation in the event of an emergency.

APPENDIX IV

Official USAAF Aircraft Accident Report & Missing Aircrew Report

500

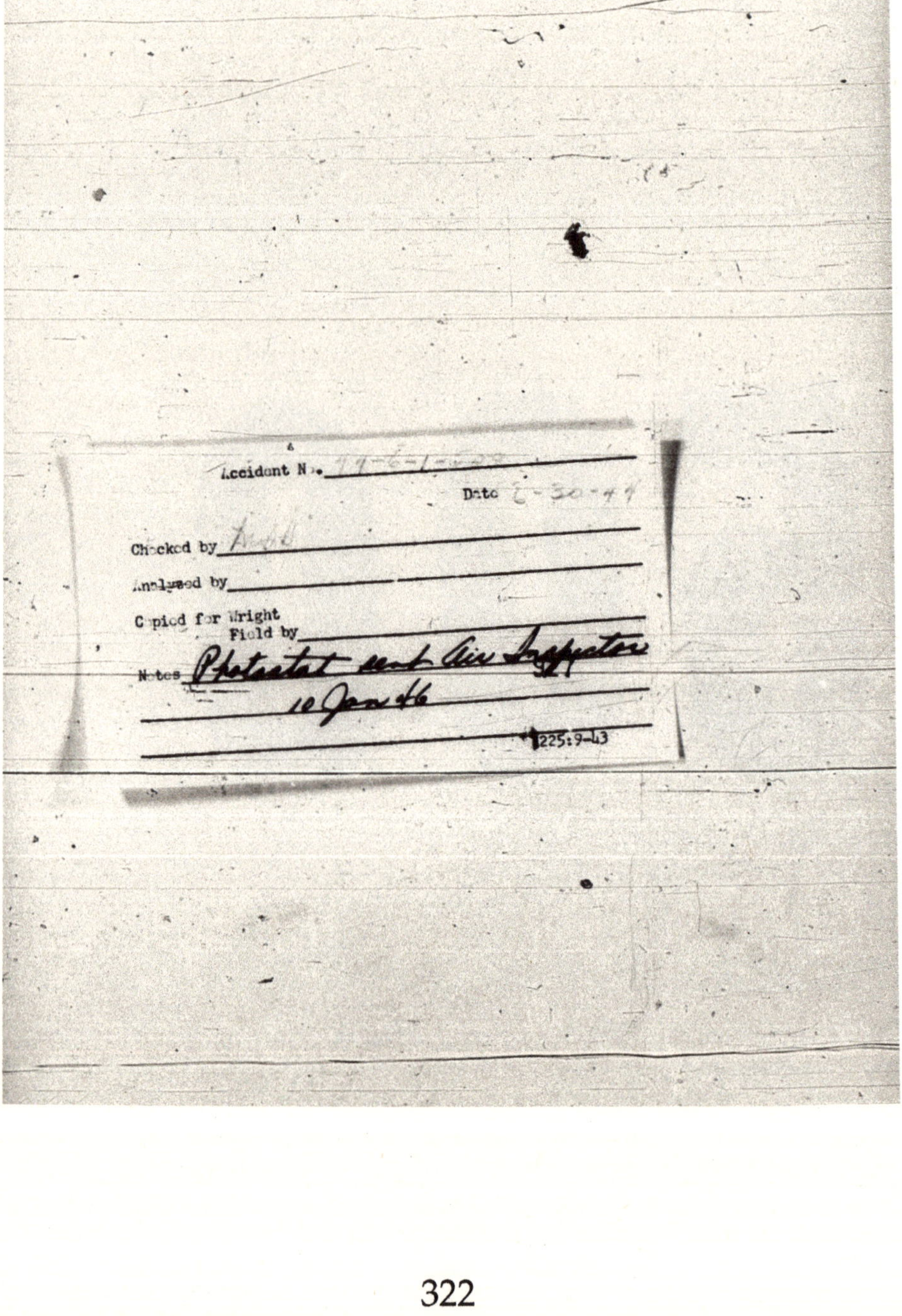

Accident No. 44-6-1-[illegible]

Date 6-30-44

Checked by

Analyzed by

Copied for Wright
Field by

Notes Photostat sent Air Inspector
10 Jan 46

225:9-43

WAR DEPARTMENT
A. A. F. Form No. 14
(Revised May 15, 1942)

Accident No. ________ Cattegard 44-6-1-500 4

WAR DEPARTMENT

RESTRICTED

REPORT OF AIRCRAFT ACCIDENT

01-565

(1) Place Cave Hill, Belfast, North Ireland (2) Date 1 June 1944 (3) Time 1030GMT

Aircraft: (4) Type and model B-17 G40 (5) A. F. No. 43-97862 (6) Station

Organization: (7) 8th AF (Command and Air Force) (8) Un-Assigned (Group) (9) 065 Y235

PERSONNEL

Duty (10)	Name (Last name first) (11)	Rating (12)	Serial No. (13)	Rank (14)	Personnel Class (15)	Branch (16)	Air Force or Command (17)	Result to Personnel (18)	Use of Parachute (19)
P	Brooke, Lester B.	P	T-61593	F/O	92		8th	Fatal	No
CP	Murphy, Jeremiah C.	P	T-62092	F/O	92		8th	Fatal	No
N	Nobilione, Joseph V.	N	0-710299	2nd Lt.	01		8th	Fatal	No
B	McKenzie, Leighton B.	B	T-123650	F/O	92		8th	Fatal	No
AMG	Brewer, Wilbur D.	AMG	16075633	S/Sgt.	20		8th	Fatal	No
AG	Hibbler, Howard A.	AG	37210378	Sgt.	20		8th	Fatal	No
ROMG	Dundon, Lawrence E.	ROMG	35692675	S/Sgt.	20		8th	Fatal	No
AG	McCrane, Lawrence R.	AG	20215468	Cpl.	20		8th	Fatal	No
AAG	Graves, Robert L. Jr.	AAG	38334100	Sgt.	20		8th	Fatal	No
AG	McGill, Edward E.	AG	10600464	S/Sgt.	20		8th	Fatal	No

[redacted]

(20) Brooke (Last name) Lester (First name) B (Middle initial) (21) T-61593 (Serial number) (22) F/O (Rank) (23) (Personnel class) (24) (Branch)

Assigned (25) 8th AF 8 (Command and Air Force) (26) Un-Asgd (Group) (27) (Squadron) (28) Y235 (Station)

Attached for flying (29) ATC (Command and Air Force) (30) (Group) (31) (Squadron) (32) W999 (Station)

Original rating (33) Pilot (Rating) (34) 11-3-43 (Date) Present rating (35) Pilot (Rating) (36) 11-3-43 (Date) Instrument rating (37) (Date)

First Pilot Hours:
(at the time of this accident)

(38) This type	240:35	(42) Instrument time last 6 months	
(39) This model	240:30	(43) Instrument trainer time last 6 months	
(40) Last 90 days	131:40	(44) Night time last 6 months	
(41) Total as of 4-30-44	493:10	(45) Night time last 30 days	

CLASSIFICATION CANCELLED OR CHANGED
TO RESTRICTED
BY AUTHORITY OF CG AAF
BY FGB DATE 2-27-46

AIRCRAFT DAMAGE F

Damage					(49) List of Damaged Parts
(46) Aircraft	W5				Complete wreck
(47) Engine(s)	W5	W5	W5	W5	
(48) Propeller(s)	W5	W5	W5	W5	

(50) Weather at the time of accident ET 4/10 to 6/10 Stratus at 600' - 10/10 at 1000' - 2000'
Visibility 3 miles, Drizzle and fog.

(51) Was the pilot flying on instruments at the time of accident Unknown 2

(52) Cleared from Gander Z313 (53) To Valley Z425 (54) Kind of clearance Instrument

(55) Pilot's mission Transatlantic Ferry of Aircraft and Crew
50

(56) Nature of accident Collision in full flight with object other than aircraft
26 927

(57) Cause of accident Undetermined
86

(58) Unsatisfactory Report submitted: No

RESTRICTED

DESCRIPTION OF ACCIDENT

(Brief narrative of accident. Include statement of responsibility and recommendations for action to prevent repetition)

1. Description of Accident:

Radio contact was made with this aircraft prior to his arrival at Nutts Corner He was instructed to hold on the radio range along with approximately fifteen (15) other aircraft, and was ultimately given permission to make his let-down in turn. The last radio contact made with him was at 10:30 GMT, when he reported himself contact over a lake. Nothing further was heard from this aircraft until some time later when R.A.F. authorities in Belfast called to report the crash of an unidentified aircraft on a hill near Belfast. It was subsequently determined that it was an American B-17 #42-97862. In the very shortest possible time American Officers and men proceeded to the scene of the crash, but there was nothing that could be done for the aircraft or the crew.

2. Findings:

a. Cause: Undetermined

b. Nature: Collision in full flight with object other than aircraft.

c. Results to personnel: All Fatal

d. Damage to material: Complete wreck.

RECEIVED
HEADQUARTERS
ARMY AIR FORCE
JUN 21 1944
SAFETY

927

Signature JOHN C. LAMBERT, Capt., AC.
(Investigating Officer)

CECIL E. HENRY, Col., AC.

ELWOOD B. STERLING, 1st Lt. AC

Date 10 June 1944.

Aircraft Accident Committee

CONFIDENTIAL

COPY:

[redacted] HOUSE,
Whitehouse.

RESTRICTED

1st June, 1944.

To:
Chief Rescue Officer,
C. D. Headquarters.

Dear Sir,

The following is a report of duties and approximate times with reference to aircraft which crashed at Hazelwood, and the Rescue party from here which assisted in recovery of the bodies.

At 12.34 approximately I was inside building when a heavy plane passed over in the immediate vicinity between Whitehall Road and Mill Road, flying very low, judging by the sound I would say roughly 300', yet engines appeared quite normal. It came from Belfast Lough direction going towards Cave Hill.

Immediately after this B. O'Hare called me stating a plane had crashed on the hill. I went out to look in that direction and could hear sharp explosions similiar to fifle fire, the only thing that could be seen was a white spot, which was the tail of this plane in question. It was impossible to gain any information by sight as the Cave Hill, Hazelwood, etc. were completely enveloped in heavy mist which extended practically to Antrim Road.

I phoned "G" District Report Centre at Approx. 12.38 informing them that a plane had crashed between Serpentine and Whitehall Roads on upper side of Antrim Road, it was impossible to state exact location due to fog and mist. By the time I got outside again flames could be faintly seen rising from what we understood to be the plane. 12.39 approx. Mr. Savage arrived and I informed him suggesting that we take action. He instructed me to phone C. D. Controller. I did so and Mr. McKibbin said send a Rescue party at once.

There was a speedy turn out of Trainees under leaders Henderson and Brennan, whilst Messrs. Savage, Duncan, Kerr and self went by the Staff Car to Hazlewood-arrived there about 12.48. I ran on, and, going in the direction of the heavy smoke arrived at the scene at 12.50. N.F.S., R.U.C. and some civilians were already there.

I made enquiries re casualties if any had been located or seen, one man said he saw one handing out of the cockpit in the middle of the flames but had now fallen back. We made a good reconnaissance but nothing could be done until flames had been damped down by N.F.S. ALL WERE DEAD

927

(Mr. McKibbin now on scene).

After flames had subsided we got to work on recovery of bodies the first 4(four) bodies were recovered, placed and lashed on stretchers by myself and R. V. Cook. A soldier (R.A.M.C.) and an N.F.S. man gave valuable assistance, Mr. Savage and Mr. Kerr directing the lowering. In the case of 5 (five) other bodies Mr. Kerr GR1, Mr. Savage, Mr. Maxwell, G.C.1, assisted Cook and I, together with Naval personnel and a band of willing helpers who gave valuable assistance in both lowering the remains of 6 (six) to the bottom of the field, and bringing 4 (four) to the top.

RESTRICTED

Incl. #6

CONFIDENTIAL

1

~~CONFIDENTIAL~~

RESTRICTED

All bodies taken out were badly burned and charred. A tenth body was removed by others from the vicinity of the left wing. Any valuables found were handed over to R.U.C. or R.A.F.

Incident cleared of bodies about 14.30.

I would like to make special mention of R. V. Cook, E.R.1., who did good work with coolness, care and without thought of himself.

Any further information that I may be able to give I will gladly do so if required.

Yours faithfully,

/s/ D. H. Elliott.
D.H. ELLIOTT.

(Asst. Training Officer)

2nd June, 1944.

From reliable eye witness information collected this morning, this plane approached from the direction of Mossley swung around in vicinity of Lough shore and was heading back to Cave Hill as already stated.

Height approx. 150' - 200'. Engines O.K. Landing carriage down.

I would say that this revised report can be fairly well relied upon.

(signed) D.H. ELLIOTT.

DHE/FBM

327

CERTIFIED TRUE COPY:

John C. Lambert
JOHN C. LAMBERT,
Capt., Air Corps,
Acft. Accident Officer.

RESTRICTED

~~CONFIDENTIAL~~

Incl. #6 (cont'd) 2

CONFIDENTIAL

CHAPLAINS' OFFICE.
R.A.F. DUNLAMBERT.
June 1. 1944.

RESTRICTED

CRASH OF FLYING FORTRESS O No. 297862

Sir,

I have the honour to submit the following report on the crash of the above machine on Cave Hill, Belfast, on June 1, 1944.

At approximately 17.30 hrs my Office telephone rang, and my wife informed me that she had heard a very large machine (she thought a flying boat) crash into Cave Hill immediately above our house, in Ben Madigan Park. I immediately informed the Controller at R.A.F. H.Q. Stormont, giving the approximate location of the crash, and then drove to the scene of the accident with Flying Officer Thompson, the Camp Commandant at Dunlambert. The climb on foot from the road to the scene of the crash is extremely arduous, but I estimate that we reached it in ten or fifteen minutes from the receipt of the news. We were the first Service personnel to reach the locality.

The machine was lying on a very steep hill side, its forward portion completely destroyed and broken away from the rear part of the fuselage which was much less damaged. The machine appeared to have hit the hill head on. A violent petrol fire was raging around the forward part of the machine, and ammunition was exploding continuously.

Several civilians who were present were taking cover behind a bank of earth. They informed me that they believed that bombs were on board the machine which they expected to explode at any moment. They also stated that there were several men in the machine and that none had been got out.

Since there was a possibility that some of the crew might be living and unable to extricate themselves, I crawled up the hillside, under the tail unit and along by the side of the less damaged part of the fuselage until I was just able to reach the point where the break had occurred, and here I was able partly to enter the fuselage. A number of bodies were visible, several in the heart of the fire itself, but they were all clearly dead and there was no sign of life anywhere.

The intense heat and choking fumes rendered it impossible for me to remain for more than a very brief space of time, and visibility was extremely difficult owing to the blinding smoke and the constant explosion of signal flares and ammunition, but before being forced to retire I was able to satisfy myself without any shadow of doubt that there were no living men in the aircraft. Before being forced back I was able to collect a few personal belongings from the interior, which I subsequently handed over to Captain Lambert of the U.S.A. Army Air Corps.

I have no doubt that all the occupants of the aircraft were killed instantaneously as a result of the collision with the hill side. This is the only grain of comfort in what is a most unfortunate and deplorable happening.

- 927
- 5-

I have the honour to remain, Sir,
Your obedient servant,
(signed) W. E. Woosnam-Jones.
Senior Chaplain

'Certified True Copy'
John C. Lambert
JOHN C. LAMBERT,
Capt., Air Corps.
Incl. #7

CONFIDENTIAL RESTRICTED

~~CONFIDENTIAL~~

RESTRICTED

10. Benmadigan Park South.
Antrim Road. Belfast.
June 1st. 1944.

STATEMENT BY MRS. M. WOOSNAM-JONES.

At approximately 12.30. hrs on June 1st. 1944 I was busy upstairs in my house when I heard the sound of a very large four engined aircraft passing at the back of the house at a low altitude. I assumed from the sound that it was a Sunderland flying boat preparing to land on Belfast loch.

Suddenly I heard the engines stop. I cannot state that the engine noise stopped completely, but it suddenly diminished very considerable indeed. Approximately seven seconds later I heard the aircraft hit the side of the hill above our home. I have checked this estimated period experimentally with my husband's stop watch, and it may be relied upon as accurate.

As soon as I heard the noise of the crash I immediately went to the telephone and with fifteen seconds I was through to my husband's office at R.A.F. Dunlambert I told him that I had heard a very large aircraft which I thought might be a flying boat, crash into the hill above our house.

I then dialled 'Telephone Emergency Call' and had a notification sent through to the police.

I then left the house, approximately a minute or so within the sound of the crash and set off climbing up the hill to find the scene of the accident. I am a qualified member of St. John's Ambulance Brigade, and hoped that I might be able to do something to help.

I reached the scene of the crash after a climb of about five minutes. When I was half way up I saw the first gush of orange flame and black smoke rise out of the trees as the machine caught fire. The machine did not therefore visibly catch fire until two or three minutes after the crash.

I was, I believe, the first to reach the vicinity of the crash. The first uprush of flame was so intense, and the explosions of the ammunition so continuous, that I could not go near, and I realised that I could do nothing to help. I looked for survivers around the plane, but saw none.

I there fore climbed back down the hill towards the road, to direct the rescue parties whom I knew must be on the way up. While on the way down I met my husband who was climbing up to the scene of the accident. I continued on down to the main road, where I directed ambulances and rescue parties until relieved.

I saw no sign of life in the machine at any time.

/s/ Muriel C. Woosnam-Jones
MURIEL C. WOOSNAM-JONES

'Certified True Copy'
John C. Lambert
JOHN C. LAMBERT,
Captain, Air Corps,
Acft. Acc. O.

RESTRICTED

- 6 -

927

Incl. #8

~~CONFIDENTIAL~~

~~CONFIDENTIAL~~

HEADQUARTERS
STATION NO 2, EWATC
APO 813, U S ARMY

RESTRICTED

OPS/JCL/dlw
10 June 1944.

SUBJECT: Aircraft Accident Report, WD AAF Form #14.

TO : Chief Flying Safety, AAF, Winston Salem, N. C.
Commanding General, Air Transport Command, Washington, D. C.
Commanding General, Sta. #1, (Hq), EWATC, APO 887, U. S. Army
Commanding General, Hq. 8th Air Force, AAF Sta. 101, APO 634, U.S.A.
Commanding General, (Hq), NAWATC, 497 Silver St., Manchester, N.H.

1. Transmitted herewith report of Aircraft Accident, WDAAF Form #14, on B-17, Ser. No. 42-97862.

2. Items 6, 9, 15, 16, 23, 24, 27-45, incomplete as information was not available this station.

3. Weight & Balance Form "F" destroyed by fire when aircraft burned

For the Commanding Officer:

JOHN C. LAMBERT,
Captain, Air Corps,
Aircraft Accident O.

8 Incls.
Incl. #1, WDAAF Form #14.
Incl. #2-5, Photographs
Incl. #6, Statement of D. H. Elliott
Incl. #7, Statement of Chaplain Woosnam-Jones
Incl. #8, Statement of Murial Woosnam-Jones

RESTRICTED

-7-

~~CONFIDENTIAL~~

927

1

AFPPA-14 (10 Apr 46)

RESTRICTED

WAR DEPARTMENT
HEADQUARTERS ARMY AIR FORCES
WASHINGTON

MISSING AIR CREW REPORT

IMPORTANT: This report will be compiled in triplicate by each Army Air Forces organization within 48 hours of the time an aircraft is officially reported missing.

1. ORGANIZATION: Location: ______ Command or Air Force ______
GROUP ______; SQUADRON ______; DETACHMENT ______
2. SPECIFY: Point of Departure ______; Course ______
Intended Destination ______; Type of Mission Transatlantic Ferry
3. WEATHER CONDITIONS AND VISIBILITY AT TIME OF CRASH OR WHEN LAST REPORTED: ______
4. GIVE: (a) Date 1 Jun 44 Time ______; And Location of Last known whereabouts of missing aircraft Crashed at Cave Hill, Belfast, N.Ireland
(b) Specify whether ( ) Last sighted; ( ) last contacted by radio; ( ) Forced down; (Seen to Crash; or ( ) Information not available.
5. AIRCRAFT WAS LOST, OR IS BELIEVED TO HAVE BEEN LOST, AS A RESULT OF (Check only one: ( ) Enemy Aircraft; ( ) Enemy Anti-Aircraft; ( ) Other Circumstances as follows ______
6. AIRCRAFT: Type, Model and Series B-17 ; AAF Serial No. 42-97862
7. ENGINES: Type, Model and Series ______; AAF Serial No. (a) ______ (b) ______ (c) ______ (d) ______
8. INSTALLED WEAPONS (Furnish below Make, Type and Serial Number)
(a) ______ (b) ______ (c) ______ (d) ______
(e) ______ (f) ______ (g) ______ (h) ______
9. THE PERSONS LISTED BELOW WERE REPORTED AS: (a) Battle Casualty ______
or (b) Non-Battle Casualty ______
10. NUMBER OF PERSONS ABOARD AIRCRAFT: Crew 10 ; Passengers ______; Total 10
(Starting with pilot, furnish the following particulars: If more than 11 persons were aboard aircraft, list similar particulars on separate sheet and attach original to this form).

Crew Position	Name in Full (Last Name First)	Rank	Serial Number
1. Pilot	Brooks, Lester B.	F/O	T-61593
2. CP	Murphy, Jeremiah C.	F/o	T-62092
3. Navigator	Nobilione, Joseph V.	2nd Lt.	0-710299
4. Bombardier	McKenzie, Leighton B.	F/O	T-123650
5. Engineer Gunner	Brewer, Wilbur D.	S/Sgt.	16075633
6. Aerial Gunner	Hibbler, Howard A.	Sgt.	37210378
7. Radio Gunner	Dundon, Lawrence E.	S/Sgt.	35692675
8. Aerial Gunner	McGrane, Lawrence R.	Cpl	20215468
9. Armorer Gunner	Graves, Robert L. Jr.	Sgt.	38334100
10. Aerial Gunner	McGill, Edward E.	S/Sgt.	10600464
11.			

12. IDENTIFY BELOW THOSE PERSONS WHO ARE BELIEVED TO HAVE LAST KNOWLEDGE OF AIRCRAFT, AND CHECK APPROPRIATE COLUMN TO INDICATE BASIS FOR SAME:

1.

RESTRICTED C6-8049S,AF

R E S T R I C T E D

WD, Hq AAF, Washington, Missing Air Crew Report.

Name in Full (Last name first)	Rank	Serial Number	Contacted by Radio	Last Sighted	Saw Crash	Saw Forced Landing
1.						
2.						
3.						

13. IF PERSONNEL ARE BELIEVED TO HAVE SURVIVED, ANSWER YES TO ONE OF THE FOLLOWING STATEMENTS: (a) Parachutes were used_______ (b) Persons were seen walking away from scene of crash______; or (c) Any other reason (Specify)______

14. ATTACH AERIAL PHOTOGRAPH, MAP, CHART, OR SKETCH, SHOWING APPROXIMATE LOCATION WHERE AIRCRAFT WAS LAST SEEN.
15. ATTACH EYEWITNESS DESCRIPTION OF CRASH, FORCED LANDING, OR OTHER CIRCUMSTANCES PERTAINING TO MISSING AIRCRAFT.
16. ATTACH A DESCRIPTION OF THE EXTENT OF SEARCH, IF ANY, AND GIVEN NAME, RANK AND SERIAL NUMBER OF OFFICER IN CHARGE HERE____________

Date of Report____________

____
(Signature of Preparing Officer)

2

R E S T R I C T E D C6-8049S,AF

CONFIDENTIAL

R-39

201 - BROOKS, Lester B. (F/O) 1st Ind. PAO/AMB/ac
ASN - T61593

HEADQUARTERS GRENIER FIELD, 1377TH AAF BASE UNIT (NAD-ATC) Manchester, N.H.
4 August 1944.

TO: Commanding General, NAD,ATC, 497 Silver Street, Manchester, N. H.
Attention: Personal Affairs Officer

Forwarded as a matter pertaining to your command.

For the Commanding Officer:

BERYL H. [illegible]SHOUR,
Captain, Air Corps,
Adjutant.

201-Brooks, Lester B. (Off) 2nd Ind. NAD/PER/PAO/EGW/jmh
HEADQUARTERS NORTH ATLANTIC DIVISION, Air Transport Command, 497 Silver
St., Manchester, N.H. 5 August 1944

PPA-8

TO: Commanding General, Army Air Forces, Washington 25, D.C.
Attn: Asst Chief Air Staff, Personnel

1. In compliance with basic communication the following information is submitted from accident report files of this Headquarters.

a. F/O Lester B. Brooks, T-61593 was the pilot of B-17 No. 42-97862 which crashed into the side of Cave Hill, Belfast, North Ireland on 1 June 1944 at 1030 GMT. Fire broke out in the wreckage shortly after the crash and none of the crew survived.

b. Cause of the crash has not been determined.

c. Description of the accident as included in Form #14 report is as follows:

"Radio contact was made with this aircraft prior to his arrival at Nutts Corner. He was instructed to hol d on the radio range along with approximately fifteen (15) other aircraft, and was ultimately given permission to make his let-down in turn. The last radio contact made with him was at 10:30 GMT, when he reported himself contact over a lake. Nothing further was heard from this aircraft until some time later when R.A.F. authorities in Belfast called to report the crash of an unidentified air-

-2-

~~CONFIDENTIAL~~

PC-8699

AC-44-140

2nd Ind. to CG, AAF, Washington, D.C. 5 Aug 44 - NAD/PER/PAO/EGW/jmh

craft on a hill near Belfast. It was subsequently determined that it was an American B-17 #42-97862. In the very shortest possible time American Officers and men proceeded to the scene of the crash, but there was nothing that could be done for the aircraft or the crew."

d. Statements accompanying the accident reports that civilian and military personnel reached the scene of the accident within five (5) or ten (10) minutes after the crash, but no sign of life was apparent and all personnel were presumed to have been killed almost instantly.

e. Mission: Transatlantic ferry of aircraft and crew.

2. A list of the crew members and their positions in the plane was as follows:

F/O	Lester B. Brooks	T-61593	Pilot
F/O	Jeremiah C. Murphy	T-62092	Co-Pilot
2nd Lt.	Joseph V. Nobilione	O-710299	Navigator
F/O	Leighton B. McKenzie	T-123650	Bombardier
S/Sgt.	Wilbur D. Brewer	16075633	Engineer Gunner
Sgt.	Howard A. Hibbler	37210378	Aerial Gunner
S/Sgt.	Lawrence E. Dundon	35692675	Radio Gunner
Cpl.	Lawrence R. McGrane	20215468	Aerial Gunner
Sgt.	Robert L. Graves, Jr.	38334100	Armorer Gunner
S/Sgt.	Edward E. McGill	10600464	Aerial Gunner

For the Commanding General:

M. H. Partridge

M. H. PARTRIDGE
Major, Air Corps
Actg Asst Chief of Staff, Personnel

CONFIDENTIAL

ADDRESS REPLY TO
COMMANDING GENERAL, ARMY AIR FORCES
WASHINGTON 25, D. C.

ATTENTION:

HEADQUARTERS, ARMY AIR FORCES
WASHINGTON

FOR VICTORY BUY UNITED STATES WAR BONDS AND STAMPS

31 July 1944

SUBJECT: Flight Officer Lester B. Brooks, T61593,
No Organization,
Killed in Airplane Crash 1 June 1944.

TO : Commanding Officer, Station #16, NAW/ATC,
Grenier Field, Manchester, New Hampshire.

1. This headquarters requests details concerning the circumstances under which the subject named was reported killed on the date shown.

2. In order to comply to this request, it is desired that information be furnished this headquarters, and if available, include a list of the crew members and their positions in the plane.

By command of General ARNOLD:

E. A. Bradunas

E. A. BRADUNAS,
Major, A. G. D.,
Chief, Notification Branch,
Personal Affairs Division,
Assistant Chief Air Staff, Personnel.

CONFIDENTIAL

IN REPLY REFER TO: AFPPA-8-JH

HEADQUARTERS, ARMY AIR FORCES
WASHINGTON

25 September 1945

SUBJECT: Flight Officer Lester B. Brooks, T61593

TO : Commanding General
NAD, ATC
497 Silver Street
Manchester, New Hampshire

Attached copies of letters forwarded for investigation, and information on which to base a reply.

BY COMMAND OF GENERAL ARNOLD:

File R-39

N. W. Reed

N. W. REED
Major, Air Corps
Chief, Notification Section
Personal Affairs Branch
Personal Services Division, AC/AS-1

360.33

360.33 1st Ind.
HEADQUARTERS, NORTH ATLANTIC WING, ATLANTIC DIVISION, Air Transport Command, 497 Silver Street, Manchester, N. H. 3 October 1945

TO: Commanding General, Headquarters, Army Air Forces, Washington 25, D. C.

1. Under date of 5 August 1944 a complete resume of the details available in connection with the aircraft accident in which F/O Lester B. Brooks, T-61593 was involved was submitted to your Headquarters by second indorsement.

2. No further information is available surrounding the death of subject officer.

FOR THE COMMANDING GENERAL:

2 Incls:
Incl 1 - Ltr dtd 23 July
Incl 2 - Ltr dtd 11 Sep 45

Allan G. Dingwall
ALLAN G. DINGWALL
Lt Colonel, AGD
Adjutant General

COPY

July 23rd

Dear Mrs. Brooks:

Am finally getting around to answering your letter. As I don't know much only what the boys at Belfast, Ireland told me, that's what I'll tell you.

Shortly after we landed there some of the boys on the field told us there was a plane that had crashed while circling the field. We inquired and found out it was Lester's plane. We were told that they, Lester's crew, radioed in that they were low on gas and could not circle the field. The Air Base told them they could not land right then so they had to stay up in the air. They soon ran out of gas and crashed in the hills just a short piece from the field. We never did find out why they wouldn't leave them land. They surely must of had a good reason or they wouldn't have done it. I'm sorry that I can't tell you more but that's all I know.

A friend

COPY

2nd Lt. Joseph V. Mobilione	Mrs. Mary A. Broccolo, (sister) Tildean Lane, Bayville, New York.
F/O Lester B. Brooks	Mrs. Lester B. Brooks, (wife) Route # 2, Carrollton, Ohio.
F/O Jeremiah C. Murphy	Mrs. Norma Murphy, (wife) 197 Madison Avenue, Albany, New York.
F/O Leighton E. McKenzie	Mrs. Guin Z. Robinson, (mother) 123 Edgewood Avenue, Mill Valley, California.
S/Sgt. Lawrence E. Dundon	Mrs. Ora R. Dundon, (wife) 219 N. 33rd Street, Louisville, Kentucky.
S/Sgt. Wilbur D. Brewer	Mr. Amos Brewer, (brother) Nepolle, Illinois.
S/Sgt. Edward E. McGill	Mr. Bud S. McGill, (brother) 812 Boscobel Street, Nashville, Tennessee.
Sgt. Howard A. Hibbler	Mrs. Susie M. Efaw, (mother) 1012 East Central Avenue, Wichita, Kansas.
Sgt. Robert L. Graves, Jr.	Mrs. Maggie Graves, (mother) Route 3, Box 72, El Dorado, Kansas.
Corporal Lawrence R. McGrane	Mr. Thomas McGrane, (brother) 50 White Oak Street, New Rochelle, New York.

APPENDIX V

RCAF Gander Operations Record Book June 1944

PLACE	DATE	TIME	SUMMARY OF EVENTS	REFERENCE TO APPENDICES
Gander, Nfld.	May 26th (Cont'd)		G.C. Johnston (C4) CB, MC arrived to invest the officers and airmen named with the following decorations: S/L A.A.T. Dorie (J3525) - D.F.C. F/O C.O. Godfrey (J26278) - D.F.C. F/O A.M. James (J21313) - A.F.C. R85802 Sgt. Giorgianni, C.E.- B.E.M. R82698 Sgt. Lyons, G.F.W. - G.M. The A.O.C.-in-C. later inspected the Hospital and Milk Plant. The Commanding Officer inspected the barracks at 1000 hours. The Roman Catholic Bishop from Harbour Grace, Nfld., arrived on the Station to hold special confirmation services this evening in the RCAF Chapel. Heavy A.A. Batteries carried out practice shots. Badminton, ping pong, pool and swimming provided sport in the Drill Hall during the evening.	
	May 27th		There were high broken to medium clouds in the morning, becoming medium overcast and low scattered clouds at the end of period; ceiling dropped by evening; some precipitation. Traffic was very heavy, both inbound and outbound. Without evident increase in numbers off the east coast of Newfoundland, the enemy showed more activity. It was noticed that on occasion, fixes on the enemy were obtained in an area well populated with Portuguese and Spanish fishing vessels. A great deal of important shipping was tracked through the same area. The A.O.C.-in-C. departed by air for Botwood at 0930 hours, returned at 1430 hours and took off immediately for Dartmouth. The ~~War~~ Command Canteen Officer arrived on the Station today, and effected several improvements in the canteens. Photographs shown as Appendix "D" show the large stock and wide variety of commodities now available in the General Canteen, which have been obtained after the untiring efforts of F/O J.H. Bourne, Station Services Officer. The Station orchestras played for dances in the Officers' and Senior NCO.s' Messes this evening. The boxing ring attracted much attention in the Drill Hall tonight. Badminton and swimming were in progress all evening.	"D"
	May 28th		It was high overcast and low broken clouds in the morning, becoming low overcast and broken clouds with heavy rain showers and thunder at the end of period; the maximum temperature was 69.8°--highest temperature for May, 1944. There was a very heavy inbound traffic. The following is an operational summary for the period 26th May to 1st June:	

	A/S Sweeps		Convoy Sorties		Monsters		Oper. Searches	
	No.	Hours	No.	Hours	No.	Hours	No.	Hours
10 Squadron	Nil		6	69:34	9	40:25	2	7:34

One Liberator departed for Africa, 47 B17's to U.K., one Catalina to Reykjavik and 19 Liberators and 3 Dakotas to Azores during the week. A large supply of canteen supplies has arrived at Central Warehouse.

APPENDIX VI

RAF Nutts Corner Operations Record Book June 1944

Appendix "K"

NUTTS CORNER TRANSAT REPORT FOR JUNE 1944.

IN.					OUT.				
Date	B17	B24	PB27	From	Date	B17	B24	PB27	To
1st June			3	Botwood	1st June	1			Langford Lodge
	19			Gander	1st "			1	Botwood
2nd "			1	Botwood	2nd "	1			Langford Lodge
3rd "		19		Goose	2nd "	15			Burtonwood
6th "	23			Gander	2nd "		4 (A.20)		Grove
7th "			1	Botwood	3rd "			2	Botwood
8th "			1	Botwood	4th "		16		Warton
8th "	23		2	Botwood	5th "		1		Debach
8th "				Gander	5th "		1		Hilsworth
9th "			2	Botwood	5th "			2	Botwood
10th "			2	Botwood	5th "		1		Langford Lodge
11th "			1	Botwood	6th "	10			Langford lodge
11th "			1	Pt. Lyautey	6th "			2	Botwood
12th "			2	Botwood	7th "	13			Langford Lodge
12th "			1	Pt. Lyautey	8th "			2	Botwood
12th "	2	26		Gander	8th "		4		Langford Lodge
13th "			3	Botwood	8th "				Burtonwood
14th "			1	Botwood	9th "	1			Burtonwood
15th "			2	Botwood	9th "			2	Botwood
15th "			1	Lyautey	9th "			1	Pt. Lyautey
16th "			1	Pt. Lyautey	10th "	1			Langford Lodge
17th "			1	Pt. Lyautey	10th "			2	Botwood
17th "			1	Botwood	10th "			1	Lyautey
18th "	16			Goose	11th "			1	Botwood
18th "		19		Goose	12th "		32		Warton
18th "			1	Botwood	12th "	1	4		Burtonwood
19th "			1	Pt. Lyautey	12th "			2	Botwood
19th "			1	Botwood	12th "			2	Pt. Lyautey
19th "	20	4		Goose	13th "		1		Warton
20th "			1	Pt. Lyautey	14th "			3	Botwood
21st "			5	Botwood	14th "			1	Pt. Lyautey
21st "			1	Pt. Lyautey	15th "	1			Langford Lodge.
23rd "			1	Pt. Lyautey	15th "		1		Warton
Total B/F.	103	68	38			68	65	24	

R.A.F. Form 540

See instructions for use of this form in K.R. and A.C.I., para. 2349 and War Manual, Pt. II., chapter XX., and notes in R.A.F. Pocket Book.

OPERATIONS

ROYA

of (Unit or Formation) CO.

Place	Date	Time	
NUTTS CORNER	JUNE, 2nd 1944.		S/LDR C.W.A. BROWN (87908
			S/LDR C. EVERITT (44647) Equip
			HEADQUARTERS NO 44 GROUP arriv
			(87908) returned by air.
			S/O S. TITCOMBE (3832) W.A.A.F
NUTTS CORNER	JUNE 3rd		F/LT REAVEY (140665) Mete
			(124953) returned by air to PR
			F/O J.N. GREENE (144671) Medic
			Aviation Medecine. F/LT W.H.
			Meteorologist, returned by air
	JUNE, 4th		W/CDR M.A. CANDLER (28180
			left by air for PRESTWICK.
			S/LDR W.C. HORDER (47669) Chie
			R.A.F. BALLYHALBERT.
			F/LT T.D.G. CARSTAIRS (85380)
			P/O T. HUNTER (170076) returne
	JUNE, 5th		F/O H.R. GLASS (148610) I
			F/O J.M. CRADDOCK (140667) Met.
			F/LT CARNELL (140451) Met., re
			F/LT N.E. HOWELL (131751) A.&
	JUNE, 6th		D DAY Invasion of Nor
	JUNE, 7th		A/P/O S. MASKELL (175773)
			reported on posting (supernume
	JUNE, 8th		F/LT H. GINN (743427) H.Q.
			Signals Visit.
	JUNE, 9th		Eighteen LANCASTERS and Se
			owing to bad weather landed on
			S/LDR F.W. CRONNE (DRI 003964)

RECORD BOOK

IR FORCE, STATION, NUTTS CORNER
RIM, NORTHERN IRELAND.

No. of pages used for day

Summary of Events SECRET.	References to Appendices
ntelligence, W/CDR M.A. CANDLER (28180) Engineer,	
t, F/LT G.S. PILLANS (113809) Electrical Engineer,	
on the Station for Staff visit, S/LDR C.W.A. BROWN	
G' reported on posting from H.Q. NO. 44 GROUP.	
logist returned by air to PRESTWICK. F/LT G. FRAMPTON	
WICK ON cessation of attachment for Briefing duties.	
proceeded by air to R.A.F. FARNBOROUGH for course in	
LLITT (122985) Navigation, F/LT W. SALTER (140737)	
om PRESTWICK.	
S/LDR C. EVERITT (44647), F/LT G.S. PILLANS (113809)	
ignals Officer, proceeded on Station Defence Course at	
urned from H.Q. TRANSPORT COMMAND and course in LONDON.	
rom R.A.F. PRESTWICK.	
lligence, returned by air to R.A.F. PRESTWICK.	
proceeded on posting to H.Q. R.A.F. N. Ireland.	
ed on posting from H.Q. R.A.F. N. Ireland.	
returned from Anti-Gas Course at R.A.F. ROLLESTONE.	
n France by British, American and Allied Forces.	
.S.D. and A/P/O A.E. COVENTON (175763) A.& S.D.	
) from R.A.F. COSFORD for Flying Control Duties.	
A.F. N. Ireland arrived on the Station for Staff	
HALIFAXES of BOMBER COMMAND diverted from home bases	
s airfield from operations in Northern France.	
.M. 8 Region, and F/LT M.W.J. STOTHERD (078252)	

APPENDIX VII

Aircraft Record Card B-17G 42-97862

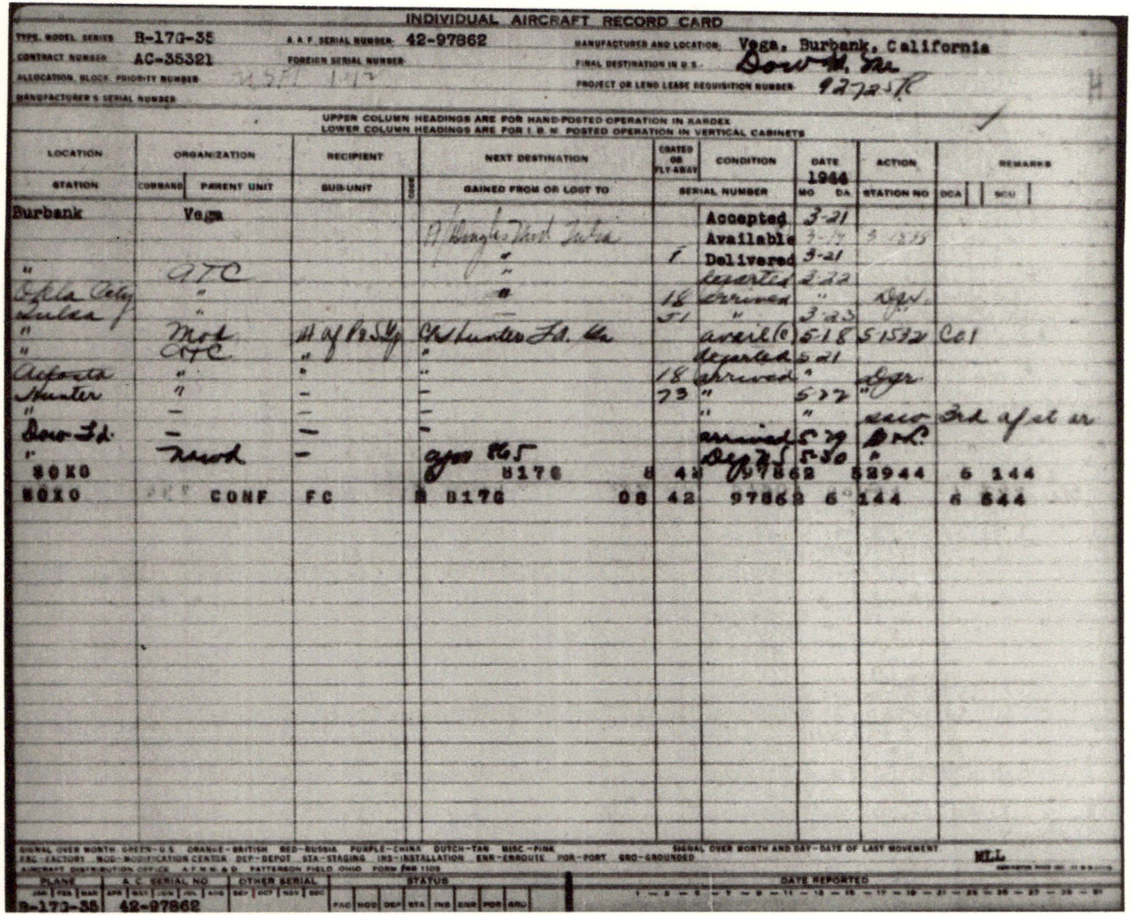

INDIVIDUAL AIRCRAFT RECORD CARD

TYPE, MODEL, SERIES B-17G-35 | A.A.F. SERIAL NUMBER 42-97862 | MANUFACTURER AND LOCATION Vega, Burbank, California
CONTRACT NUMBER AC-35321 | FOREIGN SERIAL NUMBER | FINAL DESTINATION IN U.S. Dow Fd. Me
ALLOCATION, BLOCK, PRIORITY NUMBER | PROJECT OR LEND LEASE REQUISITION NUMBER 92725R
MANUFACTURER'S SERIAL NUMBER

UPPER COLUMN HEADINGS ARE FOR HAND-POSTED OPERATION IN KARDEX
LOWER COLUMN HEADINGS ARE FOR I.B.M. POSTED OPERATION IN VERTICAL CABINETS

LOCATION / STATION	ORGANIZATION / COMMAND / PARENT UNIT	RECIPIENT / SUB-UNIT	NEXT DESTINATION / GAINED FROM OR LOST TO	CRATED OR FLY-AWAY	CONDITION / SERIAL NUMBER	DATE 1944 MO DA	ACTION / STATION NO	REMARKS
Burbank	Vega				Accepted	3-21		
			[illegible]		Available	[illegible]	[illegible]	
"			"	F	Delivered	3-21		
	ATC		"		departed	3-22		
Okla City	"		"	18	arrived	"	Dept.	
Tulsa	"			51	"	3-23	"	
"	Mod	[illegible]	[illegible]		avail (C)	5-18	51592	C01
"	ATC	"	"		departed	5-21		
Augusta	"	"	"	18	arrived	"	Dept.	
Hunter	"	–	–	73	"	5-22	"	
"	–	–	–		"	"	[illegible]	[illegible]
Dow Fd.	–	–			arrived	5-29	[illegible]	
"	[illegible]	–	[illegible]		Dep	5-30	"	
80X0			8176	8 42	97862		52944	6 144
80X0	CONF	FC	8 8176	08 42	97862	6	144	6 844

SIGNAL OVER MONTH GREEN-U.S. ORANGE-BRITISH RED-RUSSIA PURPLE-CHINA DUTCH-TAN MISC-PINK
FAC-FACTORY MOD-MODIFICATION CENTER DEP-DEPOT STA-STAGING INS-INSTALLATION ENR-ENROUTE POR-PORT GRO-GROUNDED
SIGNAL OVER MONTH AND DAY-DATE OF LAST MOVEMENT
MLL

PLANE B-17G-35 | A.C. SERIAL NO 42-97862 | OTHER SERIAL | STATUS | DATE REPORTED

Abbreviations

3rd AF Third Air Force
8th AF Eighth Air Force
AAF Army Air Force
AGRC American Graves Registration Company
ARP Air Raid Precaution
BBC British Broadcasting Company
BG Bombardment Group
BS Bombardment Squadron
Cal. Calibre
Cpl. Corporal
F/O Flying Officer
FLAK Anti-Aircraft Fire
Furlough - Leave of absence
GMT Greenwich Mean Time
GRS Graves Registration Service
KY Kentucky
Lt. Lieutenant
MPH Miles Per Hour
NFS National Fire Service
PT Primary Trainer
Pvt. Private
PX Post Exchange
RAF Royal Air Force
RCAF Royal Canadian Air Force
RPM Revolutions Per Minute
RTU Replacement Training Unit
RUC Royal Ulster Constabulary
S/Sgt. Staff Sergeant
Sgt. Sergeant
UAS Ulster Aviation Society
USAAF United States Army Air Forces
UK United Kingdom
US United States
UTV Ulster Television

About the authors

Alfred Montgomery was born in Belfast, Northern Ireland in November 1964 to Alfred and Mary Montgomery, he was to be their only child and was very much adored by both of them. He attended his local primary school along with his cousin Craig and then onto grammar school where Alfred was always chosen to play Rugby due to his sturdy build even though he hated it.

He has always had an interest in vehicles as both his father Alfred Snr. and his uncle Willy had Austin cars which Alfred used to help work at and drive from the tender age of seven. As he had grown up around vehicles and transportation, after leaving school, Alfred served as an apprenticeship truck mechanic at Felden.

Once old enough to obtain his truck and bus driving licence his vocation switched to being a driver. Alfred has driven a multitude of vehicles from car transporters to tour buses and is happiest when behind the wheel. One of the most enjoyable tasks as a driver, was when Alfred drove actor, singer and songwriter, Kris Kristofferson and his band, for five days on their all Ireland concert tour, in 1995. He has driven extensively throughout the world but one of his favourite places for driving is the good ole USA!.

Alfred met his wife Dawn in 1993 and fortunately Dawn also shared an interest in military history. Along with like minded friends, they became founding members of The Ulster Military Vehicle club which is still going today some 20 years later.

They have built up a collection of military vehicles and American trucks over the years which signify their interest and respect for American engineering. Alfred believes that a fine suit, a fancy car and a big bank account do not make a person and he himself would be the first to stop and help somebody with a broken down car or a vulnerable person in need. It is his opinion, that what is In a persons heart that matters. Alfred's driving force behind this book was to have this tragic incident recorded to inform future generations and he hopes that you enjoy reading this publication.

Will Lindsay's childhood years were spent in the city of Liverpool, in England, in the 1980's. Born to an English mother and an Ulster father, the family returned to Northern Ireland in 1994, where he was educated in primary and secondary education.

From an early age, he was fascinated with history and the past, through his Liverpool grandfather, he acquired an interest for old steam railways. His grandfather would set up his prized collection of model trains and run them for him, to a young child of five years of age, it was an amazing site to see smoke puffing out of a small engine.

His father, Alan, was an apprentice Jockey in the 1960'-70's in England and enjoyed fishing and playing golf. He would take Will and his cousins to fish on the local canals and ponds. It was something he had done his whole life back home in Northern Ireland as a young boy. During the summer months he would often take him walking on the old deserted railway lines that were close to their home, which was once part of the famous Aintree Iron. This tied in with Will's interests at the time and likely instilled a long standing appreciation he would later have for old wartime airfields.

His first interest and association with the Second World War, was when he collected up a number of coupons from a Kellogg cereal box in the late 1980's and he received two die cast models of a

Supermarine Spitfire and a Hawker Hurricane, sadly these were lost as he took them everywhere with him.

Upon moving to Northern Ireland in the autumn of 1994, the following year, he visited a former WWII airfield called Langford Lodge. The Ulster Aviation Society were holding their annual open day and fly in on the old airfield. He can vividly remember the B-17 bomber, Sally-B, flying overhead. The sheer size of this aircraft and the atmosphere of the old airfield is what ignited his interest in the U.S. forces in Northern Ireland during the war years. He is the curator of the Langford Lodge USAAF Station 597 Museum project. The museum is currently in the process of acquiring a wartime building to display the collection locally. It will likely be one of the largest collections of Northern Ireland related USAAF memorabilia in the country.

Of all the experiences in his life, he recalls that the most rewarding and enjoyable has been, in his own words *" a father to my daughter and a husband to my wife"*.

He resides in the village of Crumlin, in County Antrim, with his wife Louise and his daughter Amelia.

Will, left and Alfie to the right, at Gartree Church, Langford Lodge, September 2018. This was one of the first public open days for The Station 597 Museum. The Dawn Partrol, is Alfie and Dawn's 1942 Ford GPW Jeep. Alfie and his father restored the vehicle in the 1990's.

Acknowledgements

Alfred would like to take this opportunity to say thank you to the following people who without their input, help and guidance this book would not have been possible. Firstly my dear wife Dawn for all her hard work and giving me the love, support and encouragement to see this book become a reality. My late father for introducing me to the story and igniting my interest in this subject when I was a young boy. Ernie Cromie of the Ulster Aviation Society who pointed me in the right direction regarding information. Bob Hill from The Courier Journal in Louisville , Kentucky for his help in putting me in touch with Ruth. The Gillespie family in Kentucky who became an extended family to me. The relatives and close friends of the crew members who we have formed a close friendship with, Beverly Hibbler, Frank Fiordalisi, Lawrence McGrane, Steven Graves, Holly Poirier, Hollie Cummings, Melinda Chapman. Ray & Ellen Baxter for allowing me access to the crash site area from their property over the years. Gerard Brannigan and The Cave Hill Conservation Campaign for their help and support. The people who have passed since my journey began, my parents, Ruth Gillespie (formerly Dundon), Bill Gillespie, Jimmy Doherty, Bill Norris, Gennie Peterson (formerly Brooks). My Co author William Lindsay for burning the midnight oil on many a night and getting us to the finish line. My biggest and most sincere thanks go to the ten young American men who were on their way to fight the enemy in the skies over Europe, however they came to grief with a greater enemy "mother nature". I also extend my thanks to current and past members of both the US and British military who are still serving side by side fighting for and protecting our freedom in the western world.

" Thank you for your service"

Will would like to take this opportunity to thank the following people who have made this book possible. My very patient wife Louise and my daughter Amelia, who as a little three year old often wonders why her daddy doesn't always have the time to play as much as he would like to, when undertaking such a project. Louise has always supported my work and research, both in the field and in the office. To my two lovely girls, I offer you both my sincerest thanks and all my love, for being patient with me and an inspiration. To my late grandmother *(nan)*, who was born in 1938, to whom the war was an every day part of life, I offer my sincerest love and thanks for always being proud of me and offering support, we all miss you dearly and not a day goes by that you are not in our thoughts. To my dear parents, Alan and Sandra, I offer my sincere love and thanks for making me the person I am today, which has allowed me over the years to always chase my dreams, the culmination of which has lead me to this point of being able to tell the stories of heroes, that otherwise might never be told. I offer my sincere thanks to one of my longest and dear friends, Ernie Cromie, of the Ulster Aviation Society, who without fail has always offered his support and assistance to whom I will always be grateful. I offer my sincere thanks to my other dear friend and co-writer Alfie, for firstly being a friend that everyone in life should have and for his persistence, assistance, determination and patience in making this book a reality, you are a true gentleman and I am proud to call you my friend. To the kind hearted souls around the world, who over the years have supplied me with material in the form of documents and photographs, I thank you for taking the time out of your day to help, your kindness and generosity knows no bounds, namely Tammy Horton and Lynn Gamma, of the Air Force Historical Research Agency, located at Maxwell AFB, USA. I offer my sincere thanks to Clive Moore, who has kindly shared a number of photographs from his terrific collection. I also would like to express my sincere thanks to the families of the crew, who have supplied Alfie and I over the years with numerous documents and photographs, thank you for your assistance and I hope that this book meets with your approval as a fitting monument to your loved ones. Lastly and most importantly, I would like to thank the crew, to whom I will always feel indebted. Through such tragedy, so many human connections around the world have been made, in their memory, lasting friendships have been forged and continue to this day, a world apart. When I first visited the site, I was 19 years old, at that time, the youngest crew members on-board the aircraft would still have been older than I and I could not have ever imagined experiencing what they went through at that age, they were still young boys and they had their whole lives ahead of them. I am now 34 years of age and it is 15 years on since I first visited the crash site, in those years, I have lived a good and happy life, surrounded by good people, a job that I enjoy and most importantly I'm a father with a family of my own. I know now and I am certain, that without the sacrifice of the ten young men on-board this aircraft and all of our allied forces that made the ultimate sacrifice during the Second World War, that I would not be here today enjoying the freedom that I and my family have. For our today, they gave their tomorrow, thank you Lester, Jeremiah, Leighton, Joseph, Larry, Wilbur, Howard, Robert, Lawrence and Edward;

"Oh! I have slipped the surly bonds of Earth
And danced the skies on laughter-silvered wings;
Sunward I've climbed, and joined the tumbling mirth
of sun-split clouds, — and done a hundred things
You have not dreamed of — wheeled and soared and swung
High in the sunlit silence. Hov'ring there,
I've chased the shouting wind along, and flung
My eager craft through footless halls of air....

Up, up the long, delirious, burning blue
I've topped the wind-swept heights with easy grace.
Where never lark, or even eagle flew —
And, while with silent, lifting mind I've trod
The high untrespassed sanctity of space,
– Put out my hand, and touched the face of God."

Contact the authors

The authors would like to hear from you. Were you an eye-witness to the accident?, or perhaps a story about the crash was relayed to you by a family member?. Do you have a relic or a souvenir from that fateful crash, perhaps tucked away in your attic?, we would love to photograph it for a second edition of the book. You are more than welcome to make contact with us, you can do so by using the following e-mail addresses;

Alfred Montgomery

americanbigrig@hotmail.com

William Lindsay

willalindsay1984@gmail.com

Alternatively, you can contact us via our website contact form, which can be found at the following website address;

www.cavehillbombercrash.co.uk

Other books by William Lindsay;

Hut 203

The Wartime Log Book of Doug Eastwood, an American civilian aircraft mechanic in Northern Ireland, during the Second World War, 1942 - 1944.

Paperback: 240 pages
Publisher: STATION 597 PUBLICATIONS;
New edition (22 Nov. 2018)
Language: English
ISBN-10: 0957399391
ISBN-13: 978-0957399396

Wartime Langford Lodge

A documented account of aircraft accidents at the former American assembly, modification and repair depot, in Northern Ireland 1942-1945.

Paperback: 240 pages
Publisher: STATION 597 PUBLICATIONS;
New edition (10 Oct. 2012)
Language: English
ISBN-10: 0957399308
ISBN-13: 978-0957399303